Britain Enforcing the Peace, 1918–1923

Britain Enforcing the Peace, 1918–1923

The Royal Navy in Turkey and Southern Russia after the Great War

John D. Grainger

Pen & Sword
MILITARY

First published in Great Britain in 2024 by
Pen & Sword Military
An imprint of Pen & Sword Books Limited
Yorkshire – Philadelphia

ISBN 978 1 03612 374 1

A CIP catalogue record for this book is
available from the British Library

Typeset by Mac Style
Printed in the UK by CPI Group (UK) Ltd, Croydon, CR0 4YY.

MIX
Paper | Supporting responsible forestry
FSC® C013604

Pen & Sword Books Limited incorporates the imprints of After the Battle, Atlas, Archaeology, Aviation, Discovery, Family History, Fiction, History, Maritime, Military, Military Classics, Politics, Select, Transport, True Crime, Air World, Frontline Publishing, Leo Cooper, Remember When, Seaforth Publishing, The Praetorian Press, Wharncliffe Local History, Wharncliffe Transport, Wharncliffe True Crime and White Owl.

For a complete list of Pen & Sword titles please contact

PEN & SWORD BOOKS LIMITED
47 Church Street, Barnsley, South Yorkshire, S70 2AS, England
E-mail: enquiries@pen-and-sword.co.uk
Website: www.pen-and-sword.co.uk
or
PEN AND SWORD BOOKS
1950 Lawrence Road, Havertown, PA 19083, USA
E-mail: uspen-and-sword@casematepublishers.com
Website: www.penandswordbooks.com

Contents

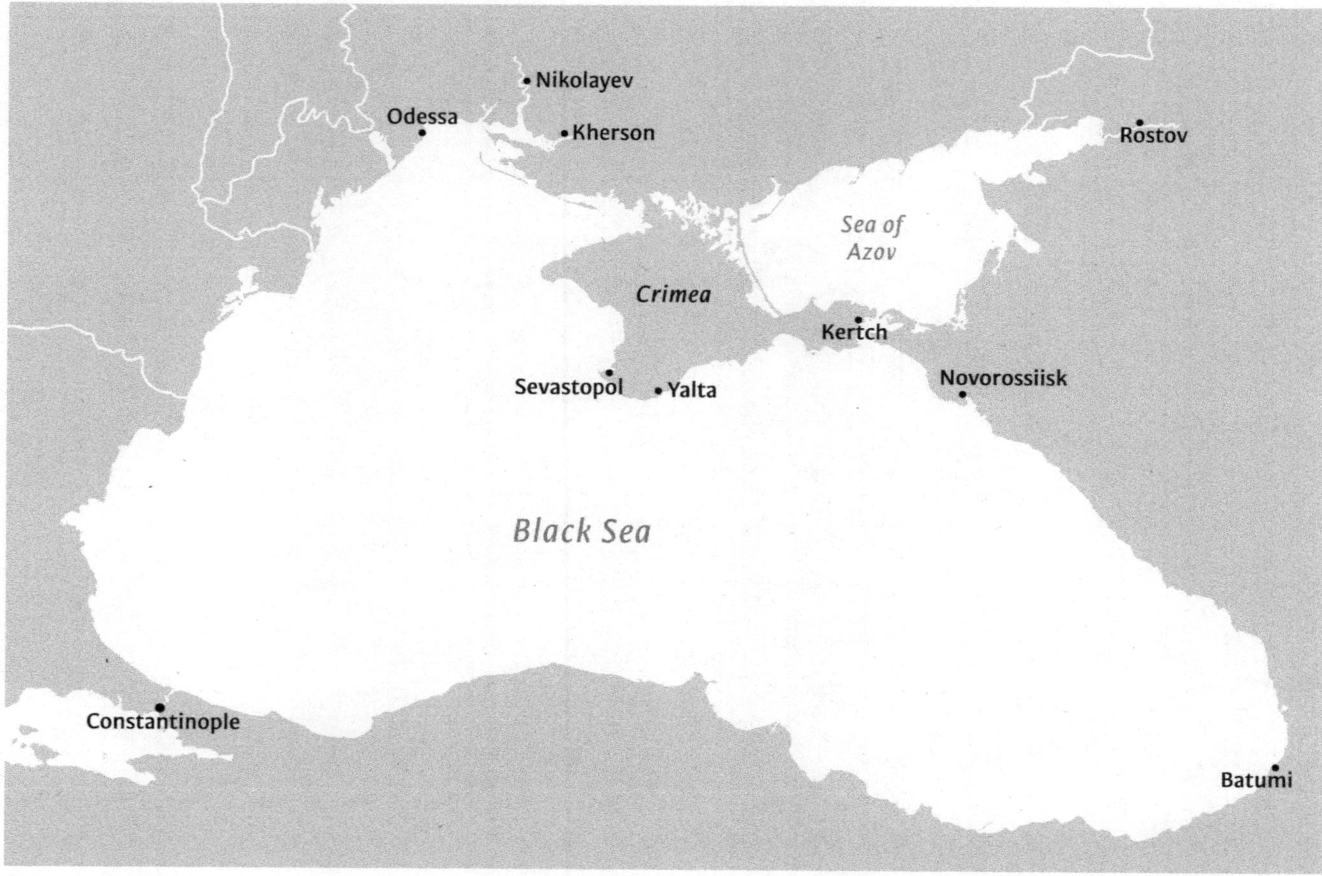

Map 1: The Black Sea.

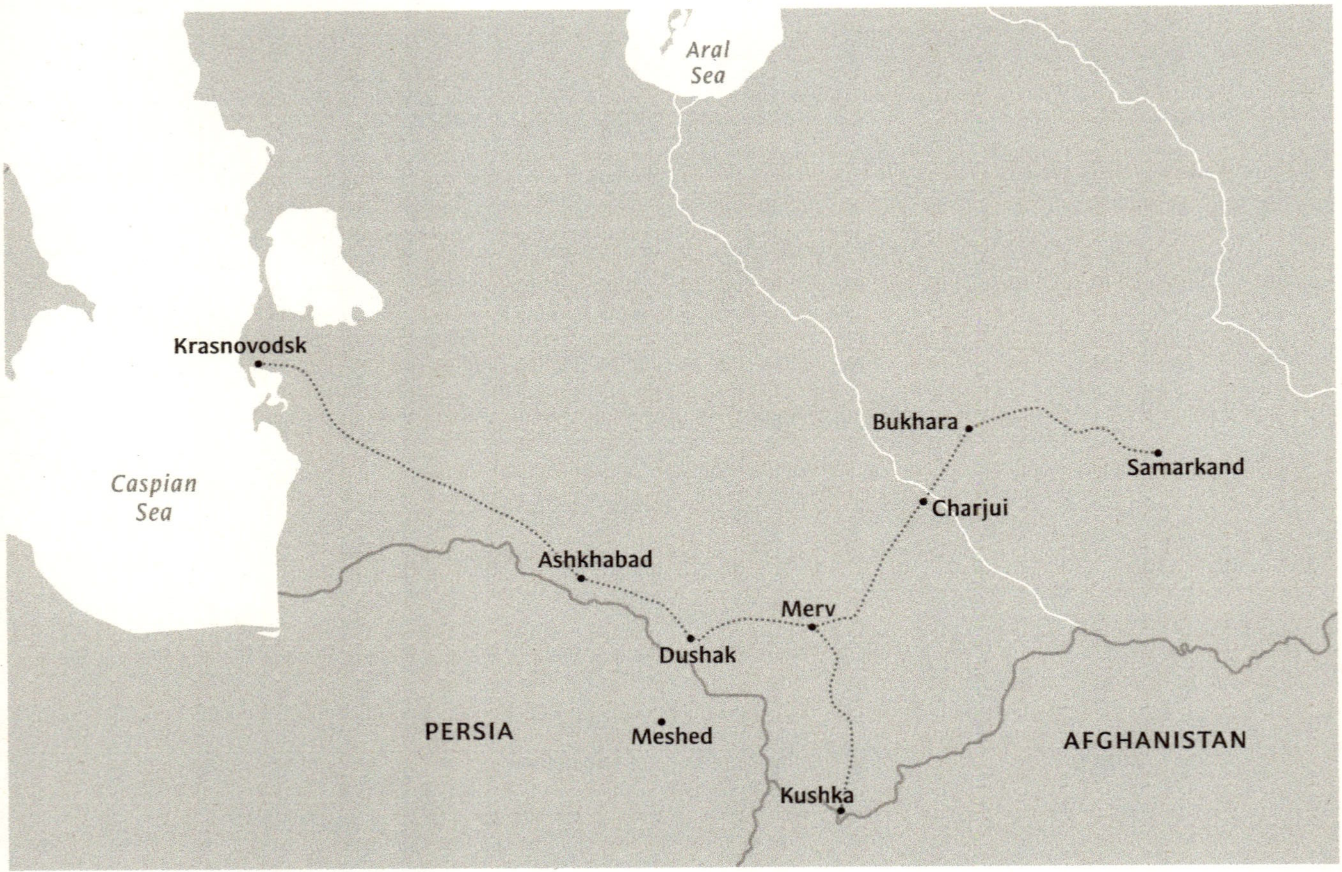

Map 2: Central Asia.

Map 3: Caspian Sea.

Map 4: The Straits.

Preface

This book is the third in a set that have the city of Constantinople at their centre. One other book considered its evolution from a nomad village to the Great City by concentrating on the history of the Straits – the Bosporos, the Sea of Marmara, and the Hellespont (*The Straits from Troy to Constantinople*) – and the second looks at its military experiences (*Forty Sieges of Constantinople*). This book takes up where that second account finished, and considers the city's role in the wider result at the end of the Great War, when the city was captured by a foreign army for only the third time in its history.

I confess that this was not my intention when I began work on this book. I was more concerned to deal with the activities of the Royal Navy in the Black Sea at the end of the Great War. As I went on, however, the subject tended to include events in a much wider area, and at the same time, the great city emerged as a major player in the story. So I found myself composing yet another book with it at its centre. So much for plans and intentions.

Introduction

The Great War ended gradually, over a period of several months. First came a series of truces, armistice by armistice, beginning with the ending of the German–Russian war, and going on to the peace conferences. But the fighting did not stop; instead, it moved frequently from a great international conflict into a series of lesser wars, civil wars and revolutions. Much of this violence centred on the collapse of Russia, but a second set of fighting affected the collapsing Ottoman Empire and its territories. From the Arctic Ocean at Murmansk and Archangel to India, from Central Asia to Egypt, not forgetting the disintegration of the international system in Europe and revolutions in Germany and Central Europe, the Great War was succeeded by five years of miscellaneous fighting, rebellions, revolutions, and other international conflicts.

These conflicts, to use a helpfully vague but comprehensive word, cannot be easily corralled into a single narration. They were too various, took place in too many geographically separate and distant places and regions, to be easily brought together, and they lasted for different periods of time. Take the greatest of the aftermath conflicts, in Russia. There were, because of the size of the country, several separate fights within it, simultaneously and successive – more than one part of the civil war happened in various places: campaigns in the Baltic lands, the North, Ukraine, the Caspian region, Siberia, all distinct fights; in addition there were Allied interventions for various purposes, and all frontiers, and invasions by those eager to cut a slice of Russian territory while they had the chance.

Very much the same complex situation developed in the dying Ottoman Empire – invasions and interventions, rebellions, civil wars, revolutions and counter-revolutions. And since Russia and the Ottoman Empire were neighbours, inevitably these internal conflicts in both countries overlapped and intersected. The interventions in this region were primarily conducted by British forces, notably the Mediterranean Fleet, and it was British forces that were involved in all the regions from Odessa to Tashkent – in Central Asia, in Iran, on the Caspian Sea, in the Caucasus, on the Black Sea, in Anatolia, on the Aegean Sea, and in the city of Constantinople.

Indeed, in many ways Constantinople was the crucial place. It was, of course, the great prize for which all combatants and interventionists had been striving, though rather more spectacular events than its quiet capture took place elsewhere. But it was the Allied capture of the great city that was the beginning of the events in the Black Sea, in Anatolia, in southern Russia, and it was the Allied interventions' withdrawal from the city that marked the end of the struggles in the whole southern region. The British interventions in Central Asia and the Caspian Sea were essentially subordinate to the events in the Black Sea, and those in the Black Sea only took place because the Allies had control of Constantinople. The interconnection of everything from the Black Sea to Central Asia was demonstrated by the appointment of a single general to oversee the whole. This was so even though events in the more distant places began before the capture of Constantinople. And the freeing of the city from foreign control brought fighting to an abrupt end in all the regions, indicating its continuing relevance.[1]

The Allied interventions had begun before the armistice with the Ottoman Empire, which was what was required to bring the Allied forces to the city, for they had not been able to reach it in four years of fighting. The original moves came from India, whose viceregal government was worried that Communist forces, seizing control of Central Asia, could well adopt a policy that had long been feared in India, of a Russian invasion of India through Afghanistan. It soon became clear, even to the quaking Indian government, that this was a fantasy, at least by comparison with its more immediate difficulties, but by then the intervention process had spread and had resulted in the disastrous encouragement of the Greek invasion of Anatolia, thus instigating what was essentially a new war. Meanwhile, Allied interventions in southern Russia in aid of selected Russian groups had come and gone.

In all this, Indian forces operated in Central Asia and in Iran, French and Italian forces in the Black Sea and Anatolia, and Greeks in the Aegean and Anatolia, but the central entity was the Royal Navy. It was the Royal Navy's Mediterranean Fleet that had the responsibility of enforcing the armistice with the Ottoman Empire, and this brought it into the Black Sea and its intervention in the Russian Civil War. This became linked with existing interventions in the Caspian Sea and Central Asia (both on a small scale), and once the Royal Navy arrived in the Black Sea, all these were automatically linked together because of its presence and because of perceived British interests. So, although the intervention in Central Asia was promoted from India, and that into the Caspian Sea from Iraq, and that at the Black Sea from the Mediterranean, they were all part of one pattern, and all failed of effect at more or less the same time.

The armistice made with the Ottoman Empire turned out to be very difficult to enforce. The Turks, like the Germans, Austrians, Hungarians, Italians, and many other nations, were disappointed and angry when the fighting ended, feeling they had made large enough 'sacrifices' that they deserved more from the peace – more rewards, more land, more loot, and more opportunities to win more territory. It was not only Germany that was to use the French term coined to describe the similar reaction in France to defeat in 1871 – *revanche*. Only the three main winners in the fighting, France, Britain and the United States, armed with fleets of battleships and prestige, could feel some satisfaction at the result, though any satisfaction was heavily disguised beneath their own griefs, costs, and losses.

Those countries who were annoyed at the result may have superficially accepted the peace, and then signed the peace treaties, but did so in most cases with the mental reservation that they would succeed next time. For it is clear that most of the defeated states looked forward to another fight; it is a truism now that the Second World War was a continuation of the Great War.

One of the countries that was defeated was the Ottoman Empire. It went through as traumatic a time as any country involved in the Great War, and more so than most. Its enemies began to seize territory from it even before the armistice was agreed, to the extent that they aimed at the destruction of the empire and a division of the Turkish homeland between them. Unlike the rest of the defeated states, however, it managed to insist on a new peace treaty to replace the original treaty; that is, to renegotiate a replacement treaty, this time on equal terms. This is undoubtedly one of the reasons it was able to settle down to avoid involvement in the second round of fighting twenty years later. And that renegotiation came out of the activities of the Turkish revolution and its conflict with the Royal Navy, the central event of which was the Allied seizure of Constantinople/Istanbul.

In tackling this subject, which had so many aspects, centres, and regions involved, therefore, some difficult issues arise. Several geographical areas saw military or naval action of various sorts, and all actively overlapped at times. The Black Sea, from the navy's point of view, entered the issue on 10 November 1918 (see Chapter 1). With the presence there of potentially hostile ships and forces, and with the navy sending major forces there, from battleships to submarines, together with Allied contingents and later also sections of the army, this area necessarily commanded attention. But that was also the date when the Turkish–Allied armistice came into effect, whose terms were almost immediately violated by the Allies, and that was the beginning of the growth of Turkish anger. So, while the navy was operating in the Black Sea, the Turks were developing their revival and their determination to resist the punitive peace treaty they saw coming. And this took place in interior Anatolia, out of reach of the navy, and effectively, as it proved, beyond the reach of the army and the Allies as well. Indeed, for long it happened without the knowledge of outsiders.

The activity in the Black Sea was first directed towards Russia and its problems, and this lasted until the end of the Russian conquest of Ukraine and Crimea in 1921. By that time, the crisis with Turkey was fully under way, and this lasted until the settlement of the Chanak part of the crisis in 1922, and the disaster at Smyrna in the same year. It then continued, diminuendo, until the new peace treaty, the Treaty of Lausanne, was agreed in 1923; only then did the navy leave the Black Sea and Constantinople.

The events concerning Russia and Turkey were therefore two of the major elements in the overall situation. The third and fourth are linked with these but more closely with each other, and had become active a year before the navy moved into the Black Sea. That which began earliest was the intervention in Central Asia, paradoxically the most distant region from the centre of these events, which was at Constantinople. When it became clear that the revolution in Russia was producing internal chaos, that is, after the Bolshevik coup in November 1917 ('the October Revolution'), the British intervened.

Early in 1918, two British expeditions – to use a rather grand expression for the small forces involved – began to move through Persian territory towards the Caucasus, the Caspian Sea, and Central Asia. These adventures started at different times and lasted different lengths of time, but are linked in that they, like the naval move into the Black Sea, were part of the British intervention in response to the Russian Revolution. The British presence in Central Asia ended in 1919 with its attention having been distracted towards the events in Afghanistan; in the Caucasus and the Caspian they lasted rather longer. By 1921, they were out of the Caspian and the Caucasus as well as Central Asia.

But we may begin the whole complex story with the voyage of a lone British destroyer to Constantinople, a guinea pig (if a ship may be so described) to see if the passage was cleared of mines and the Turkish and German forces along the shores were willing to be peaceful. It was not actually the first Allied 'force' to make the voyage, but it was the decisive one, for the ship did not sink. It is curious that the ship was called *Shark*, and that it was sent through the Dardanelles essentially as bait, to see if the way was clear for larger – and more valuable – ships. It must have been the first time and perhaps the last, that a shark was used as bait.

Part I

Seizing the City

It will, from the introduction, have been clear already that this is a complex story, politically and geographically, but the essential basis was the occupation of Constantinople by the Allied forces, and in particular by the British, whose army, navy, and eventually air force, constituted the greater part of the Allies in the city. This is the subject therefore of this first part.

There were two elements. The first is typified by the lone voyage of the destroyer *Shark* through the Straits to see if the way was clear and safe, and the second was the arrival of the massive, threatening, naval forces off the city, and the city's subsequent occupation. These are the subjects of the two chapters in this part.

Chapter 1

Shark as Bait

On 10 November 1918, the small British destroyer *Shark*, captained by Lieutenant Stuart Bonham-Carter, sailed slowly through the Dardanelles and into the Sea of Marmara. The ship was the first Allied vessel, apart from some clandestine submarines, to make such a voyage since 1915, when mines and shore-based artillery sank or severely damaged several battleships in the fleet attack aimed at capturing Constantinople. *Shark*, commissioned only four months before, and having had only a brief period of working up during the voyage from Britain to the Mediterranean, had been part of the recent attack on Durazzo in the Adriatic – claimed as a decisive Allied victory, but only so with extreme and disturbingly inaccurate optimism.[1] It had then been sent into the Aegean, to the Allied naval headquarters at Mudros on the island of Lemnos.[2] Its new task in the Straits was, in fact, to act as bait, in order to test if the recently agreed armistice made between the Allies and the Ottoman Empire was actually holding, and that it was being respected by the Ottomans – trust between enemies was in very short supply. It is not known if using a ship called *Shark* as bait produced any comments on board, but it is odds-on that the British sailors' inextinguishable black humour was fully engaged on the issue.

Shark was to check if the various enemy forces around the Straits and the Sea of Marmara were still actively hostile or not, and if the passage through the Straits was usable by bigger ships. The passage through the Dardanelles had been heavily protected by fortifications for the last four years (and for centuries before), and it was notoriously heavily mined. This is what had sunk three battleships in the great failed naval attack in March 1915. Some of the mines had certainly been cleared, but the crew was hardly confident that the passage was wholly clear. In fact, mine clearing went on for months after the armistice. There was undoubtedly a high degree of nervousness in the ship; as many men as possible were no doubt out on deck, rigged in their life jackets, and with lifeboats swung out and ready, the more easily for them to escape if a mine was struck.

Some efforts had been made, both by the Turks and the British, to ensure a safe passage for *Shark* through the Straits and the sea. The Gallipoli peninsula had now been occupied by Allied land forces, Indian soldiers and British Marines, so achieving the task for which had they had fought in 1915. Part of the Asian coast opposite had been taken over also. The artillery posts had therefore, very largely if not entirely, been seized and occupied by those Allied forces. But one could never be sure that an enraged Turk with a gun at his disposal might not fire. Almost point-blank artillery fire had been another Ottoman method – the decisive method, in fact – in preventing passage by the Allied ships. And there were other enemies than the Turks to be wary of.

From Mudros, *Shark* sailed east around the southern end of the Gallipoli peninsula, past Cape Helles, then north-east into the Strait – the Hellespont, or Dardanelles. The Anzac beach, halfway along the peninsula, was probably visible from the ship, and Cape Helles had been the site of the first landing and of the final evacuation from the peninsula in the failed attack in 1915–16; the crew no doubt noted the damage to the land which had been inflicted by Allied gunfire and the land fighting (some of that damage is still visible today). As the ship went on through the Narrows, where the naval attack in 1915 had finally stalled, it passed between Kilid Bahr and Çanakkale (Chanak). These were the great fortresses of the Ottomans, which had blocked the channel to hostile traffic for five centuries, and were still frowning at the ship from either flank. Only one fleet had fought its way through the Strait past these forts since the Ottoman capture of Constantinople in 1453 – Admiral Sir John Duckworth's expedition in 1807. (This had been recalled in the planning in 1914, fruitlessly, since it was wrongly assumed that naval warfare had so decisively changed in the intervening century that the lessons of Duckworth's visit could be ignored. The Turkish tactics proved them wrong; in fact, his fleet was subject to artillery bombardment just as the battleships of 1915, with rather less serious results, though Duckworth did lose two ships.)

Shark proceeded slowly, in part because the adverse current was strong – several knots – and also because the passage had been strewn with mines ever since 1914, and a recent sweep by Allied ships, and one by the Turks, to clear the channel may not have been fully successful. Some mines had broken loose and the swift current brought them quite unexpectedly through the Straits, where they could collide with any ship. In addition, *Shark* would also be passing close to those occupied artillery posts, which had been manned by Turkish soldiers who had been fighting for four years; and there were plenty of German and Austrian soldiers still in Turkey, neither of whose countries had yet signed an armistice, still less made peace.

The Turks had agreed to an armistice twelve days before, but no one on the Allied side was confident that all the Turkish units had been informed of this, nor that they, as Muslims, would necessarily respect a truce made with Christian states. The previous sultan-caliphs, after all, had pronounced that the Great War was a *jihad*. For the Germans and Austrians there was no reason, other than respect for the Turkish armistice, in which they had had no part, to hold their fire, and this might not be enough. Germans, Austrians, and Turks had been fighting the Allies for four years, and many individual soldiers did not feel that they had really been defeated. Enemy resentment at the sight of these Allied ships sailing through the Dardanelles might explode into violence.

Then there was the destination of the ship: Constantinople, the Great City, the Turkish capital, the object of numerous attacks for the last 1,600 years, only two of which had succeeded.[3] The city had recently been bombed from the air by Allied aircraft, an experience guaranteed to promote futile anger in the victims, as it had in London and Paris and Germany, and this anger might well be vented on any Allied soldier or sailor in sight. Even German and Austrian soldiers were subject to contempt and attack by Turks, despite being Ottoman allies, because they were Christians, and therefore infidels. The city had suffered through what had been in effect an Allied siege for the past four years, with seaborne access prevented by the Allied blockade at the Dardanelles, and by a Russian blockade at the Bosporos, and this had been tightened in the past year.[4] Trade had ended in the harbour, which was now normally empty of ships, apart from fishing boats harvesting the fish in the Straits and the Sea of Marmara, and other ships daring the enemy submarines and seaplanes and the blockade. Shortage of food in the city had been a constant problem throughout the war. The tension caused by hunger and fear had led to riots and lynchings, and to attacks on buildings belonging to Allied people and firms; neither were Germans and Austrians, who were obviously Christian Western Europeans, exempt from Turkish anger.[5]

The news of the armistice had helped to calm things down, but possibly not quite enough, and whereas there was relief at the end of the fighting, there was no immediate respite from the hunger and privation. *Shark* carried a group of Allied soldiers, officers and their guards, who were going to the city to arrange the practical details of the armistice – that is, those precise details were not yet settled, and had still to be negotiated. No one envied them their mission. There was a good deal of uncertainty all round.

The coasts of the Sea of Marmara, for example, were still under Turkish control. So the ship had to navigate its way slowly along the Dardanelles waterway, against the strong current, never certain that an unswept mine was not waiting for it, and the crew never certain that an angry Turk or German or Austrian with an anxious and nervous trigger finger would not be desperate or infuriated enough at being defeated to break the truce, and not at all sure what sort of a welcome the ship would receive at the city.

Shark had therefore been sent ahead to see if it was safe to sail to the city. If it was not safe, the earliest the ship would learn of this was when it was fired on, or when it struck a mine, no doubt hearing the cheers of enemy observers as it sank. None of these fates actually happened. Since the demining of the Strait and the sea had not been completed, it was therefore in part by luck and vigilance that the ship got through undamaged.

The army and navy officers were delivered to the city, and the ship returned immediately through the Straits to the Allied General Headquarters at Mudros. By the time it arrived, an armistice with Germany had also been signed, and the ship was sent back again to Constantinople, no doubt with this extra news, more officers, and new instructions. By that time, it had been through the Straits three times, without suffering any incident. It should therefore be safe for the fleet to follow; the bait had not caught anything.[6] But its role in advance of the fleet was not yet over.

This to and fro was fairly typical of the operations of destroyers in the war. They were often used as messengers or as scouts, just as *Shark* was acting in both roles in October and November 1918. (The ship had sailed to three different ports in the Aegean between 10 and 28 October on various purposes, so sailing to Constantinople was, in a sense, just another of those journeys.) The ship remained in the Straits and the Black Sea region for the next two months before returning to Malta for three weeks in dry dock. In that first visit it went, apart from to Constantinople, to the Gulf of Ismid, a bay off the Sea of Marmara to the east, but still close to Constantinople. This became the anchorage for the British ships when they arrived; this preliminary visit was to check on the bay's suitability.

Shark was then joined by the destroyer *Tribune*, and the two ships went through the Bosporos into the Black Sea and visited Russian Sevastopol in Crimea. They separated: *Shark* sailed west and called at the city of Odessa and the naval base city of Nikolayev (now Mykolaiev) in Ukraine, *Tribune* went eastwards to inspect the ports there, including Novorossiisk; between them, they had therefore inspected all the Russian Black Sea coast. All of these visits – it was, more or less, business as usual for the two ships – amounted to an advance survey of the region that the Allied navies and armies were to be interested in and concerned with in the next four years and more. But they were also bait, in case some hostile forces were still active.

The armistice that *Shark* was testing on its initial voyages through the Dardanelles and into the Black Sea was actually a failure. Though it led on to a peace treaty (the Treaty of Sèvres), it did not lead to a durable peace. By the time the treaty was concluded, there were two Turkish governments: the sultan's in Constantinople, and the Republicans' in Anatolia. The punitive conditions of the armistice were rejected by an insurrectionary Turkish Republican government in Anatolia even before the peace was agreed; it was accepted by the government of the sultan only under Allied armed pressure. The treaty as negotiated was therefore also rejected and denounced by that Anatolian government, which by then controlled most of continental (Asian) Turkey. A new negotiation had to be conducted, which finally reached a new agreement in 1923 in the Treaty of Lausanne – one that was much less harsh, and that lasted.

On top of that, there was the Russian Civil War, which was in fact the main reason for the Allied fleets' presence in the Black Sea, it being assumed that the Turkish armistice meant that the Turks were defeated and crushed. The Russian problem occupied much Allied attention in the Black Sea for the next two years and more. The presence of large numbers of German and Austrian soldiers all through southern Russia and in Turkey and beyond, who were essentially trapped in enemy territory, was a further complication. The British involvement in Persia and in the Caspian Sea and Central Asia, already in operation, provided an even more exotic set of sideshows. Then there were the difficulties of working with Britain's allies – France, Italy,

Greece – not to mention the regime in India, as awkward as any; and the United States, which had not been at war with the Ottoman Empire, but its ships joined in as well. Not all of these were naval problems, of course, but the whole region was in effect a single huge tangle of difficulties that turned out to be the responsibility of the British government and its forces to sort out.

This is hardly an untold story, though too often it is considered in its separate geographical parts, and very rarely is the activity of the Royal Navy discussed; other Allied navies were, fairly briefly, also present in the Black Sea. Much of the activity between 1918 and 1923 took place on land, to be sure, but the Royal Navy was deeply involved in events in the Aegean, in the Black Sea, and in the Caspian, and these adventures had their effects on the affairs of Central Asia. Yet little is ever described of the navy's activities in these areas, even though its presence was central to the events from Central Asia to the Aegean, and Anatolia; these, of course, can be, and are, all discussed separately, but the involvement of the Royal Navy in all these places provides a clear link between them. The Royal Navy, of course, did not become involved until the Straits were open – which *Shark* showed to be the case in November 1918. The British, however, had already been involved in Central Asia, in the Caspian Sea and the Caucasus for some time, coming from a different direction, before the ships got involved in the Black Sea. The Great War was over in Western Europe, at least the fighting, but it continued in the east; this, of course, is why the navy's role has been largely ignored.[7]

Yet it is impossible to compose an account of all these areas and events without taking each area in turn; they affected each other, but rarely directly. So here, as elsewhere, they have to be described separately, though I have attempted to indicate any links that can be seen.

First, then, the Black Sea, where the situation the Royal Navy faced on its arrival was as complex as was the wider political situation. To appreciate the situation in the Black Sea in 1919 it is necessary to consider in outline the naval warfare in the region since 1914, for the real naval problem in 1918 was the Russian fleet. Then, once that issue had been resolved, if it ever could be, a host of other problems presented themselves.

When the Ottoman Empire went to war against Imperial Russia in October 1914, it did so by means of two German ships, the battlecruiser

Goeben and the cruiser *Breslau*, which had escaped from British pursuit in the Mediterranean to take refuge at Constantinople, then a neutral port. It was not that the Germans bounced Turkey into the war by using these ships, which were given to the Ottomans soon after arriving, though the German crews, wearing red fezzes, remained on board to man them as pseudo-Turkish sailors. It was more a decision by the Young Turk government to join in before Germany won in the fighting in France, and so after reaping the available spoils; yet stalemate and trench warfare had already settled in by then – the Young Turks' timing was bad.

The naval attacks by the Turks on several Russian ports in the Black Sea took place without a declaration of war. And, as such decisions do, this beginning led inevitably on to a wider war in all the countries around the Black Sea. The fighting there over the next years gradually went against the aggressor, though the Russian effort collapsed when the revolution came in March 1917.

On the first day, 29 October, the *Goeben*, the most powerful ship in the region, bombarded Sevastopol and *Breslau* bombarded Novorossiisk; the Turkish cruiser *Hamidiye* fired at Yalta and Theodosia in Crimea; other Turkish ships attacked Odessa. Other targets in the next months included Poti in the Caucasus region. After all this, war was, of course, soon declared, but the joint operations by Turkish and German ships demonstrate that Turkish participation was very willing from the start. The Russian reaction to this hardly unexpected attack was to send their own ships to bombard several places on the Anatolian coast, from Batumi in the Caucasus region to the coal port of Zonguldak, which supplied Constantinople. Above all, Constantinople was the Russian target; the northern entrance to the Bosporos was mined (less than successfully) and attacked repeatedly for the next three years; the main aim, of course, was to bring pressure on the Turkish government in the city.[8]

This was a war that was largely detached from the great land fighting in Russia and France, and even from the war in Syria; the Allied attack on the Gallipoli peninsula was the great exception to this. No other power had access to the Black Sea, or had ships big or powerful enough to become involved. It took place in what was, in effect, almost a closed area. A few British submarines penetrated to the Sea of Marmara, as did a few German boats (mainly by way of the Danube). They used their position to mount attacks on the Russian Black Sea Fleet, and on the Allied ships in the Aegean. But until 1918, no outside power managed to join in this fighting on any serious scale. The Russian ships could not get out of the sea because the Bosporos remained under strict Turkish control; the Turks could not receive reinforcements, other than some German submarines, because the Allies' blockade prevented access to the Dardanelles. They could, however, receive munitions by the railway, and by barge along the Danube, at least once Serbia had been defeated and the railway and the river route reopened. The advantage in the naval contest eventually went to Russia, who had more and better ships than the Ottoman Empire, had the shipbuilding capacity in the Black Sea dockyards to build new ships, and produced more and better sailors and ships' commanders to man them. Yet by 1916, when Russian naval superiority was established, it was really too late for the Black Sea contest to have any real effect on the rest of the war. That superiority did translate into a Russian ability to invade continental Turkey by the Caucasus route, but the only worthwhile Turkish target was Constantinople.

Eventually, had the war gone on long enough, the construction yards at Sevastopol and Nikolayev, which completed three dreadnought battleships during the war, could also have produced a large enough fleet so that the Russians could overwhelm the Turkish Navy, but the revolution in Russia came first, and crippled both the fleet and the dockyard. Attacks on their enemies by both sides, of varying efficiency and effectiveness, continued while the wider war ground on, but then stopped during 1917. Both navies retained the use of their major ships throughout the last two years of the war, and the Turks could also deploy German U-boats.

The war in the Black Sea had thus gradually changed. A version of the pre-war arms race set in, with the naval balance swinging from one side to the other, with the brief advantages of new and greater vessels, or with the arrival of extra ships. Yet none of these developments were decisive enough to bring an end. For two years, until late in 1916, the *Goeben* and the *Breslau* had given the Turkish Navy an edge most of the time over the Russian threat. The *Goeben*, a battlecruiser with ten powerful guns, was more powerful and faster than any of the Russian pre-dreadnought battleships of their 1914 Black Sea Fleet, but the Russian battleships were more numerous; it was thus a stand-off among the great ships. The war therefore effectively developed into one of raids by each side. The Russians attempted to interrupt the coal trade from Zonguldak which kept Constantinople and its industries going and its supply ships and naval vessels moving; they also repeatedly mined the Turkish harbours and the northern entrance to the Bosporos. The Turks mounted far fewer raids than the Russians did, especially after the two ex-German ships were both damaged by mines. The arrival of two, then two more, German U-boats tilted the balance slightly in the Turkish favour, but they were, like most submarines, often ineffective, and as raiders menacing the land they were scarcely useful.

During 1916, however, two new Russian dreadnoughts were completed in the building yards at Nikolayev. The *Imperatritsa Mariya* and *Imperatritsa Ekaterina* were battleships, powerful vessels but less speedy than the *Goeben*, which could escape a meeting by running away – and of course, the shooting by all the ships, German and Russian, was normally abysmal. Nevertheless, the threat of the new battleships, together with *Goeben*'s own damage from the mines, which proved to be very difficult to repair, moved the naval balance back into Russia's favour. This was also a result of the Russians having a group of large, fast, and well-handled destroyers, and of the Russians' clever use of seaplanes, which were carried into battle on two converted ships, a yacht and a liner.

No decision was to be expected in the Black Sea contest, despite the shifting balance, in part because neither side was able to strike a heavy enough blow at the enemy, nor establish an effectively decisive advantage to suppress the enemy. In this, it was not dissimilar to the much larger situation in the North Sea. Had the war in the Black Sea continued for another year, the Russian dockyards might have completed more ships – there were several awaiting completion in the yards at Nikolayev, and, if they could have been manned and the crews properly trained, Russian control of the sea would have become decisively established – but this is a lot of 'ifs'. As it was, the coal trade from Zonguldak was reduced to using small sailing ships guarded against Russian attacks by the *Goeben* – an extraordinary, even ludicrous, partnership. When the situation in the city became too difficult to bear, an even more extreme expedient was adopted: the Germans were persuaded to send daily trains, each carrying 400 tons of coal, from Germany to Constantinople by rail. This could only be done because Serbia had been conquered, and so from late 1915, the drain of German resources was thereby considerable. Even so, less than half of Turkish coal requirements could be supplied in this way.

The stalemate in the sea was broken late in 1917, first by the Bolshevik seizure of power in Russia, which entailed an internal disruption of the Russian Black Sea Fleet, then with the German–Russian peace treaty signed at Brest-Litovsk on 3 March 1918. This in theory ended the war in the eastern theatre. In the year between these events, the command system of the Russian armed forces collapsed as officers were murdered or fled or deserted, or men simply went home. The Black Sea Fleet became partly immobilised in its harbours, thereby returning command of the sea once more to the Turks.

After the Treaty of Brest-Litovsk, in April 1918 German forces began moving into Ukraine, which had been made independent in the treaty. A Ukrainian government, the Directorate, had seized power under German auspices, and declared Ukraine an independent state, though its capabilities and authority were distinctly limited. The fleet at Sevastopol was not at all pleased at this; many of the sailors remained loyal to Russia. A group of fourteen destroyers and four supply ships reacted to being told that the ships were now Ukrainian by leaving Sevastopol for the port and naval base at Novorossiisk, where a pro-Russian authority, the local Soviet, was in precarious control.[9]

German forces arrived at Sevastopol on 1 May, rather earlier than expected. (Crimea had constituted itself independent of both Ukraine and Russia in the meantime.) Orders had been given by the Bolshevik government in Moscow to sink the remaining ships of the Black Sea Fleet, but the speed of the German arrival disrupted these plans. The German forces occupied the north shore of the harbour and set up guns and machine guns to threaten the ships on the opposite shore. Only one battleship, *Imperator Aleksandr III*, recently renamed *Volya*, got away to Novorossiisk unscathed. The other dreadnought, *Imperatritsa Ekaterina III*, renamed *Svobodnaya Rossiya*, was damaged by German gunfire, but then also got away.[10] The new Ukrainian Navy was reduced, even as it was initiated, to only four destroyers, one of which soon ran onshore and was then blown up.

The German command demanded that the ships at Novorossiisk be returned to Sevastopol, but Admiral Sablin, who had been promoted by the fleet to the local command, ran up the imperial flag in defiance, thus indicating separation from the Germans, the Moscow government, the Ukrainian government, the Crimean government, and the local Soviet in Novorossiisk, all of whom sought to govern in the city. The German commander threatened to march on Novorossiisk, and did in fact occupy Crimea as far as the Kertch peninsula, but no further. In Moscow, the Bolshevik government demanded that the ships be scuttled, but left the decision to the sailors, who refused. Eventually, after much discussion, it was decided that half the ships – *Volya* and six destroyers, would return to Sevastopol; the damaged *Svobodnaya Rossiya* was then sunk by torpedo fire, and the remaining ships, mainly destroyers, were scuttled.

A good deal of this change and upheaval became known almost at once to the Allies. As early as January 1918, the possibility of a German seizure of the Russian ships had been suggested by the Mediterranean commander-in-chief, Vice-Admiral Arthur Gough-Calthorpe. It was not, however, until the beginning of April 1918, when the Brest-Litovsk treaty was executed, that it was understood that German sailors – seven trains' full – were being sent to take control in Sevastopol. For the next two months the British and French sent information, conjectures, and suggestions to each other about what would or might happen, and what each thought should be done about it. Some reinforcements were sent to boost the Aegean fleet, including the French battleship *Vérité*, but the confusion in the Russian fleet reduced the energy and urgency of Allied preparations – not to mention the Allies' inability to reach the Black Sea.

The Germans were using seaplanes to watch Novorossiisk, and *Goeben* and *Breslau* came out to investigate Sevastopol at one point. But it was obvious that the ships at Sevastopol had fallen at first into Ukrainian hands, and that in effect meant the Germans would control them. There was a clear danger that, manned by the German officers and crews who had been sent in those seven trains to Russia, together with such Turkish ships as were available and armed, the ex-Russian ships could venture a raid through the Straits. *Goeben* and *Breslau* had done so in February 1918, though without any success, and had both suffered damage in the process. The potential strength of the force under German control was considerable, though the calculations varied with the news from Russia; in July, it was believed that such a force could consist of one battlecruiser (*Goeben*, when it was repaired), one dreadnought (*Volya*), three or four pre-dreadnought battleships, four cruisers (including *Breslau*, if it could be made fit), and some of the very effective Russian destroyers. (The torpedo boats and German submarines that had been sent to Turkey earlier were ignored.) It was not a particularly formidable force, and the Allies at Mudros had obviously greater power, but in the German raid through the Dardanelles, the Allied commander had let the two ships get out without his knowledge, which showed that the Aegean blockade command had become careless and lazy. Furthermore, the ex-Russian ships while at Novorossiisk had been cleaned up, refuelled, and fully maintained, and so had been brought to an efficient condition when they had been sent to Sevastopol, unlike those that had remained in the docks there. The Turkish armistice of October 1918 had no effect on all this; *Goeben*, if capable of sailing, could easily be retransferred to German possession. (The ship was being repaired at Sevastopol, and so was effectively already in German hands.)[11]

That no raids against the Allied forces occurred during these months of Russian paralysis was partly due to Russian resistance to German plans, to the deterioration in the condition of the ships while being held at Sevastopol, and to the discontent and desertion of the Russian sailors. The German high command was also preoccupied with their attempt to break the Allied line in France, and then, after 8 August, in attempting to avoid defeat. In the Black Sea region, therefore, the German intervention had left a condition of rich confusion. It was a situation that the Allies partly solved and partly compounded.

The Russian Black Sea Fleet, which had been moderately successful in the first two and a half years of the war, had thus fragmented. A part was at Sevastopol, under effective German control, but in bad condition and undermanned; a similar part was at Novorossiisk, in better condition, but under exactly whose control had become unclear; a third part had been scuttled. All this reduced the fleet to impotence by early 1918, and the presence of the German command in Crimea did not improve matters. But the ships were there, and were at least a potential force. The armistice brought the problem into the Allies' lap.

This, therefore, was the situation that was confirmed or revealed by the inspection voyages of *Shark* and *Tribune* in November 1918. The potential for hostilities was clearly considerable, though who would be fighting who was scarcely known. There were Turkish, German, Ukrainian, Russian revolutionary, and Russian monarchist forces at various places, not to mention the confused situation in the Caucasus region, where British intervention was already involved. But the first necessity was to ensure that the Turkish and German armistices were effective.

Chapter 2

Armistice – and Control of the City

The war in the Near East closed down item by item. First, Bulgaria asked for an armistice when the Allied forces broke out of the pocket of territory they had occupied at Salonika for over two years. Then victories in Syria and Mesopotamia resulted in British conquests in the Fertile Crescent as far as the southern mountainous edge of Anatolia. Then, late in October, the Ottoman government began negotiations for an armistice. Fairly soon, Allied fleets were casting anchor off Constantinople. The whole process took about two months. It was, of course, much less straightforward than this summary suggests.

On 15 September 1918, two months before *Shark* became the first Allied ship to sail directly through the Straits, the Allied forces that had been marooned at Salonika in northern Greece for two years moved to attack the Bulgarian defence line just north of the city. The Allies involved were mainly French soldiers, with a large British contingent, a Serbian army made up of refugee soldiers who had escaped the conquest of the country in 1916, and Greeks as well. The Greeks had gained the city of Salonika and its surroundings in the Balkan Wars; the Serbs and the Bulgarians had also wanted it. To all three of these Balkan states, the Great War was just another Balkan war, following on from the two previous wars in 1912–13 (and several others over the previous century). Fighting against Bulgars was highly congenial to both Greeks and Serbs; doing so with French and British help was a bonus. The Bulgars had German and Austrian 'advisers' with them.

The Bulgar defence line was heavily fortified in the Great War style, with trenches, barbed wire entanglements, interlocking machine-gun fire points, and heavy artillery zeroed in on choice targets. It had proved in the past to be a very tough line to penetrate; even now, with the Bulgars weary and despondent, it was difficult to break, but after two or three days the Allies were making progress. The French forces were commanded by General Franchet d'Espèrey, who was also commander-in-chief of the whole Allied force.

As usual, the attack against such strong defences was expensive in lives, yet after a week the Allies broke through, and by 29 September, after a fortnight's fighting, they captured the city of Skopje, where the German headquarters had been shortly before. The advance had been assisted by a large mutiny in the Bulgar army, a symptom of the Bulgar demoralisation that had already been evident in the trench fighting. A republican revolution in the country had also been attempted, and there was the beginnings of a popular rising in Serbia against the Austrian occupation – but the military breakthrough came first, and the other events followed from it. On 30 September, a Bulgar delegation arrived at Salonika to request an armistice. On the Western Front, General Ludendorff announced to his government that he had not troops to spare to combat the new offensive by the Allies in the Balkans and advised seeking a truce.[1]

Two days after the Salonika attack began, the British imperial army in Palestine launched an attack on the Turkish defences at the river Auja, just north of the small coastal port of Jaffa. The Allied forces in the line here were mainly Indian and British. Most of the British troops had been transferred to the Western Front when the major German attack in March had been expected; Indian units replaced them. A hole was neatly punched in the Turkish line by a silent night-time infantry attack, and then the cavalry poured through, in a classic example of the exploitation of victory. It was the Indian infantry that made the breakthrough; the cavalry was mainly Australian; General Sir Edmund Allenby, the commander in the theatre, believed in horses for courses.

The cavalry moved rapidly through northern Palestine and by 1 October, when the Bulgarian armistice took effect, Damascus was captured. A section of the British cavalry then moved on through the Bekaa Valley of Lebanon with only minimal opposition. They had either captured or scattered most of the organised enemy forces in Palestine, and north of Damascus there were mainly reserve troops and administrative men; the attackers rapidly moved on into north Syria. A French force landed from the sea to seize Lebanon as part of the French spoils from the victory. By 11 October, Tripoli was taken, and on the 26th, Aleppo was occupied, after a fight lasting several days. It was an advance of 400 kilometres in five weeks.[2]

At Aleppo, however, the recovering and reinforced Turkish forces withdrew from the city in good order, and took up a new and strong position at Haritan

(Katma to the Turks) only a few miles to the north of the city. Carelessly over-confident British officers sent two Indian cavalry regiments to attack, horsemen against machine guns. They reached the Turkish positions, but were then driven back, with casualties on both sides; a second attack was called off after the colonel of the regiment and his second-in-command were both killed by sniper fire. The disingenuous explanation later was that this was a probe, not an attack. The dead colonel and his equally dead second-in-command ought by now to have known better.

The commander of the force on the Turkish side was General Mustafa Kemal, who had made his military reputation by his command of a division in the fierce Turkish resistance to the Gallipoli invasion three years before, and he would soon be heard of again in only a slightly different context. Haritan was a British defeat (not usually taken note of in British histories, of course), which stopped any further northward advance in its tracks; however, the Turkish position in Palestine and Syria had been destroyed.[3]

The fighting at Aleppo and Haritan took place in the last few days of October. In the Balkans, the mainly French army, buoyed by the Bulgar armistice, drove north from Salonika into Serbia to attack the Austro-Hungarian army. By 30 October, the French and the Serbians reached the Danube, and across the river was Hungary and the Austro-Hungarian Empire. By this time, that empire was disintegrating into its constituent nationalist parts. What was left of the Austrian government asked for an armistice on 3 November.

In between these events, on 30 October, the Ottoman Empire also accepted an armistice. And then there was only one: Germany was left fighting alone. From Salonika, in addition to the main thrust to liberate Serbia and attack Austria-Hungary, a small Allied force had moved east to threaten Constantinople, but did not get very far, being held up by Turkish forces at the Turkish/Bulgar frontier, the Maritza River. This was a mainly British force, commanded by General Sir George Milne. They had occupied the Bulgarian part of Thrace and were poised to move into Turkish Thrace. The Turks could see what was coming, as their allies, Bulgaria and Austria-Hungary, collapsed, and then that the British imperial forces were ranging victoriously through Syria and others advanced in Mesopotamia; they could see that the next Allied victory would be the capture of Constantinople; they wanted to avoid that if at all possible future.

In the city the Ottoman government, which had conducted the Ottoman war, slowly crumbled, and the Young Turk leaders escaped retribution by fleeing in a German submarine. A new vizier, Ahmed Izzet Pasha, took over on 14 October and there was also a new Minister of Marine, Hussein Rauf Bey. Five days later, the first contact between the new Ottoman government and the Allies took place in neutral Madrid, where the Turkish *chargé d'affaires* asked the Spanish government to ask President Woodrow Wilson of the United States to facilitate negotiations for peace. In the Aegean, General Sir Charles Townshend, captured with his army three years before in the defeat of a British–Indian army at Kut al-Amara in Mesopotamia, was released to the Greek island of Lesbos, in order to ask the Allies for their terms.[4] He was clearly well fed and well groomed, in strong contrast to his men who had been captured at the same time, who had been starved and ill-treated, and whom he had ignored ever since his capture.

Townshend's message did bring a reaction in London, and British commander-in-chief in the Mediterranean, Vice-Admiral Sir Arthur Gough-Calthorpe, was instructed to get to Mudros and conclude an armistice. The terms to be imposed had been settled between the Allies two weeks before, so Gough-Calthorpe's task was to present them, not to negotiate around them. The Turks clearly thought that their release of Townshend would be seen as indicating goodwill on their part; the British government ordered that he stay in Mudros to provide advice. There is no sign that he was able to do so, or if he did, that his advice had any effect. He was ignored otherwise.

On 27 October, an Ottoman delegation, led by the Minister of Marine Rauf Bey in person, arrived at Mudros to negotiate the armistice terms; the delegation also included a colonel from the General Staff as an indication that the army was participating, and an under-secretary from the Foreign Office. The British had made careful preparations for the meeting, though it was not to be a negotiation, since the Allied Council of War had laid out the terms clearly three weeks earlier. So the meetings were not going to be difficult, at least between Turks and British. The terms would be, in effect, unconditional surrender, and it was already clear that the Turks would accept more or less anything that the Allies proposed. As the defeated and supplicating party, the Turks were unable to change the terms in any large way.

What was just as important to the British delegation as the talks and the terms themselves, and the reason for their careful preparations, was to be able to negotiate alone, without interference from any of their allies, in particular the French. So Admiral Calthorpe, the commander-in-chief in the Eastern Mediterranean, had been forwarded from Malta to Mudros as soon as it became clear that, with the Bulgarian collapse, the Ottoman request for an armistice would soon arrive. Calthorpe was already commander-in-chief of the British Mediterranean Fleet; by contrast, the senior French officer in the Aegean was Contre-Amiral Jean François Amet, holding a rank a degree or two lower than Calthorpe. Amet had been in overall command in the Aegean for some time, under Calthorpe's fairly distant overall command; Calthorpe's sudden parachuting into his area was perceived as a hostile coup by Amet and the French government, perfectly correctly. Amet clearly expected to conduct any armistice negotiations himself, as the established Allied commander in the Aegean, though he was certainly under Calthorpe's authority, exercised from Malta.[5]

Calthorpe had adamant instructions from the British government that Amet was not to be permitted even to join in the talks, nor was he to be consulted about the terms. The stated reason was that time was of the essence and if the French took part, so must the other delegations, those of Italy and Greece, who were also at war with the Ottoman Empire. At least the United States could be excluded, since that country was not at war with the Turks. The more delegations who were involved in the negotiations, the more would be the need for one or the other, or all of them, to refer back to their home governments over various, usually minor, terms. This was especially likely to happen with those with weak forces in the area, just to emphasise their presence. All this would simply delay matters, and possibly even prevent agreement altogether. It was also necessary, at least to the British, to avoid allowing the Turks to negotiate separately, or even all together with the Allied delegations; avoidance of this, after all, had been the purpose of the prearranged set of armistice terms.

There was another reason, of course, and one which was apparently important to the British side, and that was that the British wanted to run the show by themselves, in order to claim the credit – it was a version of the *amour-propre* of the weaker groups. David Lloyd George later, in a rant at a meeting of the Council of Four (the US, France, Italy, the UK), claimed that

500,000 British troops campaigned against the Ottoman Empire; subsequently it was claimed that 1 million troops were occupied in the campaign, mainly British, and that the others were being paid for by Britain. In the Aegean there was no doubt that the volume of naval shipping continued to be British, though the largest Allied ships present were four old French battleships.

The French, of course, were annoyed. But in a sense they had started the process by sending four pre-dreadnought battleships into the Aegean in July, which gave them a temporary maritime preponderance of local naval force. The British accepted this because it was feared at the time that the Germans, who were taking over in southern Russia, either with or against the Russian revolutionaries, were acquiring control of the ships of the Russian Black Sea Fleet. They might use these ships for a raid through the Straits against the Allied ships in the Aegean – as the *Goeben* and the *Breslau* had attempted in February. Whether the French ships would have been much use in combating the Russian dreadnoughts and the German/Turkish battlecruiser *Goeben* is not clear, but the reinforcement was clearly useful. No doubt, also the French understood that their battleship strength gave them the right to command, for the moment.

When Bulgaria collapsed at the end of September, the British decided that the situation in the Aegean was no longer tolerable. The calculation was made that 75 per cent of the warships in the Mediterranean were British, even if the French had concentrated many of their ships into the Aegean, including those battleships. This overall preponderance entitled the British to conduct the approaching armistice negotiations alone, at least in their view.[6] They had also done most of the fighting on land against the Ottoman Empire (at Gallipoli, in Egypt, Palestine, Syria, Mesopotamia, and Persia), and while the calculation of numbers of soldiers involved was dubious, the land campaigns had certainly been almost exclusively British. But to make sure, Calthorpe, who had been commander-in-chief of the British forces in the Mediterranean, headquartered at Malta at the time, was sent to Mudros, and two dreadnought battleships, *Superb* and *Temeraire*, were sent out from Britain to increase the British presence at Mudros; they arrived on 20 October, soon after Calthorpe himself. These were added to the two British pre-dreadnoughts, *Agamemnon* and *Lord Nelson*, which were already there. (The French had deployed six pre-dreadnoughts in the Aegean by that time. Thus it was that the French move was trumped almost at the last minute. It was also calculated that, of the ships of the two nations in the Aegean, the British disposed of thirty, and the French only of eighteen.[7] The British arguments were held to be conclusive, at least by the British. It also shifted the argument away from Mudros and over to London and Paris.

The two countries' prime ministers, Lloyd George and Georges Clemenceau, had a fierce row on the issue. Lloyd George had made the points about the numbers of ships and troops; Clemenceau argued that the French had great investments in the Ottoman Empire and that previous agreements were being broken. It is, however, very noticeable that Calthorpe had moved from Malta as early as 8 October, travelling in the scout cruiser *Foresight* through the Corinth Canal and had called at Piraeus on the way. He was at Mudros by 11 October. Lloyd George's letter to Clemenceau explaining his position was dated the 15th; Clemenceau's reply was dated the 21st, and was translated for Lloyd George on the 25th. By this time, all the British pieces in the game were in place, and communications with the Turks had been opened. Calthorpe and the dreadnoughts were in position, and all Lloyd George had to do was to defend the achieved position, and sturdily to ignore French demands for Amet to be involved in the talks.[8]

Clemenceau's position was that the French had large investments in the pre-war Ottoman Empire, and that this economic interest should give them preponderance. Of course, if that was so, they should have been the main participants in the fighting, but it was Lloyd George's position that it was 'boots on the ground' and ships and guns in the Aegean that really counted, not to mention Calthorpe's higher rank. The French also claimed that an Italian, and perhaps even a Greek, delegation should be included since they had also been involved in fighting the Ottomans. All this the British adamantly refused to accept. The need for the delegates to refer back constantly to their home governments at all disputed points that would stretch out the talks inordinately. The British claimed that they wished to speed up the result, and being the men (and ships, and soldiers) in position on the spot, the British argument prevailed. It was, of course, clear evidence of the continuing abrasive relationship between Britain and France, which was their normal situation, despite their wartime alliance.[9]

The French position, very much a rearguard action, was that they and the Italians should join the British in the talks, but then they dropped the Italians from their demands; even so, they were again refused participation.

Calthorpe had arrived from Malta at the Piraeus on 10 October, and was at Mudros next day. He could discuss matters with General Townshend from the 20th, and Townshend was ordered from London to stay at Mudros for that very purpose, though how useful he would be is not clear. He does not seem to have been referred to or consulted at any point.

Then, when the Turkish delegation arrived on the island on 27 October, it turned out that it was accredited only to the British. This was the final blow to the already slim French chances of being directly involved. The Turks clearly knew nothing of the inter-Allied argument, but since the British had been their constant enemy for the last four years, with a much smaller French involvement, they clearly identified the British as their obvious negotiating partners. Thus inadvertently, the British plan had succeeded by the co-operation of their enemy – that is, the Turkish enemy, though the French were shaping up as another.

The French government protested, but this was again rejected. When the talks began, on the 27th, on the British pre-dreadnought battleship *Agamemnon*, Admiral Amet was present and requested that he should be included, saying he had orders to join the talks. Calthorpe showed him the Turkish delegation's credentials, accrediting them only to discuss peace with the British, and then got on with the negotiations without him. Amet tried again the next day, equally unsuccessfully. By this time, he was simply going through the motions, and can have had no hope of prevailing. This was followed by a message to Calthorpe from Marshal Ferdinand Foch, the Allied commander-in-chief, demanding that Amet be included; this Calthorpe again refused, and by then it was too late. Calthorpe repeated all this to the Admiralty, carefully including the information that Amet, had he been included, had said that he would have to refer to the French Admiralty, whereas Calthorpe evidently had the authority to negotiate without referring to London. (This only reinforced the British position, that the armistice needed to be agreed rapidly and without argument among the Allies.) The terms were agreed by 30 October. Calthorpe had in fact reported good progress on the 28th, but even then there was little more to discuss; by that point the Turks had accepted all but one of the clauses the British had tabled.[10]

Very briefly, the terms involved disarmament on the Turkish side, and the surrender or demobilisation of all Ottoman forces. In a particularly crucial clause for the future conduct of the truce, clause 7 said that strategic positions in the Ottoman Empire were to be occupied by the Allies as they chose, 'in the event of any situation arising which threatens the security of the Allies'. No places were listed in the terms, and the clause was studiously vague as to geography. Such a list was not really necessary, since other clauses insisted that ports, dockyards, anchorages, the Taurus 'tunnel system', and telegraph and cable stations, were all to come under Allied control – there was not much else that could be included. Clause 7 was apparently included for use in emergencies, which was probably how the Turks saw it – and in case anything had been missed out; it was, however, up to the Allies to define the relevant 'situation', and 'emergency', and it became the loophole through which the Allies imposed their occupation on the city of Constantinople. Allied prisoners of war were to be released, but Turkish prisoners were to be held 'at the disposal of the Allies', an obvious precaution for the victors. The terms did not insist on an Allied-friendly government being installed, but this, with all the various parts already listed in the terms, was by then hardly necessary. Whatever government existed in the Ottoman Empire would be bound by these terms.[11]

Calthorpe, who got on well with Rauf Bey, also made several oral promises, none of which were enforceable, and which Rauf Bey interpreted very much in the Turkish favour. These included that Constantinople should not be occupied, other than the dockyard, and that Greeks and Italians should not be allowed into the city. Rauf Bey triumphantly announced this when he returned to the city, claiming that the city would not be occupied by the enemy. No wonder it took only three days to reach agreement; the terms the Allies required had been drawn up well before the armistice meeting, and the Allies were not involved in debating matters between them. In turn, the Turks had been serious only about ending the fighting. But Calthorpe did insist on the Allied fleet sailing to Constantinople. The two men toasted the agreement with champagne.[12]

This was the end of a long, hard war. Bulgaria had given in, now the Ottomans, soon the Austrians, as their empire disintegrated, and a fortnight after the Armistice of Mudros, so did the Germans. In all cases, they would stop fighting, but resentfully, without really admitting defeat; none of the Central Powers was really convinced that they had been beaten, despite the military and political evidence, as well as the fact that they had each requested an armistice to prevent even more military defeats. Of course, accepting overall defeat after all the horrors and deaths of the war was exceedingly difficult. Given the delusion of non-defeat, each would soon begin looking for new opportunities to seek revenge. For the British, above all, the end of the Ottoman war had a degree of satisfaction perhaps greater than that from any other aspect of the war as a whole. For a century, the British had dithered over their policy towards the Ottoman Empire, varying between supporting it against Russian aggression and ambition, and feeling disgust at its methods of governance. Now the empire had, it was thought, collapsed, and they gradually came to the conclusion that they could do as they wished with the remains.

The Turks had fought well, usually against heavy odds, and had inflicted grievous defeats on the British Army and Royal Navy as badly as the Germans, if on a smaller scale – Gallipoli, Kut al-Amara, First and Second Gaza, and even Haritan, were undoubted and clear victories of a weaker power against a stronger. The assault on the Gallipoli peninsula had been decisively defeated; a whole British army had been defeated and forced to surrender in Mesopotamia. The war in Palestine had begun with a Turkish invasion of Egyptian Sinai, and it had then taken three hard years to drive the invaders out, and three major battles to break through their defences at Gaza on the Palestinian border – two British defeats and one victory. After entering Palestine it had taken the British another year and three major battles to drive through Palestine and Syria as far as Aleppo, and even then, the British advance force, suffering badly from malaria, had been stopped just to the north of that city, at Haritan. (The disease had been brought under control in southern Palestine, but not in the newly conquered areas.) After all this, to be hundreds of miles inside former enemy territory was very satisfying.

On the other hand, in Syria, for the British forces the Turkish armistice had arrived very opportunely; the British Army was stretched very thin by October, occupying the conquered territory from Jerusalem and Gaza to Aleppo, and much of Iraq, as well as controlling restless Egypt, where there was revolt during 1919. If the war had continued into the next year, as had been expected, a serious Turkish counter-attack might well have driven the British back to Damascus; the armistice intervened instead.

Already another dispute was brewing with the French over which territories in the Levant each victorious country would occupy. The British deliberately moved forward in Mesopotamia to ensure their control of Mosul, which was rumoured to be sitting on a lake of oil. This was in breach of an agreement which the French thought that they had made in which Mosul would be in their section – but, again, it was the British, exclusively, who had done virtually all the fighting in Mesopotamia, while in Syria, the French had contributed only one small unit, and had landed at the last minute to occupy Lebanon. (The Turks later also laid claim to Mosul.) The Arab inhabitants' interests were being pushed aside by both British and French. The Arab contribution to the victory had been more considerable in the press, and reputation and rumour than effective in the field. Advocacy of their cause by Lawrence 'of Arabia' could be brushed aside without difficulty.

The armistice allowed the British to keep their conquests in Palestine and Mesopotamia; the defeat in Mesopotamia had been avenged, and the British Army had taken the great Muslim capitals of Baghdad and Damascus, and now Mosul, and the greatest prize of all for the Western Europeans, Jerusalem. They had therefore marked out more choice territory for the British Empire, to be secured in the peace treaty that would, it was assumed, soon follow the armistice. The French might hanker after Mosul, but they did secure Syria.

In terms of the overall war, however, neither the conquest of Mesopotamia nor that of Syria-Palestine was decisive, pleasant though these victories were. When both of these areas had been conquered, the two British armies had then faced the prospect of invading Anatolia, the Turkish homeland, where the fighting would be in the mountains, and against men defending their homes. Any soldier with imagination could see that this would be an infinitely more difficult task than that in Syria or Mesopotamia. The end of the fighting in Syria had seen the Turkish army ready and willing to fight the debilitated and stretched British advance force at Haritan, and other Ottoman forces were no longer needed to fight the Russians; the Russian collapse had enabled the Turks to recover territory in the Caucasus and to extend their conquests beyond their original boundary. There would be new Ottoman armies to fight. The armistice came just in time.

It was equally satisfactory to the British to shut out the French, allowing them only northern Syria, without Mosul. The French, however, aimed to gain Cilicia, and as much of southern Anatolia as they could seize. The blocking of the British advance force at Haritan, right at the end of the Syrian fighting, and the memories of other Turkish victories, meant that the British were quite relieved to cease their Syrian offensive. The French meanwhile had already landed forces in Lebanon and were occupying 'their' allocated section of Syria, which was a stretch of land along the Mediterranean coast.

In addition, the Italians had ambitions to gain control of the Anatolian mainland adjacent to their conquests of the Dodecanese Islands, and had tentatively marked out the coast from Antalya to Smyrna as their 'share'. And there were the Greek ambitions as well.

But the greatest item of satisfaction for all the Allies was still to come. It took a few days after the conclusion of the armistice at Mudros for the British, the French, the Italians, and the Turks to be in agreement, but by 10 November, the next step – for the British, the really satisfying one – was about to happen. One of the terms of the armistice (clause 1, in fact, the one over which the Turks had been initially in some doubts) was that naval access for the Allies to the Dardanelles and Constantinople was to be permitted. After four years of war, almost to the day, the Royal Navy was at last about to sail through the Dardanelles in force. Hence, the preliminary voyage of the destroyer *Shark* through the Dardanelles that day.

Shark's delegation of officers, however, was not the first Allied group to reach to Constantinople. At least one Allied group of officers had been sent through to the city earlier. Lieutenant Colonel C.C.R. Murphy had travelled extensively in the Middle East before and during the war, with what he called an 'amphibious staff appointment', in Persia, Mesopotamia, Oman, Palestine, and even in Crimea.[13] He was the ideal man to prospect Constantinople. He arrived at Mudros after observing the Salonika campaign late in September; once the Turkish armistice had been agreed, he was ordered to reach the city 'in charge of the first British mission into Turkey'; he refers all through to 'we' as a delegation, but never details exactly who accompanied him. They set out on 6 November, four days before *Shark*'s reconnaissance voyage.

His account of his visit to Constantinople is interesting in part because he made the voyage at all and so was in the city before any Allied officer (except prisoners of war); he also published his account as early as February 1919, before the conditions in the city became steadily more difficult and complex, at least for Allied observers. His impressions of the city in the immediate aftermath of the war certainly contrast with later, perhaps more comprehensive but also more retrospective, accounts that were produced in later books and articles, all of which ignore Murphy's account.

His voyage to the city was much more dangerous and awkward than that of *Shark* four days later. He was taken from Mudros to the island of Imbros in the destroyer *Parthian*, then he moved into a minelayer to be taken as far as Cape Helles; a Turkish gunboat, clearly by prearrangement, took him as far as Chanak, at the Narrows, where he was accommodated by the Turkish commander of the fort. The gunboat had carefully navigated the minefield: 'at least a score of floating mines ... flooded past us'; they had either been set loose by the sweeping process that was already under way, or by the strength of the current; either way, they were a distinctly uncomfortable sight. Next morning, the Turkish destroyer *Basra* collected them and they reached the Galata wharf in Constantinople by 9 a.m. on the 7th. His experience in the Straits was more harrowing than that of *Shark* a few days later; the Turks were very efficiently removing the minefields, assisted by Allied ships, but this was a dangerous process, not only for the sweepers, but when mines worked loose, and the Turks had not had long to complete the process. (They had done much more by the time *Shark* went through.) He had obtained a plan of the minefield from the Turkish commander at Chanak, though it does not seem likely that *Shark* would have received a copy when it set out. On the other hand, the fact that Murphy and his party got through safely using a variety of craft would imply that *Shark* was not facing all that much danger four days later, so long as a good lookout was kept. Lieutenant Bonham-Carter in *Shark* would have heard that the advance party had got through safely, and had arrived in the city.

Murphy's party was welcomed by the grand vizier, or at least by the grand vizier's car, and they were greeted by the cheers of some of the people who watched them arrive. Murphy spotted quickly the differing reactions of Greeks and Turks in the crowds – it was the Greeks, and perhaps the Armenians, who were cheering, but not the Turks. During his visit, he met both the grand vizier and the sultan, which is the sort of attention only the first men to arrive on a mission of peace were likely to receive. He played tourist, visiting mosques, and went to see the *Goeben*, which was flying a large Turkish naval flag. He made no reference to doing any work; perhaps the other men in the delegation did that while he skirted around it. More likely, he was keeping a discreet tongue over his actual work. It is clear that part of his purpose was to estimate the attachment of the Turkish government to the armistice, and the likelihood that it would be observed.

Murphy therefore never saw, or ignored, or failed to mention, the minesweepers, which had been busy for a week and continued to operate to open a cleared channel. *Shark*'s voyage had thus been relatively straightforward, though sailing an enemy warship through the Dardanelles was a lot more dangerous than sailing there in a Turkish warship. The minesweeping programme had clearly been largely successful in the short time since the armistice was agreed, though there were still plenty more mines to remove; the process went on for several months yet.

The Allies had ten days or so to organise their formal arrival in the city. This was to be their final joint expedition. The armistice terms included one clause by which Allied vessels would take control of the dockyard in the city; the several forts along the Dardanelles and Bosporos were to be taken in charge. This meant the forts at Chanak and Kilid Bahr on the Dardanelles, and at Rumeli Hissar and Anadolu Hissar on the Bosporos, at least. These had guarded Constantinople's approaches since the Muslim conquest by Mehmet the Conqueror; their occupation by the conquering enemies was no doubt as painful and symbolic to the Turks as the occupation of the city itself.

Shark, having navigated the Dardanelles and the Sea of Marmara in safety on 10 and 11 November after the campaign of minesweeping, the channel was clearly available; the occupation of the Dardanelles forts on both banks increased the safety factor. By 12 November, all was therefore prepared for the Allied ships to initiate the occupation of the city's 'dockyards'. All the Allied navies wanted to take part, despite Calthorpe's oral promises of no occupation of the city. It was not the only case of Allied expansion of their occupation.

The British fleet in the Aegean led the way in the procession of ships. The two dreadnought battleships, *Superb*, carrying Vice-Admiral Calthorpe, and *Temeraire*, went first, followed by the pre-dreadnoughts *Lord Nelson* and *Agamemnon* (built in the same year as the original *Dreadnought*, and so the last of the previous generation of battleships, only marginally smaller and less well armed than that so-called revolutionary battleship). The British contingent that followed consisted of five cruisers, eighteen destroyers, and the seaplane carrier *Empress*. Three of the destroyers were in fact Australian; *Shark* made the journey yet again, as part of the procession, for its third time. This was a very deliberate display of naval power; the British force was greater than the combined forces of the other Allied fleets put together.

In 1807, Admiral Sir John Duckworth fought his way through with a British fleet, but, in front of the city he was unable to compel the sultan's government to comply with British wishes, and he did not have the power to force it to do so. The fleets that repeated the journey in 1918 clearly did have the power he lacked to deal with the city; as a display of power, the British naval contingent was very effective.

There followed, in order, the French, Italian, and Greek contingents, at half-hourly intervals and progressively decreasing in size. The French sent four pre-dreadnought battleships, no doubt insisting on an equal number with the British, but only two armoured cruisers and six destroyers. The Italians sent two battleships, one cruiser and three destroyers. The Greek navy sent the armoured cruiser *Averoff* and three destroyers. As the ships passed through the Narrows, which the battleship attack had not quite reached in 1915, and where the forts were now occupied by Allied soldiers, British and Indian, the Allied troops now forming the garrisons were paraded in salute. The assembly therefore represented both the countries involved in the land war, and those who had participated at sea. Symbols counted, which was why Calthorpe had arranged for the participation of Indian soldiers and Australian ships, a further demonstration of power by land, and of the extent of empire. All the ships flew extra-large ensigns. The Romans would have called it a triumph.

From being all but deserted, with the only major Turkish warship present in Constantinople being the former *Goeben*, now the *Yavuz Sultan Selim*, the waterways of the city were suddenly crowded with monster ships and dozens of others. The battleships were almost deliberately placed in position as if ready to fire on the Topkapi Palace, which itself bristled with guns and in the walls of which gunports had been cut in 1807 to threaten Duckworth's ships – a threat that had worked then, but was now ineffective. The Greek ships insolently stood off the wharf before the Dolmabahçe Palace, where the sultan lived. He soon moved away. The Greek contingent was greeted with ecstatic cheers by the Greeks of the city, but was regarded with inveterate hostility by the Turks. The Italians, almost equally unpopular amongst the Turks, moved off by themselves, across the water to the Asian side.

One witness of the Allies' ships' arrival was General Mustafa Kemal, victor of the fighting at Haritan. He had travelled from Adana to Haidar Pasha railway station on leave, after a complaint by the British that he had stayed in position at Haritan after the armistice agreement was signed – an early indication of his dissatisfaction with the war's outcome and the conditions of the armistice. He arrived as the ships steamed through the Sea of Marmara and took station to face the city. He was then held up in crossing the Bosporos by these Allied ships of occupation. His immediate reaction was that he needed to get back to Anatolia whenever he could leave; this may be a later rationalisation of his feelings, but of his reaction to the sight there can be no doubt. It was perhaps a mercy for the Allies that they did not realise that their presence was fuelling the anger of the one man in the Ottoman Empire who would rouse the war-weary Turkish population to resistance.[14]

And all this took place on the day the German armistice, with equally harsh terms, was signed in France.

When Rauf Bey had returned from signing the armistice agreement he had announced publicly that the Allies would not occupy the city, and that he also had a promise from Calthorpe that neither the Italians nor the Greeks would be arriving. Both of these promises had therefore been instantly disregarded and broken; they were presumably quite insincere, made only to pacify an agitated Rauf Bey, who probably exaggerated and distorted Calthorpe's soothing words. Partly this disregard was due to instructions from the British government, which overrode Calthorpe's personal promises. Partly it was necessary that all the Allies who had taken part in the war on the Ottoman Empire must be allowed to participate, in the interests of the armistice and of Allied harmony. Their participation started with the triumphal naval parade, but there was also the sense that the promise had not been serious, perhaps regarded as unofficial – if, that is, anyone other than Calthorpe knew of them, and if Rauf Bey had understood them.

A promise not to occupy Constantinople was hardly realistic. This was the only serious power centre for the Ottoman Empire, and a failure to secure control of the city would be to leave the government of that empire uncontrolled – and that government was the sultan, still in office, and his ministers. The Allies never had any intention of leaving the city alone, no matter what personal promises were made. Apart from the fleets of ships now off Constantinople, the Allies had seven divisions of troops close by, in the former Bulgarian Thrace, who had been aiming to invade Turkish Thrace when the armistice was agreed. These were now available to occupy that which they had been intending to conquer.

The command of this force was complex. The overall commander at Salonika, General Franchet d'Espèrey, had General Sir George Milne in command of the subordinate British Salonika Army. Milne had three British divisions and a French division in his force (most of the French army had been directed north to liberate Serbia and then invade Hungary). The forces facing Constantinople were mainly on the line of the Maritza River, the international boundary, so were still in Bulgarian territory; there were also three Greek divisions as backup in the rear. However, it proved impossible to get the troops directly to Constantinople by land, so one division, the British 28th, was carried by sea from Salonika, another was sent to the Danube, and the third was held at Salonika. One French regiment out of the French division went to Constantinople along with the 28th Division. The army's occupation force was much less formidable than the fleet.

These contingents had not been agreed without more Anglo-French friction. Franchet d'Espèrey proposed that the British should occupy the Dardanelles forts, and the French those in the Bosporos. Both governments blocked this division of responsibility and insisted that contingents from both armies should jointly occupy the forts. In the end, when the time came for the movement, the French contingent was not ready, so the British sailed without them. Two brigades of the 28th Division landed to take over the Dardanelles forts; it was these troops and those who occupied the forts of the Dardanelles, who had saluted the fleet as they passed. The third brigade took over the Bosporos forts, joined later by the French contingent; this left just one battalion, the 3rd Middlesex, to land in the city.[15]

To the Turks this looked very like the Allied military occupation they believed they had a promise should not happen, though a single battalion was hardly a serious occupation force. A Turkish official sought out the senior Allied officer, Lieutenant General Sir Henry Maitland Wilson, to protest. Wilson had been appointed as General Officer Commanding Allied Forces, Gallipoli and Bosporos, a cumbersome description which was soon condensed to 'Commanding the Allied Corps, Constantinople', which was not quite the same (nor really much less cumbersome). The general calmly stated to the protesting official that the city had been designated as British and Allied headquarters, which left the official lacking a reply. Wilson's answer implied, however, that this was to be the limit of the Allied presence in the city. Once again, that was not so.

This was the first clear sign that the Turkish authorities' wishes would be ignored or disregarded. For a time, therefore, the city was not only increasingly the host to the Allied occupation forces (the term 'occupation' did not become official for another year), but the occupiers mingled with the various ethnic groups that lived in the city – Turks, Greeks, Armenians, Jews, and others – despite Wilson issuing an order against fraternisation. For a time there were 10,000 German and Austrian soldiers there as well (including General Liman von Sanders). These were men who had been stationed there until the armistice, or were passing through from the fighting fronts on their way home. There had been at least 20,000 of these Ottoman allies in the empire at the time of the armistice; they were now being evacuated to their homelands as soon as there were trains or ships available to carry them. Those in the city were soon ordered out to Haidar Pasha, on the Asian side of the Bosporos, where they were disarmed; the officers were interned on the Princes' Islands in the Marmara, and the men at Scutari.

Crowds of inhabitants turned out to greet, or watch, or welcome, the ships, or simply to stare in disbelief at their arrival. A certain dismay pervaded much of the crowd at the sheer power they saw in their harbour. A variety of incidents that occurred at the same time gives some indication, at least in retrospect, of the troubles that were ahead. One of these – not an incident as such – was the inevitable 'mission creep' of the occupation. Having placed Allied soldiers in the city, whether as garrison or as headquarters staff, it was inevitable that more men would arrive, that more tasks would be found for them to perform. Gradually, the whole of the administration of the city and the empire fell into the Allies' hands, whether through the resistance, obfuscation, or incompetence of the Turks, or the perception of the Allies that the occupation regime had to be extended or shaken up, or made more efficient, or made more responsive to Allied wishes. So the occupiers soon began to take over increasing sections of the administration of the city, with the result that these became problems for the occupiers. None of it could be said to be advantageous to the inhabitants.[16] When the Greek cruiser *Averoff* arrived, a crowd of Greek Constantinopolitans greeted it with ecstatic cheers. They were probably imagining that this might be the consummation of the old Greek desire to acquire the rule of the city, together with as much of the Turkish territory as their country could seize.[17] Here was a further problem for occupiers and residents.

General Mustafa Kemal checked into the Pera Palace Hotel for a few days when he arrived, before moving to a less obvious address. He was for the moment uncertain of his future – something common to most Ottoman officers, who had all lost their commands due to the demobilisation of their soldiers but were not interned as the Germans and Austrians were. It would not be long before Mustafa Kemal at least found a new purpose. He moved out of the Pera Palace, and then went to a rented house near the War College, in an area busy with politics.[18]

General Wilson took over the former English Girls' School in Pera for his headquarters, while his staff lodged in the Pera Palace Hotel and other expensive hotels, living, as occupiers always do, at a far higher standard of living than they could have afforded at home. Kemal had moved out partly because it was soon full of these Allied officers (no doubt its prices had gone up, as well). This was also the first residence of General Liman von Sanders, who stayed there for a time, as did General Sir George Milne, commanding the Allied forces in the region. Von Sanders soon moved out, like Kemal. It may have been because of the overwhelming Allied atmosphere of triumph, but it is also suggested that Kemal deliberately chose the hotel because it was full of British headquarters officers whose brains he could pick. He was, as yet, scarcely known to the British, at least by sight; few of the British troops in the city had fought in Syria, where he was known as an effective commander. Wilson's order against fraternisation between the British soldiers and the people of the city was a fairly futile instruction, being in the circumstances scarcely enforceable, and anyway would not apply to officers, whose intelligence and *savoir-faire* was assumed to be superior to those of the lower ranks, all evidence to the contrary. On the other hand, the political situation was an armistice, and the various armies in occupation of the city were still technically at war with the Ottoman Empire.

These were the most notable arrivals and residents. But there were also large numbers of people in the city who were too tired or hungry or indifferent to pay any attention to the arriving ships, for the city, besides its own large population, was also the host to many thousands of refugees. Many of them had arrived after being driven from their homes by the war, or were refugees from hostile host populations (as from Bulgaria), fleeing the Turkish massacres (the Armenians), but another main source was the peasant population of Anatolia. The conscription of men into the army had been immensely damaging to the Anatolian population and agriculture. It had left the women and children and the old men without male manual labour and this had a drastic effect on farming, since it was the men who had done the heavy work on the farms. As a result, food production had been reduced, the abandoned rural population had gone hungry, and supplies to the cities had failed, so leaving the urban population as hungry as the rural. Yet it was to the cities that the rural population had turned for relief, moving in their thousands above all to Constantinople, aggravating the situation in the cities.[19] Importing supplies of food had not been possible during the war, and this was the traditional source of relief in a widespread food emergency.

The city was therefore the scene of numerous refugee encampments, wherever temporary shelters could be placed; some were made of cardboard, others were of petrol tins battered flat, or of canvas, or simply a hole in a wall. These destitute and desperate people depended on charity to keep them alive, while the charitable organisations, principally the mosques, had as great a difficulty in finding food as everyone else. That the refugees were a mixture of Muslims and Christians, while the commerce of the city was mainly in Greek Christian or Armenian Christian control, did not subdue the mutual detestation each community had for the others. The prices went ever higher, not just because of the general scarcity but also due to profiteering. As the Allies gradually extended their control of the city and colonised the imperial administration after their arrival, they came to have some increasing responsibility for feeding these victims.

The British naval squadron did not wait long before moving away from the city. Admiral Calthorpe had more matters than command of his ships to cope with. As high commissioner, he had to concern himself in the government of the city from the start, though he could devolve as much of that as he could to the Turkish government and his officers. Similarly, the responsibility for ensuring the application of the armistice lay with the imperial Ottoman administration, though there was an inevitable reluctance to impose foreign measures, and reminders of that task had to be issued more than once. The situation in the Black Sea, however, which was confused, complicated, opaque, and problematic, and which was another element of Calthorpe's responsibilities, could not easily be left to others, though in one sense it was more straightforward since it was largely at first a naval problem, which Calthorpe as commander-in-chief could more easily tackle.

One of his first decisions had been to move the British ships away from Constantinople to take up an anchorage in the Gulf of Ismid. (One of *Shark*'s tasks in its first visit had been to make a quick inspection of the Gulf to see if it was a suitable place for the whole fleet.) Some of the ships were sent back to the Aegean and the Mediterranean, and most of the remainder were soon to be used in the Black Sea. In other words, the relative ease with which the Allies had gained control of Constantinople meant that the city as a naval and military base was quickly secured, so that ships could be deployed to other critical areas. Eventually, the Black Sea problems resolved themselves, and then the fleet would be used much closer to its anchorage, as the problem of the revival of Turkish strength developed. For the present, in late 1918 and for a year or so after the Allies' arrival, the Turkish problems were seen as essentially those of the city. They overlapped, however, with those coming out of Russia and those from the Anatolian interior, and as the first of those subsided, the second grew.

The Allies, to the dismay of the inhabitants, settled in to govern and control the city, Calthorpe's promises notwithstanding. The excuse was that the peace treaty was still under negotiation in Paris, and so the Allies were enforcing the armistice. If that was not accepted, there was the need to keep control of the city which was still the source of political authority respected in the empire, though that did not endure for long. And overall, there really was nowhere else that could be used, given that Constantinople was the only city with good communications to the rest of the empire and to the surrounding seas. The occupiers were also enjoying themselves at Turkish expense. This, of course, meant bending, if not breaking, still more of Calthorpe's oral promises, not to mention ignoring Maitland Wilson's non-fraternisation order. It could, just about, be said to be covered by the clause in the armistice agreement which gave the Allies the right to occupy strategic positions, but that was explicitly designed for emergencies, and was so vague that it could mean anything the Allies decided they wanted it to mean. Constantinople, however, was a rather more important issue than a mere 'strategic position'. This Allied unilateral extension of the terms, which they themselves had designed, was a breach of faith, and it immediately soured relations between the citizens and the occupiers, not that they were ever good in the first place.[20]

Despite that, the Turks had an unusually favourable view of the British, despite their role in the occupation, and this paradoxically continued for some years. In contrast, their view of the French was much less favourable, and of the Italians and Greeks it was even worse, amounting to detestation, even hatred. Relations with the Germans had quickly sunk even lower during the war, despite the two empires being Allies and fighting alongside each other; with closer acquaintance, detestation had set in on both sides.

Having sent a considerable force into the city, and their generals and officers having planted themselves in the best accommodation, the Allies had thereby successfully paralysed the city government, and thoroughly undermined the authority of the sultan and his ministers, so the occupation was gradually extended and became entrenched – as would have been expected from the start. The initial occupation of the dockyard and the Bosporos forts extended to the sequestration of villas and government offices for the use of the Allied forces. At first, it was possible to issue requests to the Turkish government and see them carried out. On 8 December, the Turkish government agreed to disarm the population of the city, and this was soon extended to the rest of the empire. Possibly this was done due to the practice of firing into the air in celebration, something that Greeks in particular were liable to do; more likely it was due to a lively fear of Turkish enmity, but it had been a part of the original armistice agreement. The instruction went out to other regions and for a time it was largely obeyed, though one Turkish commander flatly refused, and when the time came to resist the Allied measures it became clear that plenty of weapons had been hidden away.[21] Lloyd George, in one of his flashes of understanding, likened the situation to the Scottish Highlands after the 1745 Jacobite rebellion, and the propensity there for guerrilla warfare: President Wilson, to whom he made this observation, objected to this on the grounds that his own ancestors were Scottish, perhaps deliberately missing the point, and also ignoring the similar propensity for his own people to wave guns about all too freely.

The Allied command system was established. Calthorpe was not only high commissioner, but was also designated as the sole contact through whom communications could be made with the Turkish government, and he collected men for judicial and financial commissions. General Milne had meanwhile placed himself fully in command of all the Allied army units, soon to become collectively called, somewhat curiously, the 'Army of the Black Sea'. The naval forces, however, stayed out of Milne's grip, and remained under Calthorpe and Amet. Calthorpe received Rear Admiral Sir Michael Culme-Seymour as his second-in-command, and assigned him to act as operational commander in the Black Sea and the Aegean. Calthorpe's other task as commander-in-chief of the British Mediterranean Fleet was quite enough for one man without all the other tasks heaped on him. It was a perfect example of muddling through, inventing an administration as they went along. By the end of the year, it was clear that the Allies were in control of the city, and early in January Milne was authorised to take control of the police. In any other situation this series of developments would have been called a slow *coup d'état*.[22] (It may be pointed out that the acquisition of control of Italy by Mussolini in 1922, and of Germany by Hitler in 1933, are other examples of this same gradual process of seizing power.)

The conclusion of the armistice and the occupation of Constantinople were the start of a five-year process by which the Allies, and in the end particularly the British, came to rule the city. (The later events in the city will be discussed in Chapter 9.) But this was only one aspect of the local aftermath of the war in the Near East. The Black Sea became a British naval command soon enough once *Shark* and *Tribune* had made a quick survey, but presently, Sir George Milne was made commander of the 'Army of the Black Sea', which command in fact extended very much further than the sea itself and included the command of British forces very much further east. These forces had been active and busy in the Caucasus, the Caspian Sea, and Central Asia for a year before the occupation of Constantinople decisively changed the situation. Before discussing the events in the Black Sea, therefore, it will be necessary to consider those in these territories further east.

Part II

A Railway, Oil, and a New Fleet

To keep some sort of control over the description of events, it is necessary to dip back in time from the events at Constantinople in November 1918 to January 1919 to look at two expeditions undertaken by the British in the lands to the east of the Ottoman Empire. These are the subjects of the three chapters of this part.

One of the earliest political reactions to the Russian Revolution came from India, traditionally fearful of a Russian attack, something that would be a good deal more potent now that the threat was revolutionary, not merely imperialistic. A small expedition travelled through eastern Persia aiming to secure control of, or interrupt Russian traffic along, the Central Asian Railway (Chapter 3). A second expedition, launched from London and Iraq, made its difficult way through western Persia to secure the oil of Baku on the Caspian Sea, and so to prevent German forces from doing the same (Chapter 4); this adventure morphed curiously into a naval campaign in the Caspian Sea (Chapter 5), quite the oddest Royal Navy fleet ever. This brought British forces into the Caucasus region, and eventually the appointment of General Sir George Milne, already commander of the Army of the Black Sea, to investigate what was happening in these areas and to recommend what the conclusion of them should be.

Chapter 3

The Central Asian Railway

There were various conflicts in the Russian Revolution in the large area between the Hindu Kush and the cities of Constantinople and Odessa on the Black Sea. They are linked not only by being part of the revolution, but by the involvement of the British Empire as well. The contest can be studied in geographical sections, as in this account, but it is well to bear in mind the small numbers of men involved in two of them, for this was a conflict in which small units could have a disproportional effect. Yet, not only were these regions and conflicts separated geographically, they operated, in a sense, on differing time periods, which makes it necessary to treat them separately, noting links wherever they occur. An overall connection, in fact, besides the involvement of Britain and Russia, is the confusion at the end of the Great War.

The Black Sea region, for Britain and its navy, only became a theatre of action in November 1918, and the activities there ended with the evacuation of Constantinople in 1923; this was an entirely naval matter for the British. The Caspian Sea and the city of Baku had become an issue for them in January 1918, when it became clear that the German forces, and the Turks, were likely to launch an attack to secure the oil supplies available at Baku; this oil would then be available to fuel the German forces in France. General Lionel Dunsterville became the commander of a small force moving through Persia to pre-empt the enemy threat to Baku – but he did not reach the shores of the Caspian until June of that year. Therefore, this adventure lasted until the Soviet subjection of the Caucasus republics in 1921, though the British involvement had ended a year or more before then; both land and sea forces were involved in this section, and a Royal Navy squadron was constituted in the Caspian, and fought to gain control of that sea.

In Central Asia, the intervention was at first separate from that in the Caucasus, and was wholly by land forces from India. It began in June 1918, with the appointment of Major General Wilfrid Malleson at Quetta, and lasted until April 1919. It was followed immediately by the Third Afghan War, which proved to be a much more serious affair than the small-scale intervention in Central Asia, though the presence of Malleson's force on the western Afghan border was useful in the context of a British Afghan war. (Another adventure, Colonel Bailey's journey through Turkestan, overlapped with all these, but he is not considered in detail in this account.)[1] This chapter will discuss the events in Central Asia, and those in the Caspian and Caucasus will be discussed in the next.

The British intervention in Central Asia was a new venture for the army, especially the Indian Army, though this organisation had long feared a Russian invasion through Central Asia and Afghanistan, and had gathered a good deal of intelligence information about the region. It is worth considering just what was involved for the British in the expedition in 1918–19. They did not commit much in the way of forces to the fighting, and there was never any question of conquest – two battalions would hardly be able to control such a large region, except in occasional dreams. The events, however, do demonstrate that the British were quite willing to leave political decisions to the local inhabitants, and they withdrew readily enough in the end when it became clear that the Bolsheviks, the enemy of choice at the end of the Great War, did not have the strength for an invasion of India. Soviet forces refrained from moving south, despite the British support of their Russian enemies, and despite the outbreak of another war against the British in Afghanistan. With all their problems and apprehensions, the Soviet forces stayed behind the Imperial Russian frontiers; it was never likely they would invade India; British fears were exaggerated. They were, of course, replicated on the other side, with Russian factions fearing or hoping for a British intervention on their side.

The British intervention in the area actually grew out of their wartime involvement in Persia (as did that at Baku, in a way) and this in turn grew out of concerns about Afghanistan and the infiltration of German agents into both countries that had taken place during the Great War.[2] As a result, there were both Russian and British forces all over Persia, at first as allies, later as rivals. In particular, one force was strung along the border between Persia and Afghanistan to prevent enemy agents reaching and conducted intrigues in the latter country, where Emir Habibullah's throne was unstable (and he was to be assassinated early in 1919). This was the East Persian

Cordon Field Force, located in a dozen or more posts along the Afghan border, but within Persia. Each post consisted of a mix of Indian infantry and light cavalry, or in a few cases, only one of these. The cavalry was the 28th Light Cavalry, the infantry was the 19th Punjabis; they were backed up by local 'levies' recruited in Seistan and Baluchistan. The northernmost post, at the city of Meshed, was close to the border with Russian Turkestan, the southernmost was close to the Baluchistan (that is, the British Indian) border.[3]

The Russian confusion had brought the Bolsheviks to act in Central Asia, aiming to gain control of the old Imperial Russian territories. This involved fighting against a variety of rival revolutionaries and anti-revolutionaries, and attempts to conquer two semi-independent khanates, Khiva and Bokhara, which had survived as protectorates after the original Russian conquest of the region, back in 1880. Both of these khanates were well armed, and the evaporation of imperial power with the revolution had persuaded the khans that they were now independent once again, a reasonable conclusion since their protectorate status was agreed with the defunct imperial government, not the revolutionaries. They could be formidable enemies, for Bokhara at least maintained a substantial armed force of about 50,000 men.

Behind all this was the British fear for India, which was by no means under easy control in 1918–19. It had clearly been a target for German intrigues during the war and now for the Russian Bolsheviks. The British intervention in Central Asia may thus best be characterised as a pre-emptive move in defence of India, just as its intrusion into Persia during the war had been designed to interrupt German intrigues. The British had at no time sought to gain permanent control of any part of these territories; domination and influence was a different matter, of course.

It is not possible, as noted earlier, to treat this episode in isolation from the other British interventions in the various areas of southern Russia, particularly the western region; all were eventually responding to the military developments in interior Russia. Indeed, through the British naval control of the Caspian Sea, it was possible for the British to involve both Indian soldiers sent from India, and British troops sent from Britain by way of Salonika, the Black Sea, the Caucasus and the Caspian Sea in the fighting – a classic example of a small imperial force being highly effective.

On the Allied side, only the British were concerned about the Caucasus or about Central Asia in the contest with the Russian Bolsheviks. This was a consequence of the role of Britain as a world power – or rather, as the only existing world power at the end of the Great War. No other country had possessions and responsibilities throughout the world; only France came close, but that country was now exhausted after its exertions in the war, and the casualties it had suffered; the United States, with a strong naval force, was mainly confined to North American and Pacific waters. British predominance meant that every problem in the world landed in Britain's lap. So the consequence of the Great War was that, while Britain's pre-eminent position was superficially reinforced by the destruction of the German Empire, the exhaustion of France, and the withdrawal of the United States and Russia into themselves, it was Britain that had to cope with all the international problems. At the same time, like France, it was debilitated by the costs of the Great War, and had its own internal problems, so its power to attend to widespread and distant events after 1919 had been much reduced. The several crisis countries and regions involved here – Russia, Turkey, the Caspian, Central Asia, Persia, Afghanistan – are a good example of the difficulties, and they are a prime case for the links between apparently separate problems.

In Central Asia, the Russian Revolution(s) had a variety of effects. In the city of Tashkent, the government centre, there had been a struggle for power between imperial loyalists ('Whites') and the local Soviet ('Reds'), which was won for the moment by the Soviet in October 1917. The Soviet's oppression of the Muslim population followed. The Muslims had not participated in the Tashkent fight, but Muslim anger was now roused, and a Muslim Congress meeting at Kokand in December declared Turkestan autonomous. The reaction of the Tashkent Soviet was brutal. Kokand was besieged and taken, amid a general massacre. But the wider result was a series of uprisings against the authority of the Tashkent Soviet, including a move by the khan of Bokhara towards complete independence. He could argue that his subordinate status to in the imperial regime had ended when that regime ended. The Soviet did not agree, but was very careful not to provoke the khan to open war.

Guerrilla movements – the local term was '*basmachi*' – now preoccupied the beset Soviet. Meanwhile to the west of Tashkent, in the present region called Turkmenistan (the name at the time was Trans-Caspia), power was seized by a group in Ashkhabad, a city that was planted firmly on the Trans-Caspian (or Central Asian) Railway, and along this line its authority extended as far as the port of Krasnovodsk on the Caspian, and to the border with Bokhara at the bridge over the Amu Darya (Oxus) River to the east.[4]

The existence of rival authorities fighting a civil war, needless to say, attracted the attention of the British in India. Alarm bells rang at Delhi, fearing that the Russian problem would spill over into India's close neighbours; Major General Wilfrid Malleson was summoned to Simla, the cool summer capital of the Raj, for instructions and discussions on the issue.[5] In June, he travelled across India and Baluchistan and into south-eastern Persia, whence he could travel north along the East Persian Cordon route. He then assumed command of that force.

His headquarters were to be at Meshed, the Persian holy city in north-eastern Persia; this was garrisoned by, or contained, a detachment of the Cordon Field Force. From the city it was 150 kilometres to the crucial communications route across the Russian territory, the Trans-Caspian Railway, at a point where the line turned through almost a right angle, heading for Krasnovodsk on the Caspian to the north-west and Tashkent to the north-east. It may have been built expressly to be able to deliver Russian forces, either to conquer Central Asia, or to the Afghan border, as a means of defence or attack; this meant, however, that it was also vulnerable to the British, who were now just across the border in Persia.[6]

Meshed was in a fertile and productive area, Khorasan, and was itself connected by rail with Herat and parts east, in Afghanistan. However, it was hardly safe for British military detachments to be in Afghanistan, so supplies and soldier reinforcements had to travel by train to a new railhead at the south end of the East Persian Cordon, at the Persian–Baluchistan border, and then by marching or riding north along the rough track that was parallel to the Afghan frontier, but inside Persia. This was the route Malleson had travelled to get to his command. The distance was a good thousand kilometres from the railhead in Baluchistan to Meshed.

Major General Malleson had the use of the troops who were already present as the East Persian Cordon Force, which patrolled the Afghan border, the 19th Punjabis (infantry), and the 28th Light Cavalry, Indian units with British officers. Malleson, however, could use only parts of them, since their primary task was to patrol the Persian border.

It was not clear exactly what Malleson had to do, other than keep watch on events, and defend the British position, but British officers had recently travelled into 'Trans-Caspia' seeking political information. It had been clear, when Malleson reached Meshed in mid-June 1918, that the Bolsheviks had begun to lose their local authority, in part because of their violence. Meanwhile, in South Russia, the Germans had now advanced all across Ukraine, and it was feared that they would be able to cross the Caspian and reach into Trans-Caspia; at the time, the Bolsheviks and the Germans were operating as quasi-allies since making peace at Brest-Litovsk in March.

At Ashkhabad, on the railway, west of Meshed, the local Bolsheviks had just been driven out by a rival revolutionary group, who might be Mensheviks or Social Revolutionaries, so this looked like a moment when the British could usefully intervene in favour of this anti-Bolshevik group. They were likely to be less unfriendly than the Bolsheviks, but were also liable to be attacked by the Tashkent Bolsheviks. Malleson pushed a squadron of the 28th Light Cavalry and a platoon of the 19th Punjabis forward to the border at Muhammadabad, and another platoon of the Punjabis forward to Kuchan, on the road towards Ashkhabad; but both of these units remained within Persian territory. The Ashkhabad Executive Committee meanwhile drove the Bolsheviks away eastwards as far as the bridge across the Oxus River at Charjui.

The fear in British circles was still of German and/or Turkish forces arriving in Trans-Caspia. The Turks in particular might be able to appeal to Turkish-speaking Kazaks (who had risen in rebellion against Russian rule only three years before). These Kazaks might be persuaded to participate in a new campaign, and the British forces might well be their target. The Germans, if they could get across the Caspian Sea, might free the thousands of German and Austrian prisoners of war being held in the Turkestan camps, and so produce an instant army.

The Ashkhabad Committee and the Bolsheviks between them had shown clearly that the railway was the key to any control in the region. A small contingent had been sent by ship from the British force that had reached Enzeli on the south coast of the Caspian to occupy Krasnovodsk, the western terminus of the Central Asian Railway. This should be able to stop a landing by German or Turkish forces, so for the time being the crossing of the Caspian was thus blocked to both the Turks and the Germans.

The Bolshevik forces at Tashkent, now being called the Red Army, revived, returned to the attack at the Charjui bridge and recovered control of the section of the railway as far as Merv. The Ashkhabad Committee thereupon appealed for help to the British, whose forces were now clearly available, just across the frontier. The committee now appreciated that the British were doing more than simply guarding the Persian border. The committee had already made an alliance with the local Turkomans, dwelling in the steppeland north of the railway, and now they did so with Malleson as well. His restrictive instructions did allow him to block the railway to prevent it being used by the Bolsheviks to reach Krasnovodsk, so he could respond effectively.[7] His force was becoming subject to 'mission creep', as it was drawn slowly north into the Russian conflict.

As the Bolsheviks moved west along the railway, a formal agreement became necessary between Malleson and the Ashkhabad Committee. He sent Captain Reginald Teague-Jones to negotiate an agreement, which was reached on 19 August. By that time, the Red Army had defeated the Ashkhabad forces and had driven them back to Dushak, the closest station to Meshed on the line, only just north of the British force at Muhammadabad. The defenders retreated still further along the line to Kaahka, leaving a no-man's-land to separate them from the enemy.

The position of the whole Ashkhabad Committee was now under threat, for if the Bolsheviks took Kaahka, their next step would take them to Ashkhabad and the probable extinction of the committee. After the agreement was signed, Malleson had been given permission to operate beyond the border, though without any more troops or any extra finance, to help him. He moved a company of the 19th Punjabis across the border to give support to the men at Kaahka. They arrived there on 25 August. Two more companies of the Punjabis then arrived, and Lieutenant Colonel Knollys, commanding the Punjabis, pointed out to the defenders that better positions could be found for the defence, and his suggestions, being the man on the spot, were accepted.

The Bolsheviks attacked next day, and were defeated, in large part by the resistance of the Punjabis. Then more troops arrived, a company of the 1/4 Hampshire Regiment, and a battery of Royal Field Artillery. They had been sent across the Caspian from Baku, and had then travelled by rail to Ashkhabad. Behind this, the Turks began an offensive to take Baku, which succeeded on 15 September; this, though, was also the date of the Allied offensive that broke the Bulgars, and began the process of crumbling the enemy resistance.

At Baku, it was decided that a group of Bolshevik commissars, who had been imprisoned after attempting to carry a large part of the arsenal out of the city, had to be moved away. They were regarded as being too dangerous to be left to the Turks, who might make good use of them, but too dangerous to be released, because of the effectiveness of the Bolshevik message, and too dangerous to be handed over to the British, at least at first. So they were put on board the *Turkman*, one of the civilian steamships that normally plied back and forth between the ports of the Caspian. So far the story is reasonably clear, but whether they had been released at Baku and put on board to be disembarked in friendly territory, perhaps at Astrakhan in the north, which was where they had been heading when arrested, or were put on board as prisoners, to be handed over into another authority to be kept in another jail, is unclear. Their destination, therefore, is as unclear as the reasons for their deportation were vague, and the story becomes steadily murkier as it goes along.

They were taken across to Krasnovodsk, though the reason for this destination is again one of the uncertainties. It seems that some of the men in the ship's crew were unwilling to be taken to Astrakhan in the north, which was firmly under Bolshevik control. With this destination impossible, Krasnovodsk was about the only place they could be taken. Once landed at Krasnovodsk, the commissars, whatever their status when they were put aboard the ship, became the prisoners of the town government, and more distantly of the anti-Bolshevik Executive Committee, which was based at Ashkhabad. Both authorities were at war with the Bolsheviks from Tashkent. The executive committee was mainly composed of Social Revolutionaries and Mensheviks, and so this destination was apparently acceptable to the ship's captain and the men who had objected to going to Astrakhan. These were enemies of the Bolsheviks, and so of the commissars. Possibly there had been a general discussion on board among the crew and this destination was the consensus.

It was clear all along that the commissars were regarded as carrying some sort of politico-social disease, and no one wanted to have custody of them in case the infection spread. The composition, politically, of the population in the region was as a mixture of people of all political beliefs, from Bolsheviks to monarchists; the commissars would obviously be able to find supporters wherever they went. The complex politics of the populations in Baku and

Krasnovodsk and Ashkhabad were liable to erupt into open conflict if the commissars were released, or even if their presence was revealed. If they were detected after being kept in secret, this would probably be worse. The example of the sack and massacre at Baku that had recently taken place was a horrifying warning, as was the similar behaviour of the Bolsheviks when they captured any town – such as at Kokand not long before.

One would suppose that the prisoners were vociferous and awkward, and challenging as prisoners, and since they had plenty of sympathisers in the region they were a constant danger to the Ashkhabad government, which itself was weak and unstable. They had, after all, absconded from Baku with the armoury of the local authority, which is why they were prisoners in the first place. They might try the same trick at Ashkhabad, or mount a coup. They were certainly untrustworthy, and would be expected to break any agreement they made without a qualm of conscience. It would probably have been best if they had been taken to Astrakhan, where their fellow Bolsheviks could have dealt with their incompetence in their own way, but once they had landed at Krasnovodsk it was too late for this solution.

The commissars appear to have had no fear, at least initially, of the Ashkhabad government, which attempted to hand the problem on to Major General Malleson. Eventually, having consulted with his headquarters at Delhi, he agreed to accept them as hostages with the aim of exchanging them for some of the British officers and consuls who were being held prisoner by the Bolsheviks elsewhere in Russia. But this decision took time to be arrived at, as did every question dealt with by Delhi, and even longer to be communicated along the great distance from Delhi to Meshed. Before Malleson was able to indicate agreement to the proposal he was told that the commissars had been shot.

It emerged that they had been put on a train at Krasnovodsk, perhaps with the story that they were to be delivered to either Ashkhabad or to the British, or maybe they were told they were to be taken to their fellow Bolsheviks at Merv, but, anyway, they were under armed guard. The train was halted after 200 kilometres or so, in the middle of the Karakum Desert. The men were taken out, and then shot. When Malleson was told, he was furious, though whether it was because he was foiled of his prisoners, or by the action itself, is not clear; perhaps it was both. Captain Teague-Jones, Malleson's envoy to the Ashkhabad Committee, tried to find out what had happened. He could get no definite information at Ashkhabad, where he had been all the time; he seems to have concluded that the order for execution came from F. Funtikov, who was the president of the Ashkhabad Committee. There had been a long discussion in the committee about what to do with the commissars, lasting well into the night, but without a clear result. Funtikov is portrayed as almost certainly drunk most of the time, presumably a result of the responsibility he had assumed. When Teague-Jones probed further in attempting to discover what had happened, he found that the several members of the committee were blaming each other, and it has never become clear either who had authorised or who had carried out the murders, but if anyone was responsible, it was probably Funtikov in a drunken state.

The story, or a version of it, was collected by a Bolshevik journalist at Baku. He, either deliberately or inadvertently, or merely carelessly, elaborated the story, as journalists do, and in the end cast the blame on the British, in particular on Teague-Jones, who was actually in Ashkhabad when the killings took place, but who had made himself prominent by his attendance at the indecisive meeting at Ashkhabad, and then by his enquiries. This was a welcome story for Bolshevik propaganda purposes (they could not allow Russians to be blamed, not even Social Revolutionaries). It took a month for the story to reach Moscow, in the form of an article in a Baku newspaper, by which time it was impossible at that distance to discover the truth – not that the Moscow Bolsheviks cared. It entered the official Russian account of events in its journalistic version, as revealed truth. British denials were fruitless, for blaming the enemy was always a Soviet custom, and since they lied intentionally, they disbelieved anyone else. In the end, Teague-Jones vanished into anonymity, clearly afraid of either capture and trial, or, more likely, assassination.

This took place as news came through of the aftermath of the British evacuation of Baku on 14/15 September. The city was sacked by the Turks, or at least by the Turkish-speaking Azeris – the 'Tartars'. It was feared for a time that the Turks would be able to cross the Caspian using ships captured at Baku. Theoretically, they could thereby reach Krasnovodsk in force, then travel along the railway into Central Asia. They might well have been welcomed by, say, the Turkomans. No doubt, this was one of the reasons behind the killing of the commissars, who might have brought some sense and order into the Tashkent Committee. In itself, however, the affair of the

'26 Commissars' was only a minor item in the general unpleasantness, and it only became important when seized on by Soviet propaganda.[8]

As it happens, most of the shipping had been removed from Baku when the British left in mid-September, and a force had been sent to hold Krasnovodsk. This effectively prevented the very possibility of the Turks' crossing. So when the Turks had finished murdering the Christian Armenian population of Baku, the Turks' Army of Islam, thwarted of its possible landing at Krasnovodsk, turned north into Daghestan, another Muslim area, to indulge in more ethnic massacres.

Major General Malleson may have been annoyed at the conduct of the Ashkhabad Committee in murdering the commissars, but he was not to know how the story would be later distorted and exploited; indeed, even if he did know or suspect some future manipulation, he would hardly have expected that it would come out in the very way that it did. He could put aside the issue of the commissars – he ranted that the Russians were 'all alike, Red or White' and attended to his own issues. His real problem was that he was isolated in dangerous country, beset by enemies and/or incompetent friends; he had only a small force under his control, and was hundreds of miles from his headquarters – he was ultimately under the direct authority of the commander-in-chief in Delhi – and far from any support. The situation around him was constantly changing, and, when he had thought about it, he may well have been relieved that he did not have a bunch of noisy Bolshevik commissars to guard. To stay in his headquarters at Meshed with only about half his small force with him was to expect trouble. The time had come to make some decisions.

The first necessity was to secure his communications back to Quetta, in view of the generally disturbed situation in Persia and Afghanistan. This could be done by appointing a senior officer with the skills to recruit local forces who would then be used to guard the road and forward messengers and supplies. The man chosen was Brigadier General W.E.R. Dickson, an expert in such matters. The second necessity was to gather further troops to boost the forces under Malleson's own hand.[9] The two units he commanded in the East Persian Cordon, the 28th Light Cavalry and the 19th Punjabis, were respectively 500 and 1,000 strong. Some had already been sent to help the Ashkhabad Committee, and to gain control of the railway. He had received reinforcements from Baku, a Royal Field Artillery battery and a company of the 4th Hampshires, who had arrived by sea through Krasnovodsk, which was now also occupied by a section of the British forces who had come from Iraq. With secure communications to the south and the west, therefore, Malleson could employ his remaining troops elsewhere. These men had demonstrated their skill and capabilities in the fight at Kaahka, and had, as it proved, established a clear superiority over the Bolshevik forces.

Malleson's options were, either to abandon his position along the railway and retire, or push on to establish his own control over ever-longer stretches of the railway. This latter was beyond the capability of the Ashkhabad Committee's forces, so it had devolved onto the British troops. By controlling Ashkhabad and Kaahka, Malleson held the line of the railway, and by advancing, he could drive the Bolsheviks back to the Oxus River bridge and the Bokhara border. This became his new target.[10]

The Tashkent Committee meanwhile had become much stronger, especially since they had gained control of some of the munitions stored at Kushka, at the end of a branch line from Merv to the Afghan border, which had been designed to facilitate a Russian invasion of Afghanistan. The munitions were stored there to supply a Russian attacking force that might be used to invade Afghanistan – the Indian fear of this was not quite a fantasy after all. The Tashkent Committee, however, was scarcely better organised than the Ashkhabad Committee. In actual fact, of course, any commanding general, even one such as Malleson who had not commanded anything in the field since his time as a junior officer, neither retirement nor inactivity were options in such a situation. He had to advance.

On the railway, the Ashkhabad forces, reinforced by three companies of the Punjabis and two squadrons of the Light Cavalry, with the company of the Hampshires in reserve, moved forward from the battlefield of Kaahka towards the village of Dushak, a distance of about 40 kilometres. The force provided by the Ashkhabad Committee was badly disciplined and very difficult to control, but it did include a small force of White Russians, of which one group were a set of ex-regular soldiers who were under good discipline; they attached themselves to the equally well-organised Punjabis. There was also a group of Armenians who had not yet shown much discipline, and a cloud of Turkoman nomads who could count as light cavalry. Apart from the small group of Russian regular soldiers and the Indians – a total of perhaps 500 men – all the rest were liable to panic, or to fail to advance with any resolution.[11]

It was now mid-October. (The Germans in France were in full retreat; Bulgaria had accepted an armistice; a British force was about to retake Baku. This would make communications with the forces in the Black Sea much easier.) It was now nearly a month since the last clash with the Tashkent Committee's forces, when their third attempt to push along the railway had failed at Kaahka. Now, in retaliation, the Trans-Caspian forces were moving forward, and the two armies met at Dushak, the southernmost point of the railway, close to the Persian border. A semblance of order was imposed on the Ashkhabad forces for the occasion. The Punjabis were in the centre, flanked by the Russians and Armenians, also infantry, on their right; on their left was the 28th Light Cavalry, which at first intended to fight dismounted. The enemy was armed with a dozen guns and thirty machine guns taken from the old imperial armoury at Kushka, but they used them badly.

When the Trans-Caspian infantry force advanced, the Russians and Armenians stopped as soon as the enemy guns fired, at a distance of a thousand yards or more. The Punjabis, properly disciplined and experienced, pushed forward, commanded by Captain G.E. Shute. On the left, the Indian cavalry also advanced, at first on foot, but was soon re-horsed in order to charge; they dispersed the enemy force in front of them, using their lances, as official reports callously put it, 'with effect'. This was unnerving to the enemy, just as they had been by an earlier Punjabi charge with fixed bayonets.

The Punjabis, advancing largely alone, suffered plenty of casualties, including all their British officers, who were killed or wounded; the commander of the cavalry, Major J.A. Kreyer, sent across one of his own officers to take command. When Dushak station was reached, an ammunition train, which the Tashkent forces had stationed there, blew up, hit by a shell, probably from its own side. This stopped the advance, but the Punjabis had already driven the enemy back and had disorganised and dispersed that whole force. The Russians, Armenians, and Turkomans now joined in, since any real danger was no longer in evidence. They massacred any enemies they could find and aimed to collect the loot; in formal military terms this might have been dignified as 'exploiting the victory', if it had been actually intended. The result, when the enemy made a counter-attack by train from the next station along the line, was that the only forces left on the field of battle were the Punjabis, the Indian cavalry, and the small disciplined Russian force. These conducted a careful well-managed retreat, bringing off all their wounded, and the counter-attack was not pressed home.[12]

Casualties on both sides were considerable, as would be expected when the main weapon for both was the machine gun. The Tashkent force suffered the most in numerical terms, thanks to the ruthlessness of the nomad cavalry, but more important were the casualties among the Punjabis, who had done most of the real fighting, and were the most valuable fighting men. They were only a relatively small force, and had lost about half their manpower, almost 200 men killed or wounded. As they retreated, the Punjabis had found themselves without any sort of support from the irregular forces. They retired to their former position at Kaahka. The number of casualties amongst the Bolshevik force was guessed at about 1,000, probably an exaggeration.

The main event, however, was the explosion at the station. This in effect blocked the line, because of the wreckage and the destruction of the track. The Tashkent counter-attack, being led by an armoured train, had therefore not been able to pass the wrecked station, perhaps to the equal relief of those on board and those on the defensive. The reputation of the Punjabis as fighting men, with their bayonets, and the cavalry with their lances, was quite enough to discourage the enemy from getting out of their trains to fight.

The Bolsheviks withdrew in their trains, first to Tenzhen, about 40 kilometres east of Dushak, then to Merv, another 120 kilometres eastwards. This second move was the result of the fear of a flank attack by the Indian cavalry, which had not suffered as badly as did the infantry in the fight and still had most of its officers. This panicky reaction to a minor threat, apprehended only at a distance, was repeated a few days later when the appearance of a cavalry patrol precipitated yet another retreat, this time all the way to the Amu Darya River and the bridge at Charjui. So, despite retreating from Dushak to Kaahka after the fight, the Trans-Caspian force – that is, essentially the two Indian part-regiments – had won a notable victory, and had compelled the enemy to retire 400 kilometres along the railway line, even though they and the Trans-Caspians had technically been defeated and forced to retreat.[13]

At that point, Malleson's superiors in India and London began to worry and dither. Only after several detailed telegrams and several refusals was Malleson given permission to occupy the line up to and including Merv, which he had in fact already done. He wanted to do this because that city would provide shelter for the troops in the winter – and by late October, it was already very cold at night, while the oasis and its produce could provide supplies. He sent forward a reinforcement for the damaged Punjabis, but even here, the total British force in this Russian territory was no more than 500 men, almost entirely Indians.[14] (It is notable that the British troops – the Royal Field Artillery, and the Hampshires – were scarcely used, and the Indians had to do almost all the fighting and suffering, though the Punjabis' British officers had suffered severely.)

News of the Bulgarian collapse had already arrived, hampering the Turkish war effort by putting Constantinople in danger, and by cutting the delivery of supplies from Germany. Then the Turkish armistice followed at the end of October. These armistices certainly removed any anxiety that the Turkish forces would reach Krasnovodsk. Malleson's small force was thus now in control of the line all the way from Krasnovodsk to Merv, and faced only one semi-organised enemy, the Tashkent Bolsheviks, who were known to be scared stiff of the Indian soldiers, with their bayonets and lances, and were pleading for help from the Bolshevik centre at Moscow. They had recruited a number of Austro-Hungarian prisoners of war, partly thanks to Bolshevik persuasiveness, and partly by promising that if they fought through to the Caspian Sea they could then get home, but they were hardly motivated, and had been beaten by the Indians. The political authority which Malleson's troops were supporting, the Trans-Caspian Committee at Ashkhabad, were also pleading for still more help, being desperately short of money, and in Malleson's view, needing to instill discipline into their troops.

The Turkish and then the German armistices changed the ostensible purpose of this British intervention into Russian Central Asia. It had begun because of perceived Russian threats to India, which had thus changed to a means of preventing Turks and Germans, separately or in tandem, reaching into Central Asia for materials (oil, cotton), or to collect reinforcements for the Ottoman forces, as well as providing a possible threat to India. None of these fears were credible after the end of October and the elimination of the Ottoman Empire and Bulgaria as British enemies, and the visible fading of German and Austria-Hungarian strength. Instead, yet another new war had developed out of the old, this one now pitting British Indian forces against the Russian Bolsheviks. This conflict, of course, had been inherent all along in these events, since the Bolsheviks were linked with the Germans. But now, with Germany defeated and removed, there remained only an anti-Bolshevik war. This should have given the British a perfect excuse to withdraw, but pledges of support had been made to the Ashkhabad Committee that could not be withdrawn, at least not abruptly; then, in January, the peace conference in Paris threw a gesture of legitimacy over the anti-Bolshevik war.

By then the Ashkhabad Committee had run out of money, though Malleson fortuitously discovered that he owed it a considerable sum for the supplies that the committee had already provided, and that kept it afloat for a time. (This was an interesting case of politico-military creative accounting.) The British government, however, had decided to curtail the operation and end the occupation of the railway. The expense of the expedition was becoming steadily larger, while spending was being reined in, both in London and in Delhi. The reasons for remaining in Central Asia had changed, were now much less precise, and much less convincing, for a country that normally regarded a regime that had control of its territory as thereby legitimate – of which, Soviet communism was now one. Britain was not fighting against the Bolsheviks, the government explained in a message to Malleson – which must have been a surprise to him – but now was staying on in occupation in Trans-Caspia in order to prevent disorder from spilling over into Persia and Afghanistan. These self-serving and expansionist notions no longer seemed convincing, given the civil war in Russia.

The end of the German war had turned British official attention elsewhere. Persia had been occupied by several separate forces of British and Indian troops, to which local levies had been added (and paid for). A good deal of the expense for this was funded by India, but not all, and the government of India did not like to pay for something which in reality was a British responsibility. There were eight separate British-Indian forces in Persia, of which, as an example, the East Persian Cordon Force counted almost 500 cavalry, over 1,000 infantry, and as many local levies; and this, in March 1918 (before Malleson's expedition began), was one of the smaller commands. Such commands soon become enlarged as they got more involved in fighting north of the border, suffered casualties and required logistical support. The Malleson mission had experienced exactly that. London's accountants certainly had a point. With the Great War over, the question was why Britain was occupying large areas of Persia and Central Asia, of all places. It required investigation, which would almost certainly conclude by recommending, or ordering, evacuation.

Malleson meanwhile pointed out that the bridge over the Amu Darya at Charjui was the crucial strategic point, a condition that was obvious even to the militarily ignorant Ashkhabad Committee, but had so far apparently escaped attention in Delhi and London. He wanted to occupy the town, and so block the river crossing, but for this, he required more troops. The Ashkhabad Committee, he commented, was of little use, and required support, which meant still more troops, while the Turkoman nomads were becoming restless, and needed to be restrained. Malleson himself went to Ashkhabad to talk to the committee, and came away contemptuous. The distant headquarters in Delhi and London disagreed with each other on the issue, and the men on the spot were now pursuing goals that were contradictory to both.

The end of the Turkish war, and the occupation of the Black Sea by the Allied squadrons during December 1918, had opened up a new line of communication and supply. Instead of a long single-track railway line through Baluchistan and then a laborious journey along bad or non-existent roads for 1,000 kilometres north through eastern Persia, subject to tribal raids along the way, a more convenient route from Constantinople all the way to Merv was now available. This had come into existence gradually as the presence of the British forces' activities expanded. The 27th Division, coming from Salonika, moved across the Black Sea and into the Caucasus at the end of December. Baku was reoccupied by British forces from Persia in mid-November, and a British squadron under Commodore Norris was in control of much of the Caspian. A British force was in occupation of Krasnovodsk, and the Indian force, which included the Punjabis, controlled the line as far as Merv. And so, in December, General Milne, the commander of the Army of the Black Sea, was able to set out to travel along the whole route from west to east on an inspection of his command.[15]

Most of the action in December was in the form of telegraphic exchanges between Malleson in Meshed, the Indian Army headquarters in Delhi, and the India Office in London. The British Trans-Caspian forward position remained some distance east of Merv at a place, in a gap in a group of sand dunes, called Annenkovo. This was the only point available as a viable defensive position for a long distance – unless he could get permission to move forward to the Oxus.

The Tashkent Committee's forces made a minor attack on the Annenkovo position in early January, perhaps as a reconnaissance, and then mounted a serious attack on the 16th. Trains were used by both sides, usually with an armoured train going first, followed by ordinary trains carrying most of the infantry and the supplies. This provided both accommodation for the men, and transported them to the point of attack. At Annenkovo, there was a curiously complicated action. The Bolsheviks attempted first to cut the track and telegraph line behind the Allied armoured train, hopefully to immobilise it, and then attack the stranded Allied trains from both flanks. The cutting operation worked, but the main attacks were apparently delayed – it was a very cold and foggy day – so the track had been repaired before the main Bolshevik force arrived. This allowed the planned Allied reinforcements to move forward from the reserve and so reach their forward position without delay.

As before, it was the Indian soldiers who were the main element in the defence, both those in the train and others who were brought up in the later trains. They all leapt out to go straight into action as they landed. The Bolshevik forces attacked from both flanks, but not quite simultaneously, and both attacks were defeated. Armenian and Russian contingents fought well alongside the Punjabis. The Bolsheviks suffered about 500 casualties, dead and wounded, and the same number were crippled by frostbite. The Allied forces had almost 120 casualties. The Bolsheviks retired once again.[16]

One of the results of the continual telegraphic consultations was that it became clear that supplying Malleson's force, particularly as it was now larger than earlier, through eastern Persia was inefficient and costly. General Dickson, who had taken charge of the route early in October, had first to make an estimate of his transport needs if he was to move sufficient goods to Meshed and then further on to the railway beyond the Russian border. To transport the required supplies from the railhead just inside the Persian border with Baluchistan to Meshed, and then on to Ashkhabad was a journey of 1,000 kilometres, along a route littered with the wrecks of cars and vans, the skeletons of worn-out camels and the graves of exhausted men. By request of Malleson, Dickson put in an estimate that he would need 11,680 government camels, or 14,600 locally hired camels, or 1,450 Ford vans, to maintain an adequate flow of supplies along the route. This was based on providing supplies, after building up the British force to the estimated level along the railway and at Meshed through the winter, for a brigade of cavalry, an artillery brigade, and an infantry division, with a cavalry brigade and an infantry brigade to guard the lines of communication. These forces had been Malleson's estimate of his military manpower needs if he was to maintain his position and probably extend it; it was much larger than any force he had yet used, by a factor of perhaps a hundred. No doubt, the expense he thus estimated frightened the life of those in London and Delhi who had to pay for all this, at least politically.[17]

Two conclusions followed from such a series of estimates. First, as it was realised, now that the Turkish war was over, the troops along the railway could be supplied more conveniently from the Black Sea, by ship to Batumi, rail to Baku, ship to Krasnovodsk, and then rail again to Merv. This was a complicated journey, but it was much easier than one by foot and camel through the Baluchistan and Persian deserts. It would be quicker and more certain than maintaining a stable of thousands of camels and paying the wages of the hundreds, even thousands, of hired men who would be needed to service, care for, feed, and drive the animals. Above all, it would be conducted by, and under the control of, British troops all the way. On the other hand, it would require a considerable force of support troops along the route, and may well not have been any less expensive than that through Persia.

A further result of the estimates was the realisation that, if such a system were to be implemented, the command arrangements would need to adapt. Already Brigadier General Dickson had taken over the rearward communications from Malleson, and now Brigadier General G.A.H. Beatty was appointed as field commander under Malleson to take over command of the forces along the railway; each of these generals would need a competent staff. This effective removal of direct command from Malleson might have been because of his lack of experience of field command, but it was undoubtedly true that with the needs of administration and to keep contact with London and Delhi, he was already mainly pinned down to his Meshed headquarters, and would be the more certainly immobilised if he acquired a larger force.

There was also the continuing need for negotiation with the Ashkhabad Committee, the supervision of the thousand-mile route back to the Indian railhead, and of the similar length of the Trans-Caspian Railway under his control. It was obvious that Malleson's work had expanded greatly from merely commanding at Meshed and directing the actions of two or three companies and the cavalry squadron to block the railway. It was not, for example, until December 1918 that Malleson had been able to get to Ashkhabad to talk with the members of the beleaguered committee there. Beatty arrived with a staff, manned and organised, which would help relieve Malleson of some of the administrative work. It is notable, for example, that in none of the accounts of any of the fights that took place is any soldier of any rank described as in command – only a captain at Kaahka for the infantry, a major for the cavalry, and on one occasion a lieutenant colonel, but no men of higher rank. That is, command was at the battalion level, and the highest-ranking officer mentioned in any account of the fighting is a major; all the administration had been done by Malleson; Beatty and his staff were clearly needed.

The staff at Meshed and on the line were being elaborated and increased, therefore, in anticipation of a longer and larger campaign, and the supply system was expanding to cope. When this was finally understood, it became necessary to appoint a new overall commander, of a higher rank than Malleson or Beatty. The source of both supplies and reinforcements was now in the west, first through General Thomson at Enzeli, who worked with Commodore Norris in the Caspian Sea in the matter, and had now reoccupied Baku. At last, the Army of the Black Sea, Thomson's force at Baku and Enzeli, and the troops along the railway in Central Asia were all put under the commander of the Army of the Black Sea, General Milne. His command therefore extended along the railway from Krasnovodsk to Merv, but also back to the Caspian and Batumi, and to Constantinople. Malleson remained in command at Meshed and along the road back to Quetta, the boundary between the two commands being the international border between Persia and Russia. It was now up to Milne to decide what to do with such a strange command.

Milne finally reached Ashkhabad and met Malleson on 27 January, having travelled through the British-dominated Caucasus and across the British-controlled Caspian Sea. He arrived ten days after the defeat of the Bolshevik attack at Annenkovo, which had relieved some of Malleson's problems. It was the moment of the greatest extent of British control in these extended events, and it was the first time a general with experience of modern warfare had reached the region.

Milne made a few swift adjustments: the Hampshire battalion, no more than a weak company by now, was returned to General Marshall in Mesopotamia, to be replaced by a company of the 9th Royal Warwickshires; the 28th Light Cavalry was to be concentrated at the front – that is, at Annenkovo – in part, no doubt, because the Punjabis had by now suffered substantial casualties, and were much reduced in strength, although Annenkovo was a position that also required mainly cavalry forces. But all this was no more than Malleson could have done. Milne had a larger task.

Milne made his inspection, and talked to Malleson, and no doubt to Beatty. Then he sent a long telegram to the War Office in London. He gave his estimate of the situation and his recommendations for the future. An immediate decision, he said, was required on the future of British policy in Central Asia, which could only mean that, if control was to be retained permanently, much greater forces were needed, or, if not, all should be withdrawn entirely. He had probably seen the various contradictory, intricate, and argumentative messages sent over the past several months to Malleson from London and Delhi, and he came to the conclusion that there were only two alternatives: withdraw altogether, or support the local government of Trans-Caspia with very substantial forces, permanently posted to the area.[18]

The local authority in the area, including Ashkhabad, was now a small Committee of Public Safety, which had been constituted, and was dominated, by Malleson. It had been formed after the original Ashkhabad Committee had resigned. Support for this authority would require British troops in sufficient numbers to face possibly large numbers of Russian forces, along with the necessary arms, ammunition, supplies, and money. He put the cost at £100,000 per month, no doubt well aware of the horror this would evoke in the London accountants. He was also aware that it would grab the government's full attention and thereby provoke a decision. And he stated that the military support required to prop up the Ashkhabad Committee was a cavalry regiment, a battery of artillery, four infantry battalions, aircraft, and heavy guns – a major increase on the force already allocated to the region, which amounted to three companies of infantry and one squadron of cavalry and the Royal Field Artillery detachment. The increase would be at least fourfold. (It was, however, a good deal less than General Dickson, and perhaps Malleson, had earlier calculated was necessary.)

On the question of withdrawal, Malleson had pointed out that to do so would pull the support away from Britain's allies in the area and break faith with them. It was clear from his message that Milne himself favoured withdrawal – his telegram makes that clear – and that he cared little for the honour of the promises Malleson had made in Britain's name, or for the future of the Ashkhabad Committee of Public Safety. That is, he was prepared to pull out all British forces and let the Russians fight it out among themselves. Given that the original purpose of this intervention and been to block any support for Germany in the last year of the Great War, this was bringing the attention of the British government back to basics, with a vengeance.

Milne was considering only the military situation. Malleson, by his talk of honouring his promises, was actually talking of political matters. For the only way the British could stay in Central Asia would be to set up, and defend, independent governments. Two – Khiva and Bokhara – were ready-made; the Muslim Committee destroyed by the Tashkent Bolsheviks at Kokand could be reconstituted on the basis of the *basmachi* bands; the Kazaks, who had rebelled three years before against the imperial government, and the Turkomans, who lived north of Ashkhabad, some of whom had fought with the British along the railway, could have been recognised as local powers and independent governments. The political material was available if the decision to advance militarily was made – but given the suggested cost, as Milne and probably Malleson would surely have known, no such forward move was ever likely, just as later in the Black Sea, or in the Caucasus, the British would not support other breakaway sections of the old Russian Empire, for to do so would be to end up fighting Russia.

Milne's message was digested in London for a week. Almost inevitably, given the financial situation that the administrations in Britain and India believed themselves to be facing, the decision came down in favour of a complete withdrawal. Malleson's mission was to be drawn back to Meshed, and resume its role as the East Persian Cordon, with the extra aim of preventing any Bolshevik incursions into Persia; Krasnovodsk, which Milne had wanted to evacuate, was to be held, though for how long was not clear.[19]

Malleson was left to organise the withdrawal, though events intervened to derail his intentions. White Russian forces were sent across the Caspian to take over the defence of the British-occupied area: some of these, Cossacks, arrived at Ashkhabad with the intention of reinforcing the Trans-Caspian defence, but they quarrelled almost at once with the local Russians, and had to be 'confined'. Some Daghestani horsemen were sent across, and similarly made themselves obnoxious. (The readiness of the Russians to dispute with each other rather suggests that Malleson's manner had been much more emollient and successful.) However, as it became clear that the British ability and willingness to provide support and defence was limited, an alliance of sorts was organised between the general commanding the White forces in South Russia, Denikin, and the Ashkhabad Committee, and men from Denikin's forces were sent across, numerous enough to replace the British forces as they withdrew. This movement was one reason for holding on to Krasnovodsk. But bad relations between the arrogant Denikinites of the Volunteer Army and the rather timorous and unmilitary Ashkhabad Committee compromised the latter's efforts to survive. Hence, to the Russians' difficulties at Ashkhabad was now added bad relations between the Ashkhabad Russians and the ex-imperial officers being sent as their reinforcements.[20]

At the end of February, several more or less simultaneous developments effectively shifted British attention and forced the Ashkhabad Committee to attend to its own defence. On 28 February, Emir Habibullah of Afghanistan was assassinated, supposedly because he had refused to declare *jihad* at the recent opportunity presented by the momentary German advances in France in the summer of 1918. The implication was that any new Afghan government would actually do so, with serious consequences for all Afghanistan's neighbours. Three days later, Malleson told the Ashkhabad Committee about the plans for a British withdrawal, though by this time it was probably an open secret. Protection of Ashkhabadites would be handed to the Russian forces sent by Denikin, who were now being landed at Krasnovodsk and were moving on to Merv and the front line at Annenkovo.

The withdrawal of the British forces was carried out during March and early April. There was no fighting of any importance, but the population, which had been under, as they thought, British protection, were unhappy, even though they had done little to help themselves. The organisation of the withdrawal, of course, was a logistical exercise rather than a military one. The 28th Light Cavalry withdrew from Annenkovo to Dushak and then south into Persia to be quartered once more at Meshed. (At one point a patrol group of the regiment, fourteen strong, was caught by a Bolshevik cavalry force ten times their size; the Indians turned on their pursuers and charged them, went right through them, then returned and charged through them again; they inflicted twenty-one casualties, in exchange for one man wounded and two taken prisoner.) The 19th Punjabis left Merv on 30 March for Ashkhabad, and then went to Meshed. By 16 April, the entire British force had returned to Indian command and to its original intent and purpose.[21]

The Bolsheviks scarcely bothered to repeat their earlier attacks along the railway. The real strength of the defence, they had come to appreciate, lay in the Indian soldiers used by the British; remove them and fighting would be between two groups of Russians, and the Bolsheviks had plenty of confidence, rightly so, that they would win such a fight. The Trans-Caspian government survived only so long as it took a reinforced Red Army to march along the railway as far as Krasnovodsk, which was taken in January 1920. If there were any Russians who harboured a wish to invade India through Afghanistan, if Afghan opposition did not deter them, then the prospect of fighting several hundred battalions like the Punjabis and the Light Cavalry when they got to India would surely do so.

In Afghanistan, Emir Habibullah's successor was his son Amanullah – once he had imprisoned his uncle, who attempted to seize the throne. It was thought that Amanullah had been responsible for his father's killing. In other words, it was royalty business as usual, and he pursued a much more openly hostile policy towards Britain. He made himself emir in April 1919, and began a war with the British at the beginning of May. The war lasted until August, and can be counted as a marginal victory for Amanullah. The troops of the East Persian Cordon proved to be a helpful source of information for the British in India during the war, and in making distracting threats against Amanullah's forces, and so in restricting Afghan ambitions.[22]

This was an activity much more congenial to the Indian Army and its British officers than fighting Russians in the Central Asian deserts.

Chapter 4

The Oil of Baku

The city of Baku had become a major source of oil before the Great War, and had developed into a boomtown of Texan proportions, with the extremes of high-flying wealthy capitalist owners in palatial houses and badly paid workers living in the most squalid conditions. It was therefore a target for every revolutionary group, a target of every capitalist group, a target for the German army and for the Turkish army, and curiously, by the last part of the Great War, a target for the British Army, which had operated nowhere near it until then.

Before the war, the oil industry at Baku had been repeatedly crippled by a series of huge strikes, ethnic conflicts, and brutal repression by the Russian authorities. This had driven away the owners and many of the skilled technicians, and had left the oil industry at the city much reduced in activity and production, but still working though subject to outbursts of the workers' anger. It was still a major source of oil, which became increasingly valuable in the war effort for all sides as war became increasingly mechanised.[1]

The city had, of course, as such places do, attracted a very mixed population – Christian Armenians and Georgians, Muslim Azeris, Russians, Western Europeans, Armenians, Persians, Turks, Chinese, Americans, and others – and had a population of perhaps 200,000 in 1918. It seethed with revolutionary activity, with Bolsheviks, Mensheviks, Social Revolutionaries, nationalists of various sorts, and imperialists, all active in the city. The political and social confusion in Russia from 1917 onwards was mirrored, and even magnified, in Baku.[2] The region of which it was the centre, Azerbaijan, had been part of the Russian Empire for a century, and after the collapse of imperial rule, had constituted itself as the quasi-independent Azerbaijani Republic;[3] it was, however, in a very unstable political and social condition, not surprisingly. And, of course, at the basis of all this, it was producing large quantities of oil, and so it was a source of great wealth, producing a resource that armies and navies had come to need increasingly during the last four years of warfare.

And – again this was typical of such places – it was located in a thoroughly awkward geographical position.

During 1918, the city became the target of a British expedition sent north from Mesopotamia and of a Turkish expedition from Anatolia, and was part of the German search for oil from Europe by way of Ukraine after the Treaty of Brest-Litovsk, and then of another two British expeditions. The number of inimical forces who were avid to gain control of the city and its oil was the source of the British interest. One of the problems for German forces – and for the Turks for that matter – was that they had access to only a restricted supply of oil. The main source for Germany was Romania, and the need to gain control of that source had been one of the purposes for the German conquest of that country in 1916; British secret service agents had succeeded in badly damaging the Romanian wells and installations even as the German forces approached.[4] The damage was being repaired, but the Romanian oilfields were temporarily not very productive. Given control of the oil of Baku, however, German forces and industry would be supplied from an ample source. To prevent this the British sent expeditions against the city during 1918.

Azerbaijan was volatile; it changed governments by coups, and by invasions and conquests, all too rapidly and frequently. And all this while Baku city itself was roiling with violence, with ethnic massacres being the favourite resort of the militants.

The first British intervention was a shoestring expedition dispatched from Baghdad, commanded by an Indian Army officer, Major General Lionel Dunsterville, but on the orders of the War Office in London. He commanded a mixed group of troops. Its purpose was to deny Baku to the Turks and the Germans, who had, after the Bolshevik Russian Revolution and the peace treaty of Brest-Litovsk, moved to seize the oil of the region, or at least to gain access to it. This was part of the German exploitation by their army of the resources of southern Russia, control of which Germany had gained, for the moment, by the peace treaty. They had detached much of southern Russia from the Bolshevik Russian regime in Moscow into the Republic of Ukraine; the Caucasus peoples had also seized their independence, first as Transcaucasia, then as independent ethnic republics. The German army aimed to gain access to the several war materials available in the Caucasus region and beyond. The most pressing was oil, but this was not the only one. The German plan early in 1918 was to launch a major offensive against the Allied armies on the Western Front, and for this, an increased supply of oil was now a necessary resource. They also aimed to secure Ukraine's 1918 harvest, manganese in Georgia, and cotton from Turkestan, all vital war materials that might make all the difference to the capability of the German army.

In reply to the threat to Baku, or perhaps in anticipation of a German expedition, a small British 'advance force' – only the first of a series of these forces – left Baghdad in January 1918, on the road to the Caspian Sea port of Enzeli. This force was to be reinforced by a slightly larger force sent from Britain in February, which was referred to as 'the Baghdad party'. The aim was not necessarily to exploit Baku's oil for the Allies, but to deny that oil to Germany. The name of the commander of the whole, General Dunsterville, of the Indian Army, gave the expedition its name – 'Dunsterforce'.[5]

The plan was to send the initial British force north-east from Baghdad through Persian territory to the Caspian Sea at the Persian port of Enzeli on the south-west corner of that sea. Ships could be acquired, seized, or captured there, in which the force would sail to take control of Baku and prevent the enemy from doing so. The enemy was expected to be German or Turkish, or even Russian since the revolution. The complications were evident from the start. This was, one might say, the first of the expeditions.

The origin of the expedition was in a complex, one may say inchoate, series of proposals emanating in particular from the Persian Committee in London, which was directed by Lord Curzon, former Viceroy of India, and a well-travelled man familiar with the Caucasus, the Caspian, and Central Asia. As such plans do, the original intention was grandiose, but was gradually refined and whittled down until it was an expedition aimed at Baku. Ditched along the way was a plan to rouse Georgia to preoccupy any approaching Turkish force, and various other ideas. The basic context was a lack of manpower, given the necessary heavy concentration on the Western Front in France. Dunsterforce never had more than 1,000 men, and its aim was therefore refined down to that single item, Baku.

This expedition was to be assisted by the British commander-in-chief of the Mesopotamian force at Baghdad, General William Marshall, and to be built up by reinforcements sent from Britain. The London group was already being called 'the Baghdad party' even before it set off for London.

It was supposed to be a highly secret expedition, but the term was in use in London even before they left, and even by a salesgirl in the stores where they went for their equipment.[6] They were furthermore publicly greeted as 'the Baghdad party' at Alexandria the moment they arrived. But the term did quite effectively hide the real purpose of the group, for Baghdad was the headquarters of the British–Indian expeditionary force which had been slowly conquering Mesopotamia since 1914, but had scarcely moved for a year; referring to Baghdad as the group destination did not reveal what they were to do there, if anything.

Dunsterforce became one of a series of separate 'expeditions', which were sent by various British authorities into the region north of Persia in 1918. One, Dunsterville's Dunsterforce, was headed for Baku; a second, commanded by Major General Malleson, went into Central Asia (see Chapter 3); a third – actually a single officer, Colonel F.M. Bailey – went to Bokhara and then to Samarkand and Tashkent investigating the situation; a fourth was the projection of the British 27th Division into the Caucasus region from Salonika; a fifth was a follow-up to Dunsterforce after it had been withdrawn. These rarely linked together in any decisive way, but the whole set of expeditions does exhibit a single purpose, though they did not coincide in time and were spread widely in space. One cannot call the aims of all these co-ordinated at all.

The German threat to gain control of Baku and its oil was the main problem faced by these expeditions. But in the background of the planners' minds was the knowledge that there were several tens of thousands of German and Austro-Hungarian prisoners of war held in camps in Turkestan. If the Germans, coming from the west across the Caspian, and along the Trans-Caspian Railway could liberate these men, a large army of well-trained men and probably vengeful soldiers might suddenly emerge on the borders of India, or through Persia into Mesopotamia, or come to be used on the Western Front. With arms in their hands, they could certainly at least control Central Asia, and the disturbed conditions in that land in 1918 made such a possibility all too plausible. A small German force on the railway would have a disproportionate effect; two battalions of British Indian troops did so with little difficulty in 1918; Major General Malleson's East Persian Cordon Force quickly established control over the borderlands of Persia and Afghanistan with no more than 1,500 men.

Bailey's mission was to investigate Russian intentions and its control of Central Asia: as an Indian officer, any threat to India that he could find would have to be countered. He set out from India to reach Tashkent in Russian Turkestan, which had become the Bolshevik centre. He operated throughout alone and in disguise. His 'expedition' may have begun as a reaction to the German successes in early 1918, but it then became part of the Allied reaction to events in Russia itself and this put serious doubts on the value of his conclusions when he emerged once more, though by then his information was somewhat out of date.[7]

It may be pointed out that these expeditions were deliberately set up by co-ordination between the governments in London and Delhi, and that the leaders of all of them were Indian Army officers, while most of the men involved, the rank and file, were Indian soldiers. It was, in one sense, India reaching out to investigate its own neighbourhood, just as armed expeditions of Indian troops had been sent to fight in China and Ethiopia in the 1860s, to South Africa in the Boer War, Tibet, and China again in the 1900s, to the Western Front and to Egypt in the Great War, and, seventy years before, even to Crimea. Only under British imperial control had this Indian expansiveness happened; it would happen again in the next war; independent India has not been so expansive since the tenth century.

There was yet another 'expedition', which we can consider in its place, in connection with the British naval dominance in the Black Sea, which was established after the other expeditions had already begun. The 27th Division under Major General Forestier-Walker was sent into the Caucasus with the ultimate aim of reaching Baku, which was also Dunsterville's destination, and there was the succeeding expedition under General Thomson following in Dunsterville's footsteps. From Baku, when he gained control of it, Dunsterville made contact with Krasnovodsk at the start of the Trans-Caspian Railway, and the link was thus established with Malleson's expedition – a battery of artillery, and a battalion of the Hampshire Regiment were sent through Krasnovodsk to assist Malleson.

There were thus no less than five British expeditions going into the lands east of the Black Sea from various directions: Dunsterforce, Malleson's force, Bailey, the 27th Division, and the successors to Dunsterforce. They went to Baku, to the Caspian – for a year – into Central Asia, and into Russian Turkestan.

Considering the wide extent of the British actions, from Odessa to Tashkent, it is clear that the issue in British minds was only marginally about oil. The British had easier access to oil elsewhere; the Royal Navy had a reliable supply available in the United States and Canada and in southern Persia, with the great Abadan refinery amongst other places, including Burma (British territory) and Sumatra and Borneo (neutral Dutch country). Baku was a singularly awkward place for the Royal Navy to reach, or for the British Army or navy to depend on as a source of supply. Rather, British concern was to prevent any enemy gaining access to the Baku oil, for Russians and Germans and perhaps the Turks could well use it in the current fighting, and all these were enemies of the British Empire in one way or another. These British expeditions, several of them aimed at Southern Russian lands, were therefore tasked with short-term aims, related only to the situation in the last stages of the wider Great War. On the other hand, one of them did establish a temporary Royal Naval dominance in the Caspian Sea, surely one of the more extraordinary consequences of the Great War.

Oil, therefore, or at least access to it, was not the overwhelming issue in the several British lunges for control of Baku, and not at all in the case of those in Central Asia or the Black Sea. Maritime control of the Caspian Sea (and so of Baku) was essential to gain control of Krasnovodsk, and so access to the Trans-Caspian Railway, and so to Central Asia, but once the adventures into both were over, the Caspian could be abandoned. The British aim at Baku was not its oil, therefore, except in denying that oil to British enemies, but the defence of the threatened empire, notably the Indian Empire.

Agents of that empire had long been familiar with the outer borderlands of India – Afghanistan, Persia, Chinese Central Asia, Tibet – but Russian Central Asia was the most important and potentially the most threatening, as the old Russian threat appeared to be revived by the Bolsheviks in the region, under the specious slogan of liberation. (Bolshevism was, of course, imperialism in a new guise.) Now there was a German and the Turkish threat to add to it. What was more, the Russian rail system in Central Asia, if such a comprehensive term was appropriate for a single line, had been constructed partly with the express purpose of permitting Russian armed forces to approach the Indian borderlands as closely as possible, at the northern border of Afghanistan – the short branch line which led to a store of military materials kept at Kushka, was conveniently and most obviously placed to be available for an invader heading for India; it fell into Bolshevik hands in 1918, though the arms stored there were used in the civil war, not an invasion of Afghanistan. This was clearly a military threat. It had receded somewhat from 1907, with the Anglo-Russian Entente of that year, but since March 1917, Russia had ceased to be a reliable ally and had moved into the unreliable neutral, and possibly hostile, column.

With the Bolshevik peace treaty with Germany and Austria-Hungary, concluded at Brest-Litovsk in March 1918, Russia had become an 'almost enemy', but in social and revolutionary terms was a clear threat with its anti-imperialist rhetoric. Hence, amongst other things, the activity of the British fleet in the Black Sea, whose purpose in the British view was essentially defensive, aiming to promote political stability in Russia and in the Near East. The Mediterranean Fleet was able to gain access to the Black Sea by mid-November 1918, hence the renewed pervasive interest displayed in London and Delhi by the British towards all the southern Russian lands from Crimea to Chinese Central Asia – and hence also all these various expeditions.

The original purpose of the intervention by Dunsterforce aimed at Baku was to counter the late Turkish invasion of the Caucasus region, which came in 1918 when the Russian defences had vanished. The Turkish move had been inspired by the Russian collapse in 1917–18 after the successive revolutions, and the consequent end of the Turkish–Russian War. With Russia removed from the Turks' active enemies, Enver Pasha had constructed a new army, the Army of Islam, commanded by his brother Nuri Pasha, and containing a high proportion of experienced and well-motivated Turkish soldiers. This was his vehicle for this campaign, which was aimed at rousing the fellow Turks in Central Asia and reviving the mediaeval Turkish empires. Turkish control over the Caucasus region, and Baku, was to be the first step – the Azeris and the Daghestanis could be counted as fellow Turks.[8]

Russian authority had evaporated throughout the southern region with the revolution, and it was unclear what would replace it; in the Caucasus region, though, this meant, for the moment, the locally independent states of Armenia, Georgia, and Azerbaijan. The oil reserves at Baku were tempting for many reasons. Germany planned new attacks in the West, and the Germans in Eastern Europe wanted their Turkish allies to secure the oil. At the same time, the German army was sending troops through Ukraine and southern Russia towards the Caucasus to gain access for themselves to these riches. (There were other, less important, sources of oil in the region, at Maikop, for example.) The Turks were very willing to take control of this region, partly because they would be perfectly happy to secure the oil themselves, but also because the Azeris, who were the majority population in the Baku area, were Muslims, and could probably be counted on as Ottoman supporters, or at least as fellow Muslims (they had also been fellow massacrers of Armenians). Baku would provide access to the Caspian, and therefore to the port of Krasnovodsk and its railway, and to the lands of Central Asia, inhabited by more Turkish-speaking peoples. Enver was aiming to build a new Turkish empire to replace that lost by the independence of the Christian states in the Balkans, and the British conquest of the Arab lands in Syria and Mesopotamia.[9]

The British, besides perceiving a threat to their Asian possessions, were also concerned that any German forces that overran southern Russia would then be able to transfer their forces, fully supplied with oil, to the Western Front, there to mount yet another new attack using their victorious and fresh forces from the east. If they reached Baku, the oil from there would be part of that reinforcement, increasing their mobility on land and in the air. If they reached Central Asia, they could secure supplies of cotton, and perhaps liberate the thousands of Austrian and German prisoners held in camps in that region.

During the years of fighting since 1914, all armies had become mechanised, and so increasingly reliant on oil; furthermore, the cotton of Turkestan would be more than useful, for cotton was a constituent of explosives, while the wheat of Ukraine would allow the Germans to survive the increasingly oppressive Allied blockade. The Germans had already, on a much smaller scale, achieved the same mutual reinforcement of wheat and oil in their conquest of Romania. There had been German agents active in Persia and Afghanistan during the war, seeking to rouse the local rulers against the all-pervasive British; the ground had in part been well prepared.

Facing such a threat in the West (which became real in the successive German attacks between March and July 1918), the Allies had no surplus of forces that could be deployed so far from their bases as Baku. The nearest of their forces to the crucial area were the British armies in Palestine, Egypt, and Mesopotamia, all of which faced formidable Turkish armies, and none of which could spare men for the distant Caspian Sea. There were, however, considerable reserves of military manpower in India, though most of these were needed to keep control there where unrest, partly caused by the war's effects, was becoming serious. The Indian government was also well aware of the German and Turkish intrigues in the Muslim lands between the Mediterranean and the Khyber Pass, and had been busy countering them in Persia, where several Indian Army forces were active. By 1918, also those British armies in Palestine and Mesopotamia were very largely composed of Indian soldiers. It was not only the German armies that were suffering from a shortage of manpower.

These considerations meant that mounting the expeditions from Baghdad and Quetta would allow them to use only minimal forces sent from India and Britain – Malleson in Meshed used only forces that were already in Persia, and Dunsterville similarly used forces already in Mesopotamia and Persia. They were given quite specific objectives – to cut the Trans-Caspian Railway, seize and hold Baku for a time to deny the oil to the enemy – but they were not aiming to conquer territory, for this would require garrisons and further campaigns to secure the new conquests. The British (and even more, the French) were at the end of their manpower resources by 1918, and no Americans would be available to help out in imperial matters; plainly, it was India that had to provide the required military manpower to operate in its own backyard.

The British had begun their move to contain the Turkish attack on Baku as early as December 1917 (a month after the Bolshevik *coup d'état* had overthrown the imperial regime). General Dunsterville was called away from his command on the North-West Frontier of India to go to Mesopotamia and assume command of the expedition aimed at Baku. He was to march north through western Persia to the shores of the Caspian Sea at Enzeli, in the south-western corner of that sea, where he would find ships to carry him to Baku – or that was the plan in outline. He was given an independent command, even if there was only a small force of about fifty men under him at first. He at once ran up against the commander-in-chief of the British forces in Mesopotamia, General Marshall, who was not at all pleased to find that Dunsterville was to be independent of his authority, nor that he was demanding that extra forces to be detached from the army in Mesopotamia for his use. He also required considerable supplies.

At least so Dunsterville indicated, when he reached Iraq to take up his new command. It took some time for the Baghdad party (a minimal reinforcement from Britain, mainly officers and NCOs) to reach Baghdad, and even then, Marshall held them back. It seems likely that those who chose Dunsterville for the Baku expedition fully appreciated the contrasting characters of the two generals: Dunsterville was adventurous, a risk-taker, though ultimately very careful of his men – just the man to have in command on the volatile Indian frontier. Marshall was extra cautious, a by-the-book commander with little or no initiative in him; he had to be pushed to move his fighting forces north from Baghdad when the Turkish command facing him disintegrated. On the other hand, Marshall's caution – due as much to the need to surrender men to other theatres of the war – might be expected to exercise some restraint on Dunsterville's adventurousness. Marshall resented losing control of even the few men Dunsterville took with him in his first attempt to fulfil his orders, and he failed repeatedly to send supplies and reinforcements after him – for, after all, he could point out that Dunsterville's command was deliberately made independent of his.

Not that this was altogether Marshall's own fault, though his cautious bureaucratic mind happily fell in with the concept of doing nothing. Dunsterville does not mention Marshall by name in his account of his 'adventures', clearly preferring to ignore him. Donohoe, a journalist who chronicles in detail his voyage from Britain to Basra and his stay in Iraq, similarly does not mention Marshall, though he does contrast his office regime with that of his predecessor, Sir Stanley Maude, who made his officers work through the heat of the afternoon rather than take their expected siesta. Elements of conflict between the generals did reach print in the *Official History*, however.[10]

In addition, by 1918, when Dunsterville arrived, Marshall was being pressed to advance north in Mesopotamia. The British forces were still only a little way north of Baghdad, and had been stuck there for a year. He had lost forces for the crisis on the Western Front and to Allenby in Palestine, and could clearly plead manpower poverty, even if the estimates he made of his weakness were exaggerated. So Dunsterville's arrival was therefore another blow to his reduced command. He had advanced forwards early in 1918 as far as Hit, on the Euphrates, 100 miles from Baghdad, but only because the Turks had evacuated it first. He therefore exercised his talent for finding excuses for doing nothing, even though the demands made by Dunsterville were relatively small, at least at first – but Marshall was bureaucratic enough to recognise that a small early request could well balloon later into a much greater demand.

No matter how small the force Dunsterville started with – he had only fifty-five men at the beginning – he had to travel 700 miles through difficult country, which was destitute of any sort of supplies, and the men found evidence all along the route of starvation in the Persian population. As a result, everything would have to come from Mesopotamia in an endless stream of lorries. The land he marched through had been ravaged by brigands, Turks, and other enemies, and he found people dying of hunger by the side of the road. Marshall could clearly see that this was a project that would gobble up men and supplies endlessly and possibly strangle him, leaving him unable to conduct the other operations he was ordered to make. He was right, even though he was using Dunsterforce as an excuse.

Marshall had in fact been strongly urged to participate in a new advance in Mesopotamia, by which he would eventually link up with Allenby from Syria as they both advanced north. The ultimate intention, or perhaps hope, was that Marshall's own left flank would link with Allenby's right, and his own right flank would rest at Baku, so linking with Dunsterville. It was the sort of plan dreamed up in a London office by an inexperienced staff officer, after considering a small-scale map of the region in question. It ignored any and all physical obstacles or difficulties – there were several mountain ranges between the Mesopotamian base and Baku, not to mention plenty of human obstacles, as Dunsterville discovered. Marshall, not surprisingly, was sceptical, and was extremely reluctant even to attempt such activity. On the other hand, in late 1918 he did advance suddenly, on orders of course, to seize Kirkuk and Mosul. It had been realised in London that the French might go for Mosul from Syria, which had been assigned to them by the Sykes–Picot Agreement back in 1915. The British could claim that this agreement was out of date, but that would hardly stop the French lunging for Mosul if they got the chance. The British thus had an uncertain claim to the area; actual control at the time of the peace conference would be crucial – and both areas were probable sources of oil, and therefore wealth. Marshall eventually achieved the goal, showing he could move when he was pushed hard enough.

The Dunsterville expedition counted forty-one soldiers, two NCOs, and fourteen officers when it began from Baghdad, though the numbers slowly increased as the Baghdad party caught up, and as other groups were roped in, either as volunteers or conscripts. There were some elements in its favour: it was motorised, and included an armoured car, which impressed all who faced it; the roads were good, if only relatively speaking; and Dunsterville could collect accurate local intelligence from the various British and French consuls and vice-consuls along the route. The route, in fact, was more or less clear for most of the way, though travel was hindered by the presence of numerous Russian soldiers, who had been stationed as controlling garrisons in northern Persia before the revolutions, and who were no longer required there; they were thus moving north in the general direction of home. These men were usually without any discipline, the officers' authority having evaporated with the Russian imperial regime's collapse, though one particular unit of Cossacks did retain their discipline, understanding the dangers of their isolation, and being devoted to their commander, General Lazar Bicherakov.

The retreating soldiers were being fleeced of their weapons by the local brigands and chiefs, who might well also object to a British force passing by; Bicherakov's cavalry, retaining their discipline and their weapons, did not suffer this indignity. The individual Russians were, on the other hand, friendly and cheerful, since they were going home, though they were very liable to steal food and to demand transport with menaces.[11]

Dunsterville got his small force most of the way to his Caspian Sea destination reasonably quickly. However, he found when he got to Resht, a city only a few miles short of Enzeli, that he was separated from that destination by a mountain range, and that a local dissident Persian group called the Jangalis, who claimed to be Bolsheviks, and were thoroughly hostile, blocked the way. They also held hostage a British officer, Captain Noel. Even with the reinforcements who had joined him on the journey, Dunsterville was heavily outnumbered. Most of the Baghdad party had been held up in Baghdad by Marshall's inability, or unwillingness, to provide transport for them, and they had trickled in only slowly. As a result, Dunsterville failed to get to Enzeli. He found his Jangali enemies too numerous for his small force to confront; they were also being advised by a couple of German officers, hence their unusually good organisation. He withdrew his force back to Hamadan, about halfway back to his Mesopotamian starting point, and looked again for more reinforcements, or at least for the troops who had been assigned to him to be allowed to join him, and for others to come along as well. Marshall's apprehensions were coming true.[12]

It may be pointed out that all this was taking place in a neutral country. The authority of Persia's central government, the Shah, was weak, so that it had become a playground for intrigues by Turks, Germans, Russians, and British since 1914, not to mention local tribes and chieftains, who had become accustomed to acting independently. The German aim had been to stimulate a war that would threaten India, either by Persia or by Afghanistan. They were sure this would distract the British from the Western Front, and tie down some of their forces. This had not worked out, but, situated between British India and Turkish Mesopotamia, Persia became an intriguer's playground. By treaty, both Britain and Russia had been able to station troops in the country since 1907, and the fighting between them and the Persians was low level but continual. It was never on a large scale, but the Russians in the north were preoccupied all the time, and in the south, the British had forces at Abadan, where there was a great British-owned oil refinery, other forces in Fars province, and the East Persian Cordon Force along the Afghan–Persian boundary. In the south, as well, Sir Percy Sykes had recruited a force called the South Persian Rifles, which policed the area.[13] All this was in a country where fighting was often against the tribal chiefs rather than the imperial Shah; as a result, Persians and Persia had suffered severely, as the Dunsterforce troops noted on their march.

From Hamadan, Dunsterville visited Teheran, the Persian capital, partly to gather information from the British ambassador. He was also busy recruiting Persian troops, in the same way as Sykes had done. It was May by this time, and Dunsterville had been on the way from Baghdad since February, without reaching his goal. And now the Turks from Anatolia had sent a force into north-western Persia and occupied Tabriz. The matter was becoming steadily more complicated.[14]

Marshall was now given direct instructions to assist Dunsterville. He sent on a cargo of captured Turkish rifles to arm the militia recruits. It had been understood that a Turkish advance would likely overrun the Caucasus region, including Baku. (This was Enver's Army of Islam, commanded by his brother.) Marshall was therefore ordered to provide Dunsterville at Hamadan with the materials and reinforcements he needed; there he could establish a base against German intrigues in North Persia, and hopefully deter a Turkish attack. Marshall was also instructed to push forward in Mesopotamia at least as far as Kirkuk in order to distract the Turks from their probable invasion of Persia – Kirkuk, by coincidence (of course), was believed to be a major source of oil. Marshall advanced on Kirkuk; a month later, he was reminded that he should give support to Dunsterville as well.[15] Dunsterville decided he had enough soldiers and supplies to leave Hamadan and return northwards, at least to Kazvin.[16]

Having failed in his attempt to reach the Caspian at his first attempt, Dunsterville found that his instructions had changed; he was now to promote the stability of north-western Persia, though on consideration it must have been realised that it was a task highly unsuitable for anyone except a Persian. It was actually little different from the earlier situation, since such groups as the Jangalis, and their German advisers, were the prime causes of the instability. When the Turks began moving eastwards into the Caucasus and north-western Persia in the summer of 1918, partly in pursuit of the oil of Baku, his original mission was then restored. It was now known that the Russian Bolshevik government and the Germans were negotiating about Baku's oil, which would imply that the Germans were expecting to gain access to it, and that the Turkish advance was in part aimed at thwarting a further German advance by seizing the area first. And yet, a Turkish seizure of Baku would certainly allow oil to be delivered to the Germans, if at a likely higher price.[17]

Dunsterville revived the existing forces he had originally commanded, received some more troops, and made an alliance with the only Russian force still under discipline that was left in the area, Bicherakov's Cossack regiment; this was about 1,200 men, all cavalry. Marshall's reluctant support at last delivered a contingent of British officers and NCOs, designed as the foundation for the locally recruited militia force. By the beginning of June, five months after he had started from Baghdad, Dunsterville had enough forces to return to the north, and to fight and defeat the Jangalis.[18]

The Jangalis attempted to block Dunsterforce's way at the pass through the Western Elburz Mountains. This time, Dunsterville had an adequate force with him to tackle them, and Bicherakov's Cossacks could do much of the fighting. The Jangalis, advised by their German officers, had constructed an entrenched defensive position at Manjil. Their trenches were stormed, and then a second battle had to be fought to open the route. The object of the fighting was to secure the city of Resht, which was occupied by the Jangalis, though most of their forces were largely hidden in the surrounding forests. Dunsterville had a force of 450 troops, with two armoured cars, and he was able to call in aircraft, whose bombing and machine-gun fire from the air had a powerful effect. The route back to Kazvin was patrolled by a larger force, consisting of a battalion of the Hampshire Regiment and one of Gurkhas. General Bicherakov's Cossacks had pushed forward into Enzeli, where some occupying Jangalis were pushed out. The whole position of the British force was precarious, spread all along the road for many miles, but this second defeat brought the Jangalis to a peace agreement. By the end of June, the expedition had at least reached Enzeli.[19]

General Bicherakov transferred himself and his men from Enzeli to Baku, claiming that he had become a Bolshevik – but Dunsterville sent a group of British staff officers with him, which rather undermined such an assertion. The main threat at Baku was now Nuri Pasha's Army of Islam. Bicherakov, on his 'conversion', had taken over command of the local Red Army forces, but he found that they would not fight. In consequence, he and his local Cossacks were driven back into Baku. At that point a coup took place in the city.

A message went from Baku to Dunsterville at Enzeli that a coup had overthrown the Bolsheviks, and a governing committee calling itself the Centro-Caspian Directorate had assumed power. The prospect of a more friendly reception in the city now existed. Dunsterville was requested to send help in order to maintain the new regime and to defend it and Baku against the approaching Turks, who had retreated after reaching the outskirts as a result of a momentary panic.[20] By this time, the road south of Resht and Resht itself had been cleared by the defeat of the Jangalis, so Dunsterville could move on; it had taken him six months to reach this far.

Turkish and German intentions were to some extent at cross-purposes, since the Germans feared that, if the Turks gained control of Baku, they would keep it and, if they were attacked, they might damage the oil installations to deny them to their enemies, either the British or the Russians (or even the Germans). Bicherakov and his men in the city were Dunsterville's own contribution to its defence. Other groups intending to be part of the defence included, for a time, a Soviet Russian force of about 3,000 men, local Armenians and Tartars (whose mutual hatred was on hold in the face of a greater threat to both), and now the Cossacks and the British. All these were only united in opposition to the Turkish Army of Islam, whose aim was less to gain the oil than to preserve and extend the Ottoman Empire. Across the sea from Baku in Central Asia were plenty of Turkish-speaking people, who were expected to welcome incorporation into the empire.

The decisive defeat of the Jangalis at Manjil and the anti-Bolshevik coup at Baku happened at much the same time (22–25 July). In France, the latest, and last, German offensive, towards Paris, had expired, and the Allies could see their way to victory at last. The Germans who were in Baku meanwhile made attempts to hinder the Turkish advance on the city, and it may have been their influence that inhibited the Turkish attack when they came close to the city for the first time. The German commander in the area was General Kress von Kressenstein, a man familiar to the British from his work with the Turks in Palestine. He had made an alliance with the Georgians, who agreed to supply manganese for the German war effort in return for German political support for their independence and to stiffen their republican government.[21] The Turks nonetheless reached close to Baku by 31 July, but then pulled back in the face of the Dunsterforce's local support. General Marshall in Baghdad, instructed to assist Dunsterville, had at last produced some real help; he had a great column of lorries now moving along the road northwards through Persia, carrying supplies and reinforcements, and incidentally using up all the supplies of petrol on the way.

The reinforcement consisted of the 39th Infantry Brigade, and included the 7th Service Battalions of the Gloucestershire and the North Staffordshire regiments, and the 9th Service battalions of the Worcestershire and Warwickshire regiments. (He already had a battalion of the 4th Hampshires and the 2nd Gurkhas.) These new forces were all 'New Army' battalions, and they constantly outfought the Turks, despite the latter's greater numbers and experience, but Dunsterville was very careful in his use of them, knowing well that he depended entirely on them.[22]

One of the passengers in the convoy through Persia to Enzeli was Commodore David Norris, who had held a naval command in the Persian Gulf and was now sent north along with four naval guns, forwarded from the Indian Navy at Bombay, with which he was to equip and command any suitable ships he could find at Enzeli or Baku. Dunsterville had already gained access to ships held in the harbour at Enzeli, some of which he commandeered, while others he hired. The harbour had been partly blocked by the Bolsheviks; the Hampshires and the Gurkhas had turned to and cleared it. It was known that there were armed vessels elsewhere in the Caspian, relics of the earlier Russian domination of the sea. They were presumably under someone's control, though exactly whose was not clear; some were based at Astrakhan, a city on the Volga River controlled by the Bolsheviks; the river gave it access to the Caspian. Norris was to form an armed squadron, which was as much predatory as aggressive, aiming to secure Baku and impose its own dominance over the Caspian; gaining control over any armed Russian ships would also be very useful.[23]

Norris was a good choice for the task he faced. He had commanded an armed merchant cruiser in the 10th Cruiser Squadron, which had been part of the blockading force in the northern Atlantic Ocean based on the Shetland Islands, so he knew the capabilities of civilian ships converted to war and manned by largely civilian crews. His new fleet would be, when armed, essentially a group of armed merchant ships, though generally of a smaller size and in much poorer condition than he was used to. In the Caspian there already were a number of similar armed vessels; they were usually small, of up to 1,000 tons, and usually British built. To get to the Caspian they had been sailed along the Russian rivers, hence their small size and shallow draught – this last consideration was essential in the northern part of the sea, where the average depth was only 20 feet. Many of the vessels had been armed as the times became threatening with whatever guns were available, and they were commanded poorly. Norris's fleet, when organised, should have no difficulty in dominating the sea.

Dunsterville at Enzeli was also conscious of the approach of the Nuri Pasha's Army of Islam. He understood that their numbers and experience made it very likely that they would capture Baku in the end. That therefore raised a further issue. He knew about the German advance through southern Russia, and information had arrived that they were interested not only in Baku's oil, but in manganese from Georgia (one reason for Kress's alliance with Georgia), and in Turkestan's stores of cotton, which had accumulated in store through lack of markets.

Turkestan also held those thousands of German and Austro-Hungarian prisoners of war. Some of these men had been moved to camps in Siberia, but there were still about 38,000 of them in Turkestan, in a string of twenty-five concentration camps spread along the Trans-Caspian Railway from Tashkent to Krasnovodsk, though the westernmost ones had been evacuated. If Turkish or German forces reached this region, and freed and armed this many enemy soldiers on the borderlands of Afghanistan and India, the old British nightmare might become a reality.

There was a Danish Red Cross delegation in Turkestan from early 1918 attempting to get the prisoners released and sent home in accordance with the Treaty of Brest-Litovsk. It was commanded by Captain A.H. Brun, a patient and diplomatic man, but he was having little success, partly through lack of transport – the Trans-Caspian railway line was of course unavailable – and partly because of the confusion in Russia. The delegation suffered harassment and interference by the ever-suspicious Bolshevik officials, who did not play by the old diplomatic rules, and who had adopted the obstructive tactics of the old imperial bureaucracy.[24]

If or when the Turks gained control of Baku and its port, they would capture a number of ships that would then be available to reach across the Caspian to the port of Krasnovodsk on the eastern coast. If such a communication link could be established, the cotton could be exported along the Central Asian Railway, and the prisoner of war camps along the railway might also produce several thousands of trained military soldiers for the invaders. (The Bolsheviks did recruit a number of Austrians from the camps into their local forces on the promise of letting them go home if they could get control of the railway; they did not in the end fight very well.)

Dunsterville made contact with General Malleson, who was now in north-eastern Persia, based for the moment at Meshed, close to the railway that ran alongside the Persian border there. Some of Malleson's officers were already in informal contact with plotters across the border in Turkestan, where a civil war was developing. Malleson's aim was to interrupt the railway to prevent communications between Tashkent, the local Bolshevik power centre, and Krasnovodsk; this would inevitably block exports through the latter even more thoroughly. But Dunsterville and Malleson had diverging aims, so their mutual communications were of limited use to either of them.

General Bicherakov's Cossacks fought the Turks. He had British armoured cars with him and the use of some aircraft. The fighting remained essentially at a stalemate for some time, though this did mean that Baku and its oil remained out of either Turkish or German control, which was Dunsterville's object. The local militia forces in the city were inefficient, and were quite happy to relax and leave any fighting in defence of the city to the foreigners, British, Indian, and Cossack. By the end of July, however, the Turks were in a position to encircle the city. Bicherakov, no doubt recalling his original purpose in getting his own men home, and being short of supplies, now left the city by marching off northwards, where he established himself at Petrovski on the western Caspian coast and there gained control of a number of small armed ships of war.[25] This in fact was useful to Dunsterville and Malleson, since this was another useful port that was now out of German and Turkish reach.

Bicherakov's defection, if that is what it was, weakened the defence of the city decisively. The Soviet Russians and the Bolsheviks who had been unseated by the Centro-Caspian Directorate (enemies of Bicherakov, the Turks, the British, and the Germans) had sensibly already left to go to Astrakhan. They were retreating there by sea, and they attempted to take as much military equipment as they could collect in the thirteen ships they had seized. The new government discovered this after a short time, and sent their own ships in chase, forced those in flight to return, recovered the armaments, and the captured commissars were then jailed, though the men were expelled, and were sent in a ship as planned to Astrakhan.[26]

They did not reach that Bolshevik stronghold. They were taken by the crew of the ship to Krasnovodsk, became known as the 26 Commissars, and were later shot. (See Chapter 3.) It will be noted that all through their fatal experiences, these men were imprisoned and judged and executed by their fellow Russians. Both the flight and the capture showed unusual initiative by both sides; the Bolsheviks at Astrakhan clearly retained a degree of energy, but the Baku Directorate lapsed into inactivity when Dunsterforce arrived. Now desperately short of skilled soldiers, the Directors applied to Dunsterville for support once more.

In response, Dunsterville now sent small groups of his forces into the town over several days, using whatever shipping was available at Enzeli and at Baku. The British – there were only 1,000 of them, which was no doubt why he had not used them earlier – were intended to provide support and training for the local forces, who were amateurs and militiamen, but the locals actually expected them to do the fighting, as they had Bicherakov's Cossacks, while themselves relaxing. Dunsterville himself reached Baku on 10 August. The defence was already well engaged against the more numerous Turks of Nuri Pasha, and the fighting continued indecisively for the next month.[27]

The population of the city largely stayed out of the fighting, though the Armenians did produce a militia force, which was notably inefficient. There were also many German and Austrian released prisoners of war in the city, and a large 'Tartar' population, all Muslims. Dunsterville noted 'the enemy should have been able to obtain much detailed information' about the British numbers and their dispositions. Whether they did or not is not known, but it is notable that many of these groups took no part in the fighting for their city. The fact that the released prisoners of war did not participate may suggest that the prospect of the many thousands of their fellows in Turkestan being recruited to fight was to attempt to do so in the face of widespread disinterest in returning to the fray.[28]

Once the Turks actually started to attack seriously, however, some of the locals did join in to defend the city, but in an undisciplined and haphazard way. Dunsterville directed the defence against several Turkish attacks during August and into early September, but the numbers against the British force were far too great, and local participation had been less than enthusiastic. On 14 September, Dunsterville admitted defeat. He skilfully withdrew almost all of his men (a few men were left behind, having been forgotten or were out of touch). He had carefully prepared for this withdrawal, by keeping several ships fuelled and ready in the harbour so as to be able to embark and remove his retreating forces.[29]

The Turks made short work of the remaining defenders, and having broken into the town, let loose the local irregulars, the Tartars, on the unfortunate population of Baku. A massacre of Armenians took place – yet another massacre of Armenians by Turks – in which several thousands were killed.[30] There had been a massacre of Muslims by Armenians in the city earlier in the year, but the Turkish menace had forced the two to co-operate. The Turkish capture of the city liberated the local Tartars from their forced alliance and they transferred their support to the conquerors; their massacres were a good deal more thorough than those by the Armenians. The Turks were also at this time slowly moving their forces in northern Persia into a position that threatened the British supply lines and their base at Enzeli, but this movement was not in any real strength.

The British withdrawal was the end for Dunsterforce. General Marshall seized the opportunity of Dunsterville's retreat to take away most of his men for a different task in Persia. This was quite justified. Dunsterforce had accomplished its main task in foiling the German plan to get at Baku's oil. His withdrawal had permitted the Turks to seize the city; the German attempt had therefore failed – and the steady retreat of the German armies in France for the last month made it clear to observers that the war was coming to an end. Supplies of oil from Baku would be no use to them now.

Marshall had new orders to advance again in Mesopotamia, where Mosul (oil again) had to be seized before any Turkish armistice went into effect. Dunsterville was returned to India, where he wrote his own account of the events, then retired. His aim, it may be recalled, had been to prevent the enemy, Turks or Germans or Bolsheviks, from gaining control of Baku and its oil. The danger to the Allies of such a coup had been quite real. A German party had in fact turned up in the city while the British were in control and had found themselves arrested by a second lieutenant; to their great surprise, they had become prisoners of war.[31] Until the Turkish conquest in September, this was the only enemy 'force' to reach the city, and it was the closest the Germans got to gaining access to Baku's oil. When Dunsterville withdrew his force, he had completed his task. Not the least of his achievements was to keep the original purpose of his expedition in mind, and to retire before becoming involved in a much wider war.

Dunsterville's British force withdrew from Baku on 14/15 September, retreating to Enzeli. Their presence in the city had held the town and its oil out of Turkish and German hands for a month and a half, during which, on the Western Front, the German attacks on the French line had been stopped, and the final British offensive had begun. According to General Ludendorff, 8 August was 'the black day of the German army', characteristically putting the German army before the German state and people. (It had been Ludendorff who drew attention to the possibility of securing oil at Baku; in a sense, he was one of the original begetters of all these events.) The Germans had been driven back steadily in France in a series of battles in August and September, convincingly underlining their progressive defeat. The Baku oil and Turkestan cotton had both been denied them, and the troops they had sent into southern Russia, who were vainly attempting to secure these resources, were unavailable for the more vital

Western Front. The withdrawal of Dunsterforce in local ships from Baku had also denied the Turks the chance to use Baku as a launching pad for their ambitions in Central Asia. (Bicherakov's control of the small port of Petrovski on the Daghestani coast was another obstacle to German/Turkish attempts to cross the Caspian.) Dunsterville had therefore succeeded in his primary mission, despite hindrance from Marshall, the Persians, the vanished Centro-Caspian Directorate, and the War Office's changing orders, and in preventing these further Turkish ambitions. The investment of 1,000 men in the Baku expedition had paid off handsomely.

Having got rid of Dunsterville's unwelcome and awkward presence, General Marshall then found he had to continue supporting new attempts to recover Baku. The Russian Bolsheviks had now emerged as an active enemy in Central Asia and elsewhere, and it became evident, at least in London, that securing Baku was now once again an important political objective, not (again) for its oil but to control it as a useful base on the Caspian. General William Thomson was given Dunsterville's command, extended and enlarged to include North Persia and the road from Hamadan to Enzeli, so suggesting that some lessons had been learned from Dunsterville's difficulties in Persia and with Marshall. He also had a considerably larger force than Dunsterville had ever commanded – two full infantry brigades (one of which was Dunsterville's 39th Brigade) with attendant supplementary machine-gun squadrons, artillery batteries, and armoured cars, 2,000 men in all, and plenty of munitions. The 36th Brigade included a battalion of the Hampshire Regiment, two battalions each of Sikhs and Gurkhas, and two of Punjabis, plus the 14th Hussars.[32] It is reasonable to suppose that, if Dunsterville had had such a force from the start – and fewer hindrances – much of the fighting could have been avoided, and Baku could have been held for much longer.

Events in Syria and Mesopotamia, as well as the Bulgar collapse, which put Constantinople in danger, eventually produced the Turkish armistice at the end of October, but there had been a series of military withdrawals beforehand. Some of the Turks were withdrawn northwards from Mesopotamia, and others from Syria, where both Marshall and Allenby were advancing. Marshall had finally been stirred into action by the War Office, and he duly gained control of Kirkuk and Mosul. This was to prevent either place falling to the French (or kept by the Turks), just as Baku had been seized to prevent it falling to the Germans or the Turks. At times, one has to stop and remember that the French were British allies in this war. Marshall, of course, grumbled but complied, without the difficulty he undoubtedly expected.

In October, Turkish defences crumbled, less than a month after Dunsterville's withdrawal. General Thomson was able to advance, only to find that much of his force, about 2,000 men, was incapacitated by the worldwide influenza epidemic, and much of the rest were immobilised in garrisons throughout Northwest Persia. The Turks gradually withdrew during October as greater threats to their heartland developed. The armistice at the end of the month included a clause by which the Turks were to evacuate all the Caucasus area, though it took more than another week, and a fierce prod from General Marshall, to get Nuri Pasha to begin moving his Army of Islam troops out of Baku, and the Caucasus as well. At that point, Thomson's forces were able to move in, without having to fight. The British occupation – or reoccupation – of Baku finally took place early in November, just as the Turks and then the Germans, who had been competing to reach the city, finally ceased to fight.

At Enzeli, General Thomson now had a reasonably strong force to defend the town as his base, and firm control of the route back to Hamadan and Baghdad. Dunsterville had sent some of his forces to hold Krasnovodsk, which had enabled him to deny the use of the Central Asian Railway to the Germans and the Turkish forces, even though they had held Baku and its port; he had also, of course, removed most of the ships. Nuri Pasha had therefore directed his attacks northwards.

At Baghdad, General Marshall had made yet another attempt to close down Dunsterville's – now Thomson's – command, claiming that the forces at Enzeli were outnumbered and that it was impossible to control the Caspian. He wanted to withdraw from both Enzeli and Krasnovodsk. In this, he demonstrated a wilful ignorance of what was happening in the regions involved, as well as a fundamental failure to understand the purpose of holding those places. He also came up against Commodore Norris, who had reached Enzeli and there assumed command of the ships. He explained, no doubt forcefully, in the naval way, that he could man three or four ships at Enzeli so long as his base there continued to be safe and available. Dunsterville, who was at Baghdad, joined in, confirming that the town could be held: he had spent some time fortifying it while there. Both men, unlike Marshall, spoke from first-hand knowledge of the situation, of the geography, and of the need to hold the place, whereas Marshall was primarily concerned with the position in Mesopotamia, where, after the end of October, he was immobile again. Then he had been given orders to advance northwards. He seems to have been totally ignorant, possibly wilfully, of what was going on in the Caspian area.

The War Office in London had not been convinced that the threat to Thomson's communications from a nearby Turkish force was really serious, no doubt seeing that the British advances in Syria, and against the Bulgars, and the Allied progress on the Western Front, would significantly damage Turkish morale and their capacity to move. Four days after his alarmed and alarmist message of despair, Marshall found that the Turkish force he feared was withdrawing out of reach.

The Turkish threat disappeared. Thomson and Norris's forces reigned supreme at Baku, in the southern Caspian, and at Krasnovodsk. The 4th Hampshires and a Royal Field Artillery battery went to reinforce the meagre troops who were campaigning along the Trans-Caspian Railway. But all this produced a new and different political situation, one that had to be resolved. Here the British naval forces in the Black Sea and those in the Caspian were as potent as the soldiers occupying the Caucasus and Central Asia.

Chapter 5

The Royal Navy Caspian Sea Flotilla

Enzeli on the Persian coast of the Caspian Sea remained in British hands even after Dunsterville retreated from Baku and was then dismissed to return to India. General W.M. Thomson took over, with a much larger force than Dunsterville had commanded; it was now called the North Persian Force. Thomson arrived in September 1918, at which time some of the Turks in the area were beginning to withdraw as General Marshall in Mesopotamia pushed forward to secure Kirkuk and Mosul, and General Allenby moved north to conquer Syria. More withdrawals took place once Constantinople was directly threatened by the Allies' Salonika Army early in October. Thomson also had with him Commodore David Norris, whose protest against Marshall's plan to evacuate northern Persia was in part successful in preventing it.[1] Norris had set about arming the ships in Enzeli harbour with the naval guns he had brought from the Gulf (they had been sent from Bombay earlier). There came also Colonel F.J.F. French, direct from Whitehall to the Caspian, assigned to the British Caspian Flotilla.[2]

Norris had taken Dunsterville on a cruise from Baku to consult with Bicherakov at Derbend, halfway along the western coast. He aimed also to visit Krasnovodsk, defying the risk of the 'Bolshevik pirate ships' which were reported to be active in the sea. The plan comprehensively failed: near Derbend, the ship they were travelling in, the *President Kruger*, was driven away by a Bolshevik ship and had to return directly to Baku. (Dunsterville had some fun with the name of the ship, named after the South African president the British had fought against in the Boer War; it still had a picture of Kruger on the wall of the mess room.)[3] At Baku, Norris took charge of preparing the ships chosen for the evacuation. He had three, the *President Kruger*, *Kursk*, and *Abo*, to convey the soldiers and a smaller vessel, *Armenian*, which would carry the explosives. It had been difficult to escape from Baku in the face of demands from various members of the Centro-Caspian Directorate to stay and defend them, and their guard ships fired on the escapees.[4] But the result was a considerable concentration of armed ships at Enzeli. The town was taken over by General Thomson when he arrived, and with several useful ships Norris could mount the naval guns he had brought from the Persian Gulf, donated by the Indian Navy.

By October, Thomson had a considerable force under his command: two infantry brigades (36th and 39th), the 14th Hussars, two Royal Field Artillery batteries, a Mountain battery, and the 15th Light Armoured Motor Battery; plus two flights of the Royal Air Force, manned of members of the former Royal Naval Air Service, and so accustomed to working with the navy. However, this force was spread over a large part of North Persia, from Hamadan to Enzeli and beyond.[5] And soon, Thomson had to send a part of his Enzeli force to Krasnovodsk (the 44th Royal Field Artillery and part of the Hampshire battalion), who went on further east to join Malleson's forces. They sailed in Norris's ships from Enzeli.

The loss of Baku in mid-September had made the Caspian available to the Turks, at least in theory; however, by placing a British force at Krasnovodsk, which Dunsterville had seized and Thomson reinforced, that port was blocked to the Turks and any Germans who arrived, and the landing place was blocked. The British could also make use of the expertise of the mechanics in the railway workshops, and, of course, were in control of a long section of the Trans-Caspian Railway.[6] No Turkish move to cross the sea could be made without a secure port at which to land. (The Turks' method of conquest at Baku – massacre – left them badly disorganised, and their Tartar auxiliaries were thoroughly undisciplined. They probably had had a good chance of crossing the Caspian if they had moved to do so as soon as they took Baku, but they were slackly commanded as well as disorganised.)

The Army of Islam, under Nuri Pasha, having therefore been foiled – or had foiled itself – in its (presumed) original intention of crossing the Caspian, then turned north into Daghestan, the territory north of Azerbaijan, and bordering on the Caspian, to drive out the Bolsheviks who were fighting the local Daghestani Muslims.[7] There, along with some German officers who had reached the area, they began seeking to hire shipping, and in particular to gain control of a group of Russian ships in the Chechen area, but these ships had come under the control of General Bicherakov; he was, in theory, politically anti-Bolshevik, but the Germans were now in collusion with the Bolsheviks, even though the Turks were German allies. Bicherakov, therefore, stood independent, and the ships remained out of the Turks' hands. Foiled again.[8]

Norris reported all this back to Marshall at Baghdad, and pointed out that the Russian fleet in Baku and elsewhere was disorganised; he proposed simply to ignore it until it revived. He had, he said, the use of thirty-seven ships at Enzeli, plus two more at Krasnovodsk.[9] There was a Russian fleet, which was now under Bolshevik control and was held at the northern end of the sea in the Volga River Delta and further upstream at Astrakhan. There were thus at least four separate groups of warships in the Caspian, and perhaps more – such as those 'Bolshevik pirates' Dunsterville had been bothered about. Norris's report on his strength, and the possibility of using his ships, came during his protest against Marshall's announced intention to withdraw from northern Persia. The War Office's reply to both of them was that Norris was instructed to gain control of the Caspian Sea by whatever means would produce success. Marshall in Mesopotamia was, even so, still in overall command.

While the Centro-Caspian Directorate held Baku, it also held control of the squadron of ships there, some of which were armed. They included the two up-to-date Imperial Russian gunboats, *Kars* and *Ardahan*. Dunsterville's occupation of the city had allowed Norris's naval party to begin chartering other ships at the port, either as transports or to be armed with the guns Norris had brought, and he was recruiting sailors to man them. Needless to say, Dunsterville's withdrawal had ended this process, but he had brought away a considerable number of Baku's ships on his retreat. Norris's thirty-seven ships thus included Dunsterville's contribution from Baku. He had virtually all the useful ships in the southern Caspian under his control.

Other vessels had also escaped from Baku as the Turks moved in. So Norris had even more ships available to charter to supplement those he had already armed. When the Turkish armistice was signed at the end of October, he had five ships ready, fuelled and crewed, and equipped with guns and ammunition. Norris was concerned that Enzeli did not have the facilities for maintaining his ships, but at Krasnovodsk, there was the railway workshop, and therefore skilled engineers, workmen and machinery. He took his ships there, headed by the *President Kruger*, which had been armed with four field guns. He decided to make Krasnovodsk his base, but then Baku, when the Turks withdrew, became available as well. Given that the

Bolsheviks became the enemy of choice when the Turks withdrew, and they were based at Astrakhan, Krasnovodsk seemed the best strategic location for a naval force to dominate the sea.

However, the Centro-Caspian Directorate, abandoned by Dunsterville, now found themselves once again threatened by the advancing Turks, who seized and sacked the city two days after the British had left. This marked the end of the Directorate; six weeks later, the Turkish armistice included instructions for the Army of Islam to withdraw back to Ottoman territory, and this allowed Thomson's troops at Enzeli to reoccupy Baku on 17 November.[10]

It had taken some days for Nuri Pasha's Army to decide to obey the instructions to retire; also there were several battalions of German troops in Georgia, and a German party in Baku, which would have to leave after 11 November. Norris's ships were then able to make use of Baku harbour and the ships there came under his command. He brought his ships across to Baku from Krasnovodsk, but left the Hampshires, the artillery, and some vessels as garrison at Krasnovodsk – some of them went on to Ashkhabad. With Enzeli, Baku, and Krasnovodsk under British control, Norris's ships dominated the whole southern half of the sea and he could use these bases to make an attempt to gain control of the northern half.

The reluctant removal of the Turks from Baku and the Caucasus, forced back by hard words and threats from General Marshall, by the armistice agreement, and by their essential military isolation in the Caucasus, opened the way for the British military occupation of all the Caucasus area, from Batumi to Baku, with the 27th Division moving in from Salonika.

The situation was immensely confused. Agreements made with the Germans, for example by Georgia, were immediately cancelled. Georgia was controlled by a fairly stable regime, but Armenia, with great ambitions, was internally much divided between several parties and several sets of bandits, and Azerbaijan was the host to a vast variety of political groups. In a sense, the confusion was epitomised on 4 January when the Georgian war minister gave a farewell dinner to General Kress von Kressenstein, while the Georgian government gave a welcoming dinner to a British delegation – and then Kress did not leave for another month.[11]

British policy towards the Caucasian republics was just as confused. Every senior minister – Curzon, Balfour, Churchill, Lloyd George – advocated a different aim. On the ground, General Forestier-Walker, commanding

27 Division, did not agree with General Cooke-Collis, who had installed himself as a sort of governor general at Batumi, then he was blocked when he found that his Georgian staff went on strike.

The British priority on the ground, and therefore the decisions by Forestier-Walker, were to gain control of the Transcaucasian Railway, which linked the Black Sea ports of Poti (where his division had landed) and Batumi (Cooke-Collis's headquarters) with the Georgian capital at Tbilisi and with Baku. One of 27 Division's battalions was detailed to join Malleson on the Trans-Caspian Railway. Norris was in control of the southern part of the Caspian Sea and Malleson held the railway from Krasnovodsk to beyond Merv, so with Cooke-Collis at one end and Forestier-Walker along the line of the railway, and Thomson at Baku, the whole Transcaucasian and Trans-Caspian region was now under some sort of British control.

This, together with the slowly advancing 27th Division in the Caucasus, was all part of the new command regime for the whole region given to General Sir George Milne as commander of the British Army of the Black Sea, which largely consisted of these several units scattered from the Black Sea to Annenkovo. Milne came through on a tour of inspection, visiting the units in his command, during December and January, reaching Malleson at Meshed on 21 January, as noted in Chapter 3. He was disgusted at everything and everybody, except the British Army, finding the inhabitants 'loathsome' and expressing the view that if 'the whole of the country cut each other's throats' the world would be better off.[12] Not a diplomat, then; not a man tolerant of foreigners. All this was irrelevant, for he was, of course, principally concerned at the military position of the British forces and its problems.

He certainly found a region close to chaos. Georgia was under a Menshevik-oriented regime, though it was also principally nationalistic. The government was veering from being briefly a German protectorate to now seeking British protection instead – in other words, it was aligning itself with the most powerful authority within its reach.[13] There was a considerable German colony still in the country, and this included Kress von Kressenstein, who had withdrawn to the mountains, and who had originated the country's initial link to Germany. He had the ability to mobilise the substantial colony of Germans in the area, if he felt it necessary or advantageous. The country had decided it was now to be an independent republic, but this was not recognised by anyone else. Armenia had chosen the same status, but also claimed a much wider geographical area than was currently inhabited by Armenians, a relic of a momentary mediaeval empire. This claim was for territory from the Black Sea to the Caspian, an area far beyond their capacity to realise, and which put them at odds with the Georgians in particular. Meanwhile, the Armenians and the Turks were still busy fighting each other, a continuation of the conflict between them from 1915 and the great Armenian massacres. Azerbaijan had claimed republican status also, but its main port, Baku, was first occupied by Dunsterforce, then by the Turkish Army of Islam, and was then taken by Thomson's troops from Enzeli; its internal politics were complex, violent, and unstable, based mainly on the several ethnic groups, with various Communist groups mixed in.

Another arrival from Britain was Lieutenant Colonel F.J.F. French. He was one of the first to publish an account of his experiences in this expedition, even as Dunsterville was publishing his story. On the other hand, it bears all the hallmarks of a rushed job, replete with mistakes and omissions. He appears to have come direct from the War Office, though this is one of his omissions, but his title is *From Whitehall to the Caspian*.[14] He does show that General Bicherakov was induced, once Thomson had regained control of Baku, to return to that city after the Army of Islam drove him out of Petrovski. His wife set up her salon in one of the most prestigious hotels. This is something that nobody else seems to mention, which rather suggested that Bicherakov had ceased to have any real importance, once driven from Petrovski.[15] French was carried to the little port in a convoy of five of Norris's ships. He also purports to describe the activities of the Caspian Flotilla, but omits significant details and events. For example, he omits all mention of Commodore Norris, though several other Royal Naval officers are named. Finally, he makes no reference, still less gives an account, of the only real battle by the flotilla, at Fort Alexandrovsky. He can only be relied on for direct personal testimony; otherwise, he seems to have reported, badly and inaccurately, gossip and third-hand reports.

All these fragments of the Russian Empire in the Caucasus had declared their independence in May 1918, Georgia and Azerbaijan on the 26th, Armenia on the 28th. This unfortunately immediately gained them the enmity of General Denikin's Volunteer Army, which was gathering to the north of the Caucasus, and whose programme was the restoration of the Russian Empire, both its monarchy and its old boundaries. The Georgian government was Menshevik in political flavour, the Armenian, insofar as it had a government, was purely nationalist, the Azerbaijani similar but Muslim, and liable to frequent *coups d'état*. The whole region was threatened by Bolsheviks from inside each of the new states, by General Denikin's Volunteer Army from the north, by the Turks and the Georgians, and by the British. Denikin was anxious to gain control of the Caucasus because it had been Imperial Russian territory, but this was an expensive distraction, for his real enemies were the Red Army to the north, and the Turks from the west.

General Milne travelled right across to visit Malleson in Central Asia on his inspection tour, though he had only superficial authority in the Caucasus for a time – his official appointment to that area dated from 1 January 1919. In the meantime, General Thomson made attempts to calm the region down, though with only a small force in Baku (most of his command remained inside Persia to control his communications back to Baghdad), he was reduced to sending out officers on missions of persuasion.

Moberly's *Official History* of the British war effort in Persia lists the difficulties:[16] Kress at Tiflis controlled the German radio station and was intriguing with both the Georgian Mensheviks and the Bolsheviks, who were, of course, opposed to each other; the Turks dragged their feet over their withdrawal from the area and spent their energies in looting and murdering Armenians in Baku; the Armenians and the Tartars (who had been responsible for the massacre in Baku) fought each other, and the Armenians pursued their territorial claims, and so fought the Georgians as well as the Turks. The Armenians were perhaps in a state of collective shock after the massacres of their people during the Great War, but they were building up a dangerous number of new enemies by their claims and their appetite for revenge.

The Bolsheviks were a minority in all these areas. They used workmen's strikes as their main weapon, especially in Baku, where there were plenty of sympathetic workers in the oil fields. The advance of the 27th Division, whose size and efficiency would have a properly calming effect, was slow, in part due to political distractions – they landed and stayed for a time at Batumi and Poti first, of which the first became their base – but also because the Batumi–Baku railway was disorganised; it was still not working in mid-December.[17] In his attempts to induce a calmer atmosphere all round, Thomson sent out officers to Tiflis, to Batumi, and to Elizabetpol and Petrovski north of the mountains, but he really had very little success.

The Bolsheviks had control of a flotilla of ships at Astrakhan and in the Volga Delta. The British flotilla under Norris at Baku went on patrol into the northern part of the sea in early December. One of the ships went into the far north-eastern corner, to the small port of Guryev, in order to make contact with the Ural Cossacks, who were under pressure from the Bolsheviks, and to deliver supplies for them.[18]

The strategic point for dominating the northern half of the sea was Chechen Island, a detached part of a long, narrow peninsula on the west coast north of Petrovski. It was about halfway between Baku and the Volga Delta; it was also, in most years, the southernmost point to remain free of sea ice in the winter – a good place for a naval base, in other words.

On 8 December, two of Norris's now British ships, *Zoroaster* and *Ala Verdi*, were anchored near Chechen Island when a Bolshevik force of three armed ships was sighted. They are described as 'destroyers', though they were, like the British ships, armed merchant ships, and no more powerful than the British ships. They were aiming to continue the work of setting up a base on the island, which was a surprise to the British, who hadn't noticed the work already done. (French says they were three in number and were convoying three transports; he shows no knowledge of the Bolshevik base.) The two forces fired at each other, one of the Bolshevik ships was set on fire, and *Zoroaster* was hit three times, but with no casualties. The Bolshevik ships withdrew, and their base, which was now searched for, was found, but was unfinished. It was bombarded and supposedly destroyed three weeks later.[19] Activity at sea ended in mid-January as the northern part of the sea iced up as far south as Chechen Island; the northern third of the sea remained inaccessible to either force until March, but the southern three-quarters of the sea remained clear.

This little British victory discouraged further Bolshevik naval patrols, and then ice closed the Volga River and Astrakhan, and the northern third of the sea. The British ships returned to Baku, leaving one ship stationed at Petrovski, just south of Chechen Island. This had formerly been General Bicherakov's headquarters, and was the most northerly port available during the winter. The ships made an occasional patrol along the edge of the ice. At Baku, Norris put the men to work on maintenance and repairs, and on preparing more of his ships for war. The mixed crews were composed of British naval officers and some British ratings, with Russians and other locally recruited men forming the rest of the crews, particularly the engine room staff; the British sailors manned the guns and operated the wireless sets.[20]

During this winter period of 'rest', however, many of the British sailors, who were a mixture of regulars recalled to the service for the war's duration or retained after their service had theoretically expired, and 'hostilities only' men, were due for demobilisation. Both groups much resented being retained when they could see others, who may have enlisted later and so to them were less entitled, being discharged before them. In the end, they were replaced by men seconded from the Mediterranean Fleet, to the annoyance of the captains who had to surrender them, and received replacements much later, if at all. On the other hand, the locally recruited men responded to a different grievance, notably Bolshevik complaints, voiced through their unions. The British were compelled to agree to a minimum manning of ships, which the union usually put much higher than the British would normally have accepted.[21]

The result of the winter work employed a considerably expanded force of armed ships, though it was still composed of a variety of formerly civilian ships, now armed with as wide a variety of weapons. The *President Kruger*, taken over originally by Dunsterville at Baku, was a small merchantman armed with four 4-inch guns, and was the flagship of the little fleet. The flotilla's largest ship, *Emile Nobel*, regarded as its 'dreadnought', was a former oil tanker armed with three 6-inch guns and one 4.7-inch, capable of heavier fire than any of the rest. The two ships that had been used at the Chechen Island fight were soon regarded as unreliable: *Zoroaster* had two 4-inch guns, but became relegated to reserve status; *Ala Verdi*, with defective boilers, was soon paid off. (Boilers in these steamers were a constant trial, for it had been usual to use Caspian seawater in them, and while the Caspian water was almost fresh, with the salt content much less than seawater, it was still capable of progressively damaging the boilers by constant use.)

Other ships that were taken up at Baku or Enzeli were the *Bibiabat*, fitted with three 4-inch guns, the *Slava*, with one 6-inch and one 4-inch gun, the *Ventuir* (called by the British the *Venture*) with three 4-inch, and *Asia* with four 4-inch guns. A flock of coastal motor boats was sent across from Batumi to supplement this small force; these were formerly Imperial

Russian boats and were of fairly modern construction. Two of the larger ships, *Soyous* (renamed *Edinburgh Castle*) and *Sergie*, were used as carriers for these motorboats, and were armed with one 12-pounder gun each. The fleet had two seaplanes, which were carried into action, or a patrol, on a carrier, at first on a ship called *Orlionoch*, then on another called *A. Yusanoff*, though this latter was not in good condition. There were various other vessels left with their original purposes unchanged, but were available usually for transport use.[22]

There were other naval forces based at Baku. The Centro-Caspian Directorate had mustered a squadron (with which it had chased and captured the fleeing larcenous commissars, and which had fired in their attempt to prevent Dunsterforce from leaving). Denikin's Volunteer Army had a naval section, and Bicherakov had seized some ships at Petrovski (these two groups were actually the same). Supposed allies of the British, Denikin and Bicherakov's ships' crews were liable to decide not to take part in any particular operation, or rather, in most operations. There had been two Centro-Caspian ships meant to join the *Ala Verdi* and *Zoroaster* at the Chechen Island patrol, but they had refused. The problem, of course, was not cowardice, or political preference, but lack of food and pay, and the unpleasant living conditions on board. While the local crews in the British ships were paid regularly (and therefore very unlikely to feel the need to strike), those on the other ships with Russian or Azerbaijani crews were often only able to survive by nefarious means, selling supplies, stealing, smuggling, and so on.

In addition, it emerged that some of the men on the ships were in clandestine radio contact with Bolshevik forces elsewhere, presumably at Astrakhan. So long as the sea was partly closed by the ice, this situation of the flotilla was not serious. The radio messages implied that the Bolsheviks knew all about the strengths and resources of the Caspian Flotilla. As it became clear that there would be action in the spring – intelligence clearly travelled in both directions, and the Bolshevik preparations were known about – Norris, in March 1919, and on instructions from London, closed down both non-British flotillas, and seized their ships. The Volunteer Army men were sent away to join Denikin, the Centro-Caspian men (whose government had long vanished, of course) were disbanded, or possibly re-recruited. Their ships were added to the British fleet, or, if not seized, immobilised. Until then, as a political gesture, much resented by Bolsheviks and Mensheviks, the British ships had flown the Imperial Russian ensign. Now they hoisted the white ensign of the Royal Navy and were regarded as, and described as, His Majesty's Ships. (So there was now a ship called HMS *President Kruger* on the Admiralty's lists.)

The Caspian Flotilla gained, by this action, only three usable ships, though it removed a possible threat and closed down an intelligence leak. The *Orlionoch*, converted to a seaplane carrier and carrying two aircraft, was one of them; it was armed with two 4-inch guns. The others were renamed, and armed more efficiently: *Windsor Castle* (formerly *Lieutenant Smidt*) was armed with four 4-inch guns, and was reliable enough and well armed enough to be a 'half-leader'; the *Dublin Castle* (formerly *Jupiter*) was given two 6-inch guns. As a result, the fleet, when the ice retreated and the northern part of the Caspian became available, consisted of 7 armed civilian ships, 12 coastal motor boats, and 2 seaplanes. The motor boats had a good turn of speed, and were transported on their two carriers; the seaplane carrier similarly carried the aircraft to the scene of action; one ship was held in reserve as another seaplane carrier. It was a curious, but varied, little fleet.

While the ships are being renovated and repaired, and the ice prevented any naval activity in the north of the sea, the 27th Division occupied Batumi at the end of December, once the Turks had removed themselves, and gradually began to occupy other places in the Caucasus region. In Central Asia, General Milne had completed his inspection and at the end of January had established himself in his command, which spread from Constantinople to Merv. General Malleson was full of suggestions for pushing the Bolsheviks ever further away, arming the Ashkhabad Committee, and so on, apparently under the impression that the British government was interested in extending its own authority well into Central Asia. In this, he had a good geopolitical/military argument to make, since, by extending British control as far as the old Amu Darya bridge at Charjui, he would link up with the lands of the emir of Bokhara, whose territory spread south to the Afghan border, and north almost to the Aral Sea. Securing alliances with the khan and the Ashkhabad Committee could be seen as making Bokhara a useful buffer against the Bolsheviks in Tashkent. The khan had a large armed force, though it had been recently fairly easily defeated. Perhaps it, and he, were looking for revenge.

This arrangement would thus have extended British authority decisively at the expense of the Tashkent Committee, which would likely collapse in the face of the challenge. The Turkomans of the steppe-desert area even suggested that they should become a British protectorate, an idea that evoked no interest in either London or Delhi, despite the alluring imperial possibilities. All these ideas, including the question of finance for all of them, including improvements to the East Persian Cordon route, came up against a thorough disapproval from both headquarters. Clearly, this was one of the reasons Milne had been appointed, to examine the British involvement in Central Asia, and to rein in the various military ambitions.

It is not uncommon for historians to remark disparagingly on the financial problems of the British government at this time, but it is a fact that it was a shortage of government resources that was the basis of the cutbacks in commitments. In the case of the expeditions into the Black Sea and as far as Central Asia, this meant the abandonment of any further activities outside the Indian boundaries (including accepting defeat at the hands of the Afghans in the war of 1919) and an eventual withdrawal from the Black Sea and the (former) Ottoman Empire. The problem also affected other interested parties in the area; both France and Italy, who had ambitions to take control of parts of Anatolia, drew back, partly because they faced serious opposition on the ground, but also because of the cost that would be involved. Even the United States drew away from any commitments, as when a mandate for Armenia was suggested.[23]

General Thomson from Enzeli had sent troops to occupy Baku back in November and they set about reducing the city to order. He imposed martial law and under that condition, he appointed British officers to be in charge of the police, and put others to running much of the economy. The Batumi–Baku railway was operating again by the end of December, and production of oil revived, helped by bringing the pipeline to the Black Sea back into use.[24] Thomson deliberately restricted his own authority to the city, surely a difficult enough task in itself, leaving that part of Azerbaijan outside the city to the local Azerbaijani government. At the other end of the Caucasus Valley, the 27th Division established control of Batumi when the Turks withdrew, and sent a small force on as far as Tbilisi, where its presence was not liked by the Georgians, principally because the soldiers were Indians. Milne was thus able to pass through all his command during

January, and approved the arrangements that had already come into existence. His approval, however, was only provisional. He clearly discouraged any further Central Asian ambitions, and his report to London recommended withdrawal.[25] This was accepted, and the withdrawal began in February, but took two months to complete.

In the spring of 1919, forward bases for the ships and aircraft in the Caspian were established at Chechen Island, perhaps close to where the Bolsheviks had started to build their base the year before – it would make sense to use the same site, and perhaps the same buildings, if they had survived the bombardment in December. The ships used Petrovski on the mainland as their operating base. There they were in contact with Bicherakov's force and with Denikin's Volunteer Army. The RAF contingent was established on the island, airfield and all, and the RAF strength was gradually built up to forty de Havilland DH-9 aircraft; the commander was Lieutenant Colonel F.W. Bowhill. This expansion was taking place just at the time that the British commitments in the area were being reduced.

In April, the ice in the Caspian had sufficiently retreated to allow patrolling, by ships and by air, to be resumed, by both the British and the Bolsheviks. At first, only a few ships were available at Petrovski for Norris to use, but others were sent on from Baku as they became ready. The bases at Petrovski and Chechen Island represented a considerable investment of time, manpower, resources, and finance, and at Baku there had been developments of the same sort. An old paddle steamer found at Krasnovodsk was brought across to Baku and was converted to provide accommodation for 130 officers and men, and so it was designated as 'R.N. Barracks Baku'; in the city, a depot for stores and ammunition was established, also a seaplane base, and a base for the coastal motor boats. The whole establishment was beginning to look both large and permanent. There were almost 1,100 Royal Navy officers and men at these several bases, with over 300 Russians also employed.[26]

The opening-up of the sea as the ice melted did not only allow British patrols to take place, the Bolshevik ships at Astrakhan were also able to sortie by mid-April. The advantage lay with the Bolsheviks, if speed, firepower, and the number of ships were counted; their destroyers were old, but they could still outsail all the British vessels except the coastal motor boats, whose range was short and armament was insufficient to face the larger ships. There were supposedly six or eight Russian destroyers, which were faster, operated better in the shallow waters, were better armed, and even better manned. The rival patrols occasionally sighted each other, but the Bolshevik ships always withdrew, sometimes after a brief exchange of shots; perhaps the memory of the clash at Chechen Island in the previous December had had its effect in establishing what the British fondly regarded as their 'moral superiority'. More likely, it was a deliberate policy decision at the Bolshevik headquarters to avoid a serious clash with the British, which would gain them nothing; a British withdrawal from the Caspian would seem to be the most likely eventual result, so fighting in that case was pointless – they were already leaving Central Asia. The Bolshevik ships were also usually tasked with a particular job, and fighting the British force was a distraction. It was very rare in the whole intervention episode that Russian and British forces actually fought each other – the Caspian and Central Asia were two of the few places where direct battle occurred, and, at least at sea, it was usually because the British attacked; on land they were usually on the defensive, as in Trans-Caspia and in Baku.

The airfield on Chechen Island became the base for bombing raids on the Bolshevik ships at their bases at Astrakhan and on the Volga, usually without any effect, other than to provide a spectacle for the intended victims. More helpful were reconnaissance flights, which detected between six and twelve Bolshevik destroyers, six armed merchantman, and possibly two or three submarines. This was the Russian Caspian fleet, though it is evident that these figures are all either estimated or exaggerated, and that the reconnaissance took no account of readiness to sail. On paper, therefore, the Bolshevik naval force was superior in all respects, but it never tried to exercise that superiority. It was, of course, not in the Bolshevik interest for a row to develop with the British forces, hence probably the reluctance to fight.

At Baku, one of the results of Thomson's clampdown was to clear Bicherakov and his Cossacks out of the city. This left them without a base and with no real purpose. In April, the group disintegrated. Bicherakov decided to retire, possibly, as he once suggested, to Britain to breed horses. His men were encouraged to join General Denikin's forces, and they were sent to Petrovski by rail, no doubt to the relief of the population of Baku. Most of them, however, chose simply to go home.[27]

In April, Norris went to Petrovski, where he could oversee the establishment of the new British naval base and hold talks with the Volunteer Army commander General Przevalski. Norris made it clear he did not wish the White Russians to do anything at sea, and that it was the British who would establish naval control. This was not a popular decision amongst the Russians, and one officer told him bluntly to leave fighting in Russia to the Russians.

It is quite possible that news of this vocal disagreement reached the Bolsheviks at Astrakhan, for in May they made a dual naval sortie in force. They were also taking advantage of the weather, for the Caspian is often fogbound in spring. One force sailed to Fort Alexandrovsky (now Fort Shevchenko) on the Mangyshlak peninsula on the east Caspian coast, 500 kilometres north of Krasnovodsk. There they set about founding a new base, directly across the sea from Petrovski and Chechen Island. This was thus a well-chosen spot, where Bolshevik ships could sortie to interrupt the communications between the Volunteer forces in Petrovski and those which had been, and were being, transported from there by way of Krasnovodsk to fight the Tashkent Bolsheviks. However, it was also an easier reach to intercept the British ships at Baku and Petrovski than the Volga estuary.

Air reconnaissance of the Volga delta and Astrakhan discovered that the Bolshevik fleet, or part of it, had sailed. Some of the ships were discovered by a patrol at Fort Alexandrovsky. The weather was difficult, with much fog. A sea reconnaissance of Alexandrovsky was mounted, and the patrol met a Bolshevik convoy consisting of a destroyer and three armed merchantman escorting two barges. The escorting ships turned and left; the barges were sunk; they had probably been carrying supplies to Fort Alexandrovsky, and this suggests that the base had already been fairly well established, and this had certainly taken place since the ice broke up. The Bolshevik ships were actually withdrawing northwards, and they were now followed by the British ships – 'chased' is not an accurate characterisation of the limping progress which was all that the British ships were capable of achieving. The fog closed in and both sides lost sight of each other. It had also hidden a second Bolshevik force, which was at sea intending to attack the Chechen Island anchorage and probably the air base there as well. This was the second part of the dual sortie by the Bolsheviks, and the small convoy with the barges may well have been an attempt at distraction, though since those ships were heading north, it would seem that they had already delivered their supplies. This second raid was abandoned because of the weather, and most of the ships went on to Alexandrovsky. Thus, the full Bolshevik force was gathered in that harbour. It was clearly the intention to found a permanent base there.

A seaplane reconnaissance from Petrovski finally located the new Bolshevik base accurately on 18 May. It was clearly intended to be a major installation: there were eight destroyers, five armed merchantman, fourteen coastal motor boats, and two gunboats in the bay; the plane missed seeing other vessels – two or three submarines, a minelayer, and two depot ships – but what was seen was of considerably greater strength than anything the British could put to sea, and it was quite enough to disturb Norris. It was also clear that the British were well behind the game already. Presumably, the area of the bay and the new base had not been surveyed earlier by any British force, though the existence of an imperial regime fort – which was now being redeveloped by the Bolsheviks – should have been a clue. It is not clear if the considerable Bolshevik force was intended to be based there permanently, or if the ships were only there overnight and on their way elsewhere. Some of the ships were those that had failed to raid Chechen Island earlier, and a second attempt on that was obviously possible. It was also possible that Krasnovodsk, still in British control but about to be abandoned, was another ultimate target, with the aim of severing the developing connection between the White Russian forces at Petrovski and those in the Trans-Caspian region, for which possession of Krasnovodsk was crucial. The number of ships with the Bolshevik fleet could probably put a considerable armed force on shore, certainly large enough to defend itself against anything Norris could have brought against them, and to defeat the small British force at Krasnovodsk.

Norris took his ships to sea on the 20th. He had five of his armed merchantman with him (*President Kruger*, *Windsor Castle*, *Emile Nobel*, *Asia*, and *Ventuir*) and carriers for the seaplanes and the motor boats – effectively, his entire naval force. The Bolsheviks were anchored in a 6-mile-long bay, protected on the west by a narrow peninsula. The two seaplanes searched for but failed to find the Bolshevik ships, and one plane was lost when it crashed into the sea on take-off. Norris was expecting three more ships to join him, but one of them was *Zoroaster*, which suffered an engine breakdown and returned to Petrovski. Norris sent the now useless carriers away, and took his armed ships into the entrance to the bay, to make a reconnaissance from the sea. This was now 21 May.

Norris's force, as they moved into the entrance to the bay, found that there were three destroyers already outside the harbour; these quickly left, presumably obeying earlier orders to return to Astrakhan. The remaining ships exchanged fire with the British vessels, but most shots on both sides missed their targets. Norris took his ships further into the bay, but only two of them, *Emile Nobel* and *Ventuir*, were able to get within firing range, and *Emile Nobel* was hit in the engine room. One of the Bolshevik barges, this time with two guns on board, was sunk, and one of the Bolshevik armed merchant ships was set on fire and abandoned; its cargo exploded, damaging several nearby ships. The other Bolshevik ships retired further up the bay. This put them under the protection of a shore battery, and also gave them the ability to concentrate their fire on the British ships, which were now moving into a small and constricted area. An attack into the narrow bay, where manoeuvring would be impossible and all his ships would be easy targets, would be suicidal, and Norris called off the attack. The action had lasted a little over an hour. The Bolsheviks had lost another of their barges and one of their ships, with others damaged in the explosion, but two of Norris's important ships, *Emile Nobel* and *President Kruger*, had been damaged, the former in the engine room, the latter in the steering gear.

Norris tried to contact the carriers with his coastal motor boats (*Sergie* and *Windsor Castle*), but could not get through on the inadequate wireless sets. He sent away his damaged ships with an escort, and was left with only the *President Kruger* and *Ventuir*, the motor boat carriers, and the *A. Yusanoff* with the remaining seaplane. This was used next day on repeated bombing runs. The pilot made five such raids during the day, before being lost in the fog and crashing into the sea. (He was found and rescued next day.) Also that day, *President Kruger* and *Ventuir* suddenly met two of the Bolshevik destroyers. Both sides were evidently surprised by the encounter, and fired at each other unsuccessfully; the Bolshevik ships retired into the fog, or so at least the British said. Perhaps the fog simply closed in. The bombing raids on this day had been fairly successful for once, and it was later discovered that one of the opposing destroyers, a depot ship, and some small craft, had been sunk. It may have been this that persuaded the Bolshevik commander to abandon his venture; he had lost at least half his fleet, sailed away or sunk. On the next reconnaissance, it was found that the harbour was deserted. The Bolshevik ships were never encountered again.[28]

Norris could perhaps claim that his ships had won a victory because of these late sinkings, and because the Bolsheviks had withdrawn; the Bolsheviks also claimed a victory, because the British ships withdrew next day. But it was an expensive success on both sides. Norris had lost both of his seaplanes, and most of his bigger ships were damaged and had to return to Petrovski. His usable ships went out on patrol afterwards, while those of the Bolsheviks did not, as far as anyone knew, so Norris could claim to have driven them back to their initial base, but this only worked because the Bolsheviks never seriously challenged him again. It seems evident that the Bolsheviks had not any feeling for sea warfare (though the Bolshevik plan had been ingenious and, until discovered, had been well under way to being implemented), or possibly the commanders at Astrakhan had more pressing concerns once the bases at Chechen Island and Fort Alexandrovsky failed to be established. Norris certainly displayed a grasp of essentials, attacking the Bolshevik ships in their new base before they could get settled, all in the best Royal Navy style.

It is worth considering, however, what the Bolshevik strategy was. They had attempted to establish bases at Chechen Island and Fort Alexandrovsky; if they had succeeded this would have given them full maritime control over the northern third of the Caspian, and bases from which to move further south, either on patrol or to establish other bases. Possibly, therefore, the next move would have been to seize Krasnovodsk on the east coast – which was now in White Russian control, and so a legitimate civil war target – and perhaps Derbend on the west. This would be a viable strategy if they had managed to succeed in their first steps and so gain control over the northern part of the sea. It was, in fact, the mirror image of Norris's strategy of securing control of the southern part. Note that in the spring of 1919 their intent was apparently to return to Chechen Island and to establish a base there at the same time as at Fort Alexandrovsky.

After the Bolshevik withdrawal, the British ships kept up their patrols for a while, but it was gradually realised that the Bolsheviks were not going to come out again. Astrakhan came under a distant siege from Denikin's Volunteer Army; probably all the military energies in the city were devoted to resistance to Denikin's pressure, though this again was a waiting game, until the central Bolshevik authorities could organise a relieving expedition.

The British were, in theory, more or less allies of the Denikin's Volunteer Army, but friendship of any sort between their forces was absent, as was any real co-operation. The White officers came up with a variety of impractical schemes and were annoyed when the British pointed out their impracticality and refused to be involved. No doubt, the British officers treated these suggestions with disdain, and this attitude would come through. Denikin was given guns and the use of the motor boats, which were the most useful vessels in the northern part of the sea, which is shallow and so is inaccessible to anything much larger, except apparently the Bolsheviks' custom-built, formerly imperial, destroyers at Astrakhan; the motor boats, of course, were originally Imperial Russian vessels as well.[29]

By this time – the battle at Fort Alexandrovsky was in late May – the British involvement in Central Asia had already ceased, except for holding Krasnovodsk (and the Afghan War had begun), while the reinforcements from the Volunteer Army who were supposed to help defend the Ashkhabad region against Bolshevik attacks from Tashkent were seen to be unsuccessful. The Tashkent Committee had been reinforced, or perhaps superseded, by a larger Red Army, a more professional force, which advanced along the railway and gradually rolled up the opposition – though to be fair, this had been the committee's intention earlier, and the Red Army did not have to fight the Indian soldiers of Britain's Indian Army.

Across the sea to the west, the Caucasus region continued to be disturbed. Plans out of the peace conference in Paris for a mandate for Armenia, for Italy or for the United States got nowhere, and this would leave Armenia on its own facing the Red Army or the resurgent Turkish army, or both, but this was not Britain's business. By July 1919, it was clear that there was no more point in maintaining the rather ridiculous Royal Navy squadron in the Caspian Sea. Its original purpose had, as usual, changed, and then changed again. In fact it was constituted so late that its original purpose, to prevent German access to the sea, to Baku, and Central Asia, was over before it began. Since the British government was still clear that they were not going to get themselves involved in the Russian civil war, even its later, rather weak, anti-Bolshevik purpose had quickly expired. Nevertheless, the Bolsheviks were seen as an enemy, so when it was decided to withdraw the naval contingent – which had reached 1,200 officers and men by this time – the equipment was handed over to the Whites, and that included the aircraft at the RAF base on Chechen Island. The final naval action was to clear some Bolshevik forces from a number of offshore islands, and to suppress a Bolshevik gunboat that was being used for 'piracy' at a base at the Persian port of Ashurada (now Bandar e-Torkaman) in the south-east corner of the sea.[30]

In the Caucasus region, the 27th Division was gradually being withdrawn westward – it had expanded its area quickly even closer to Petrovski, with a detachment in Central Asia; now it receded. The last army units left Baku on 24 August. In the Caspian, the last ships in the armament were handed over to the White forces at Petrovski on 2 September, together with the aircraft. The men then travelled to the Black Sea by rail to rejoin their original ships there or their RAF units. The last of these British forces left through Batumi early in September. Only the Black Sea remained as a British naval interest – until two more such concerns emerged.[31]

The pressure on the Bolshevik government in Moscow during the summer of 1919 was intense, and it only just survived the several attacks made upon it and its territory, which came from all directions. Norris's exploits had been curious and interesting, but scarcely central to Russian affairs, and once the decision had been made to cease to support the Ashkhabad Committee in Central Asia, his fleet had become irrelevant to any wider war; as in Central Asia and the Caucasus, their withdrawal took several months.

There was, however, a curious aftermath to this Caspian adventure. The Admiralty was concerned at the ships Norris had used, which were presumably on their books somewhere, even though they were largely clapped-out merchantmen. In January, Admiral de Robeck, Calthorpe's successor as Mediterranean commander-in-chief, was told to be prepared to send a 'party of officers and men' to recover the ships in the Caspian that had been delivered to Denikin's command a few months earlier. This would 'bring the Caspian squadron back to full strength' – but no Caspian squadron had existed since that sea had been abandoned months before.[32]

This was provoked by a move by the First Sea Lord, Admiral Beatty, who suggested that the government plans for the Near East required the re-establishment of the Caspian Flotilla.[33] A link with the Azerbaijani government was suggested. Presumably, the order was intended to reactivate the Royal Navy in the Caspian so that it could dominate the sea in the face of the approaching Bolshevik conquest of the Caspian coasts. De Robeck called for volunteers to man the putative ships, but in the same message to the Admiralty he described the condition of Norris's ships in detail. He was clearly suggesting that someone at the Admiralty should look at a map, and perhaps at the previous correspondence on the issue. There is no sign that de Robeck made any further move to comply.

The party of Royal Naval sailors, commanded by Commander Bruce Fraser (later Admiral of the Fleet) was sent by rail to Baku on the way to Enzeli and the ships, but at Baku, another coup returned the city to a Bolshevik regime. The naval party were made prisoners and held as hostages for the next several months. The Georgian government, not yet taken over by the Bolsheviks, acted as intermediaries, and the men were at last released in November 1920. The British involvement in the Caspian Sea, which had begun in a curiously ragged way, thus ended three times, with Norris's withdrawal, with Admiralty mistakes, and with the withdrawal of Commander Fraser's hostages.[34]

Part III

The Black Sea and its Problems

The story so far has very largely ignored the Black Sea, though this was central to it. The armistice in October 1918, and the fleet's move through the Straits in November, certainly opened the way into the sea, but then it had been necessary to divert the story to consider the other British activities in the wider region – the expeditions into Central Asia and into the Caspian Sea – which were perhaps somewhat peripheral to those in the Black Sea, but were also briefly of importance to the wider war. These had begun in late 1917, a year before the Allied armies and navies reached Constantinople, and they continued for several months while most attention was fixed on events in the Black Sea area, and they ended before the activities in the Black Sea did. But they, the Black Sea, the Caspian, the Caucasus, and Central Asia, were all of a piece, and were linked together, as the appointment of General Milne to command them all from Constantinople to Merv shows. The next chapters therefore return the story to the essential centre, to the events in the Black Sea. Their conclusion, at least temporarily, in 1919, forbids further distractions.

Chapter 6

Into the Inhospitable Sea

The Black Sea was called, by the Greeks when they first reached it, the *Pontus Axeinos*, 'the inhospitable sea', but that was before they explored it and settled colonies of Greeks in cities all around its coasts. Some wit then changed the name to *Pontos Euxeinos* – 'the hospitable sea' – though the name became Black Sea in the mediaeval period (*Kara Deniz* in Turkish). With the Ottoman capture of Constantinople in 1453, the sea became largely closed to non-Turkish shipping – those castles in the Straits guarded the entrance well. Only in the nineteenth century, with the growth of Russian power and presence along the north coast, was it possible to reach the sea from the Mediterranean, and for Russian ships to come out. For a time there, 'hospitable' seemed appropriate, but by November 1918, 'inhospitable' could once more be said to be a reasonable description, though perhaps 'hostile' would also fit, for since 1914 it had been an active war zone; the states around the sea were at odds with each other, and so were their navies.

From Constantinople, reading clockwise round the sea, the coasts were Turkish in Thrace, then Bulgarian – both allies of Germany – as far as the plateau of the Dobrudja and the delta of the Danube, which were Romanian, an Anglo-French ally, but occupied by German forces until 1918. All of these coasts were therefore certainly hostile territory towards the Allies until the armistice of 11 November. The north coast was in Russian control, but which Russian party controlled that region in late 1918 was unclear; the political changes in the land north of the sea during the past year meant that authority had declined and fragmented. German occupation had been imposed in southern Russia during the summer of 1918, as far east as Kherson, and Nikolayev and Crimea, so extending German control even further. In Odessa, a Ukrainian governor held office, for the Ukrainian government claimed independence, though it was dominated by the German army. Beyond Crimea to the east, the coast could be counted as Russian as far as the Caucasus Mountains, and from the Don River to the mountain barrier it was under the rule of the White Russian Royalist forces of General Denikin, the Volunteer Army, composed of imperial officers taking all ranks. South of the Caucasus Mountains there were, as noted in the last chapter, several independent or revolutionary states – Georgia, Armenia, Azerbaijan; then along the south coast there was the Ottoman Empire. The governments here were weaker, and even after the Turkish armistice the Ottoman army went on fighting the Armenians and refusing to surrender its weapons.

The British were particularly interested in Crimea, and it was to look into Sevastopol that *Shark* and *Tribune* had begun their joint but separate voyages around the sea in November 1918. This was the major Russian naval base, and to the west was the city of Nikolayev, where there was the major dockyard, which was actively building new warships, including dreadnoughts. To the east was Novorossiisk, the naval headquarters of Denikin's forces. There were warships in all these places, but it was unclear whose authority, if any, they answered to, still less whose orders they might obey. In the eastern corner of the sea was Batumi, also of uncertain political allegiance, but it and the port of Poti were the gateways to the Caucasus area, the termini of the Caucasus railway to the oil port of Baku and a route through Batumi into north-eastern Turkey.

In the Caucasus, a series of political changes had eventually resulted in the emergence of a group of republics claiming independence, but with Turkish and German troops intervening – and British forces had, of course, intervened at Baku, arriving from Mesopotamia. British control was only secured in Baku by the Turkish armistice, which compelled Enver's late venture of the Army of Islam to pull out. This was, altogether, a hugely complex situation, which was discovered only when it became possible, from 13 November, for British forces to gain access to the Black Sea as a whole through the Bosporos. There were certainly problems enough to be dealt with.

For a year before the Turkish armistice was agreed, the British government had a policy of sorts in place for the Black Sea region, co-ordinated to some extent with the French. They would intervene in Russia in favour of the enemies of the Bolsheviks, though the Treaty of Brest-Litovsk meant that Ukraine as a whole would become, at least nominally, independent. So in the Black Sea in late 1918, the first task for the Royal Navy was to investigate who had power locally, and what was their attitude to the Bolsheviks. A policy originally made in late 1917, in response to the Bolshevik coup, was quite out of date by late 1918. The *coup d'état* of the Bolsheviks in October 1917 had been the trigger for a new attitude of more intense hostility, but since then other events had overtaken both the Allies and the Bolsheviks.

The new Russian (Bolshevik) government gained an armistice and then made a peace treaty with their German and Austro-Hungarian enemies – the Treaty of Brest-Litovsk in March 1918. The Russians had been compelled to surrender huge swathes of territory – Finland, the Baltics, Poland, Ukraine, Crimea – though they had mental reservations about the permanence of that surrender. In South Russia, Ukraine became an independent state, with a plethora of political groups competing to rule, though its independence was severely circumscribed by the government's dependence on German forces, who marched in to occupy and exploit the country during the summer, aiming to fuel their own country from Ukrainian and Caucasian resources, and so defeat the British naval blockade.[1]

In the Caucasus, local authorities emerged – three or four separate and mutually hostile successor states; this division rendered the whole area vulnerable to outside intervention and conquest – by the Bolsheviks, the Turks, the Germans, the 'White' Russian forces, all of whom aimed at conquest and busily intervened. The Germans aimed at exploitation, and the British intervened to deter the Germans and Turks – Georgia accepted a German protective force of several battalions, Baku was held by the British for a time, the Turks fought the Armenians, and the Armenians had aspirations for Georgia. Both outsiders were interested in the local resources, either to acquire them (Georgian manganese) or to prevent others from acquiring them (Baku oil, Turkestan cotton). The local sentiment was probably mainly in favour of independence, in which case all were to be disappointed.

In April 1918, German forces, army and navy, marched into Crimea and just missed seizing the Russian Black Sea Fleet at Sevastopol.[2] In August, the Germans moved in strength through the south of Russia and Ukraine, aiming to secure the Ukrainian harvest for their own use, and so help to sustain the main offensive on which they had embarked on the Western Front. They had in mind also gaining access to the oil of Baku, and a German cadre went to the city, only to become prisoners of the British. The Ukrainian Republic succumbed to occupation at once, but rival groups then emerged, each claiming to be the true government, pro- and anti-German, pro- and anti-Russian.

The Transcaucasians were threatened by Russian forces, Red, White, and others, and some, especially in Georgia, welcomed German support; the Germans were willing to provide it, since it gave them access to the local resources. So the oil of Baku became a major target for the German invaders, but also a major target for the British, who aimed to prevent the Germans succeeding. Others welcomed Russian interventions, and that included some who welcomed Bolshevik support, or were, or claimed to be, Bolsheviks themselves, like General Bicherakov. The net result was a great fragmentation of authority throughout the region, with the appearance of unstable republics and general disorder. From August to November 1918 in South Russia, the most potent authority was the German army. Some of the warships that had moved from Sebastopol to Novorossiisk returned to Sevastopol, where German engineers and sailors set about making them seaworthy again.

The Bolsheviks could claim no political legitimacy until they could enforce it, install a credible local government, and achieve some international recognition. They were holding Moscow and St Petersburg (now Petrograd), and thereby could lay claim to a certain internal legitimacy by virtue of ruling from the cities that were traditionally the capitals of Russia; since the Russian railway system fanned out to the provinces from Moscow, they had a strong logistical foundation that gave them the ability to reach out to the provinces. But Russia was big, and the Bolsheviks would have to gain genuine legitimacy, and not just the recognition sought by the conquest of the traditional territory of Russia. (They also, of course, had ambitions for revolutionising the whole world, and it was this that bothered non-Russians the most.)

The Bolsheviks had several major weapons in their ideological armoury: their promise of power for the working class; their denigration of imperial and aristocratic inherited authority – which in many countries had become particularly obnoxious in the generation before the war; and their achievement in seizing power in the largest country in the world, and in fighting hard to retain and extend it. All this gave them a strong appeal amongst the people of Russia, and those abroad, if not among the more wary governments. They could usually count on an active minority of supporters in every city and region, even beyond Russia's borders. These would welcome their arrival, in whatever form, military or civilian or political, and many were liable to announce themselves as Bolsheviks, opportunely. This made for a very potent political and social appeal, difficult to counter, though that appeal was limited by their own inability, and by the need to find food – which had often been confiscated by one or other 'authority' – for much of the population. The Russian fleet in the Black Sea had thus, not surprisingly, been subject to changes and conflicting orders and had to cope with a very fluid situation, several deliberating authorities, several Bolshevik parties, the emergent states, new and old, and several foreign interventions. And it was the control of the Russian fleet that particularly exercised British concern.

A great deal of this general situation was known to the British, of course, and antipathy towards the Bolsheviks was strong, at least in British ruling and property-owning classes; these, of course, included the entirety of the officers of the navy and the army. The British working class had a greater degree of sympathy for Bolshevik aspirations, if not for their methods. However, having now gained access to power in Britain, through trade unions, the Labour Party, and the right to vote, they were less attracted to Bolshevism, seen as a competitor. The complex mixture of naval, military, diplomatic, and logistical issues in the Black Sea area meant that, for the British fleet arriving into the Black Sea in November 1918, much depended on orders from London, which could take some time to be formulated and to arrive, and which were liable to be out of date when received. The precise policy to be pursued was never altogether clear when seen from London, and so was even more obscure in the Black Sea.

And, of course, the naval authorities – the Admiralty and the commanders-in-chief – had their own agendas, specifically to ensure that the surviving ships of the Russian Black Sea Fleet were not used against them. This was a fleet that had been generally successful and inventive during the war, and since then, many crews were liable to announce themselves as Bolsheviks, opportunely; the officers had often been killed or driven away, seriously compromising the ships' abilities to be fought. Until the German armistice, in fact, the ships were to come under German control, as a result of the Brest-Litovsk treaty; German forces had seized both the Nikolayev construction yards and the Sevastopol naval base. Some ships had been moved from Sevastopol to the Novorossiisk base to escape such a fate. The treaty had established a technically independent Ukraine, but the German invasion had stultified its ability to establish itself.

The arrival of the news of the German armistice from 11 November thrust a new element of confusion into the situation. It spread even before the Allies' ships had entered the Black Sea. The Allied fleet would, in theory, therefore be sailing into a calm sea, politically at least. An early task for Admirals Calthorpe and Amet and their ships was to ensure that the Bolsheviks did not seize those Russian ships. No Russian authority was well enough established to be trusted with such weapons, in the admirals and their governments' views, and the arrival of the Bolsheviks to replace German authority, if that happened, would be no improvement. Germans and Bolsheviks might be seen as allies, and this would very likely mean the Bolsheviks' acquisition of the old navy's ships that the Germans had seized. The British, after all, had been fighting against the Bolsheviks in North Russia for a year already; similar hostility in the south was virtually guaranteed.[3] The Bolsheviks, as the new government of Russia, could therefore argue that they were fully entitled to use the ex-imperial ships against the Royal Navy.

Admiral Calthorpe, commanding the Mediterranean Fleet, and now in overall command of the Allied naval forces entering the Black Sea, made the first exploratory review of the Black Sea situation as soon as he arrived in the sea. A year earlier, he had written a paper speculating where the Russian Black Sea Fleet in German hands might be used.[4] Now he sent his ships in all directions to discover the actual situation. *Shark* and *Tribune* and other destroyers visited for a quick survey of the main ports along the northern coast, from Odessa round to Batumi; two of the British cruisers, *Grafton* and *Canterbury*, joined in as temporary command centres for the reconnaissance.[5]

Calthorpe commanded a mixed Allied force. There were two British battleships, *Superb* (his flagship) and *Temeraire*, the scout cruiser *Skirmisher*, some cruisers and destroyers, the submarine depot ship *Adamant*, and one submarine, *E.21*; there were also two French battleships, *Justice* and *Démocratie*, with a destroyer; Rear Admiral R.A. Lejay was in command; an Italian battleship, *Roma*, with the gunboat *Agordat*; and two Greek destroyers. In addition, the cruiser *Liverpool* had sailed with a British Military Mission to establish contact with General Denikin, commanding the Volunteer Army in the Don province; Calthorpe was anxious to find out more about this force and Denikin's intentions. This was located east of Crimea, and

Denikin's headquarters were at the city of Ekaterinodar, and he controlled the port of Novorossiisk.

A base for the British ships had been established in the Gulf of Ismid in the Sea of Marmara – reconnoitred earlier by *Shark* – and close enough to Constantinople to be intimidating. He had other ships under his command in the Aegean and the Mediterranean. Having ensured that the ships were not required at Constantinople, which was quiet, he had taken the larger part of his mixed fleet through the Bosporos into the sea.

The Black Sea was thus only one of the responsibilities heaped on Calthorpe, who was also high commissioner in charge of relations with the Ottoman authorities. One of the early British measures, still in November 1918, was to send a force of soldiers – 800 British and 1,200 Indians of the 27th Division, taken from the Salonika Army – right across the Black Sea to the Caucasus area, where Batumi was occupied. This was also at the western end of the railway from Baku – though by this time, the line was in poor condition and such use as there was remained intermittent. Batumi itself was for the moment a constituent city of the independent Republic of Georgia. This was the neighbour to Armenia and Azerbaijan, also newly independent but much more unstable than Georgia. All three were under threat from Turks and Russians, and perhaps from arriving Germans, who had been retained in Georgia, as well as internally from monarchists, other Republicans, and Bolsheviks.

This was one concern. Baku was another, a town gripped by party and ethnic warfare, murder, and massacre. Dunsterville's expedition had attempted to intervene, without permanent success. He had accomplished his original purpose of preventing the Germans gaining access to the oil before having to retreat before a strong Turkish attack. A second British–Indian expedition under General Thomson arrived in the city on 17 November; Commodore Norris, with the Caspian Flotilla, was also under Calthorpe's rather distant orders. Further east, there was confusion in Central Asia, where General Malleson's expedition from India had been attempting to block Bolshevik progress there for almost a year. This was a region on the borders of Afghanistan, always a highly sensitive subject for the British in India, and the tradition of invasions through Afghanistan to that country. (And in Afghanistan in April 1919, a British expedition sought, vainly as usual in that country, to impose foreign control.) All this, except Afghanistan, technically fell under Calthorpe's remit. That authority was soon to be curtailed by the appointment of General Milne to command the Army of the Black Sea (which included the forces in Baku and Central Asia). Confusion, with a variety of independent expeditions and several sources of ultimate authority, was the inevitable result.

In the Caucasus republics the internal disputations were conducted between the several communities, places, and parties, local and outsider (including now the British), but the main concern of the British was that one party in every dispute was composed of Russian Bolsheviks. They had a proven record of seizing power illegally, and retaining it with violence, not that they were unique in this. This was a concern in Central Asia, and in the lands north of the Black Sea, since part of the Bolshevik creed was to recover control of Imperial Russian territory, after which their further aim was to spread their revolution to the rest of the world. The British, being the most powerful and most prominent world power, and specifically a naval power, were immediately the Bolsheviks' enemy; the British returned the enmity. As time passed, the problem of Turkey was added to all this, and eventually overwhelmed it.

Admiral Calthorpe took his main fleet into the Black Sea on 25 November. It was, with five battleships, a powerful force. The voyage was exploratory, as much political as naval, aiming to visit the ports of the Russian coast and assess both the local political situation in each place, and particularly the presence and condition of Russian or ex-Russian naval vessels. The local reaction to the British arrival was also to be assessed. Beneath this surface information, Calthorpe needed to know the intentions and capabilities of the various authorities, forces, rebels, brigands, generals, political parties, and so on, throughout the whole of southern Russia. Underlying everything was the Allied antipathy towards the Bolsheviks, an antipathy fuelled by the fear of a wider revolution.

There had been a preliminary division of responsibility between the British and the French, arranged before the fleets entered the sea. The French were to be active in the western part of the sea, the British in the east, with Sevastopol, which had the best naval harbour, under some sort of joint control, though technically in the French zone. This put the French in charge at Odessa and the British at Novorossiisk and Batumi. Nikolayev, between Odessa and Crimea, was a major naval shipbuilding base, and so of interest to both British and French; it was in the latter's portion, but Calthorpe's ships were soon involved in investigating the city. On land, the dividing line between the two zones was the Don River, putting all of Ukraine in the French region, and Denikin's White Russian area between the Don and the Caucasus in the British. The French, however, though they had men and ships available, soon found that Odessa was a large and very turbulent city, and for a time it absorbed their forces and all their attention.

The French government in Paris, or rather the French high command, had made elaborate plans for their intervention in the region, beginning their planning in the summer of 1918. The fundamental purpose was anti-Bolshevik, but also there was an intention to put any succeeding government under an obligation. But then, as the size of the problem became clearer, and as it became obvious that the French on the spot would not have anywhere near enough troops available to implement their elaborate plans, the plans themselves shrank. By the time of the Allied entry into the Black Sea, the French were still intending to deploy a large mixed force, including several more battleships and five army divisions, but the commanders were already busily pointing out the deep unwillingness of their men to indulge in any more fighting, quite apart from the fact that even five divisions was nowhere near enough for the huge area to be controlled. There was also a certain sympathy among the republican French for the anti-aristocratic, anti-monarchic Russian Revolution. Then the influenza epidemic arrived; it could knock out whole battalions and whole crews almost instantly. It was clear that the French ambitions could not be realised.[6]

Calthorpe took his mixed fleet directly to Crimea, the main Russian naval base; Nikolayev would soon require his attention, and the French would concentrate on Odessa. It was the British intention to gain control of all the warships in the sea, pending a decision at the peace conference (which had not yet convened) on their future ownership. The Russian ships had been ceded to Germany in the Brest-Litovsk treaty, so they could now be seen as legitimate war booty by the Allies. The contrast between the ambitions of the British and the French, between securing (and eliminating) the Russian Navy, and securing Russian land, is not surprising, given their differing politico-military sensitivities.

For the French, even more was at stake. Clemenceau all along had emphasised the French interests in Russia (and in the Ottoman Empire) in the form of their extensive pre-war investments – he had used this interest as the basis of his argument that Admiral Amet should take part in the armistice talks. So the French were in part intervening for their own economic interests – just as the British were interested in eliminating Russia as a threat to India, and as a competing sea power. The divergence of aims, together with the difference in enthusiasm of their soldiers and sailors, soon brought separation in action.

It took some time for the varying intentions of the Allies to be implemented. It was in a sense easiest for the British, who were using ships, and so were more mobile than the French. Again, as with *Shark* at the Dardanelles, Calthorpe sent a ship, in this case the light cruiser *Canterbury*, accompanied by a destroyer, ahead of the main fleet, arriving at Sevastopol on 24 November. The British arrival was welcomed, but in the short term, they essentially merely added yet another element to the complex situation. The main fleet, with Calthorpe, arrived on the 26th. German and Turkish ships were to be secured in accordance with the armistice terms.

Half a dozen and more groups were claiming some authority at Sevastopol, but there was also a large part of the Russian Black Sea Fleet in the harbour, one dreadnought battleship (*Volya*, formerly *Imperator Aleksandr III*), and six destroyers. All of these, particularly *Volya*, had had the advantage of a campaign of maintenance, first at Novorossiisk, where it had been in White hands, and then by the German sailors and engineers when they returned to Sevastopol. This had brought *Volya* to a reasonable condition, and the several armistices had arrived just in time to prevent them from being used against the Allies. There were also four German U-boats in the harbour, making it clear that Sevastopol had become an active German naval base in the last two months. (*Goeben* had been repaired there after its unsuccessful foray in February; it was, as Colonel Murphy noted, now in the Constantinople dockyard.) All these ships were now taken over by the Allies; the British manned *Volya* with a skeleton crew from *Agamemnon*. The destroyers were distributed, two to the French, and one each to the Italians and Greeks; the British took the remaining two. The U-boats were also seized. They all counted as Allies' booty. For *Volya*, this was the fifth change of ownership in the past year, and the changes were not finished yet.[7]

There was an argument over the inclusion of German merchant ships in the armistice terms. The British insisted that they were to be transferred to the

Allies as further items of booty. The Germans claimed that German merchant ships were not to be included as 'material' for confiscation. Calthorpe, bolstered by an interpretation from London, insisted that it did, but also agreed to refer the issue onwards and meanwhile he accepted that some of those ships should be used for the evacuation of German and Austrian soldiers. This evacuation was to take place as quickly as possible, and German and Austrian troops in the Caucasus region could be brought to Crimea for moving onwards. This would prove to be difficult; already the railway north from Odessa had been cut by Russian forces; hence the promise to use the recaptured ships. The German Vice-Admiral Albert Hopman accepted this, under protest; at least the men would get home in relative safety.

There were also considerable numbers of Allied merchant ships, which had been seized by the Germans; some of these had been trapped in the sea when the Straits had been closed in 1914, and claimed by Germany under the treaty. (The Germans had taken Allied ships as booty, but now complained when German ships were also claimed as booty by their enemies.) Fourteen German ships were taken over by the French, and the Italians seized several more; the British were in fact contented with recovering the British ships that had been marooned in the sea.

The British sailors who manned *Volya* were reported to be disgusted by the filthy conditions on board. It seems that the Germans had concentrated on getting the ships into fighting trim, but had ignored the conditions in the living quarters. Before that, the Russians had neglected both living and working parts when the officers' authority had collapsed with the revolution. Neglect had been general and maintenance ignored, so recovery had clearly been limited. But the battleship was able to move, and the Germans had succeeded in producing a fighting vessel, which the British command confirmed. Had the Germans been faster at this maintenance, or had more time, the ship might have been able to come out to challenge the British and French blockade of the Straits' entrance. A powerful dreadnought and the repaired battlecruiser *Goeben* would certainly have been a serious threat to the antiquated ships and lazy command of the blockading squadron at Mudros. Of the four German submarines in the port, the British and French took two each. The British manned them with detachments from their own battleships. There had therefore certainly been a viable German–

Turkish raiding force coming into existence at the moment of the Turkish and German armistices.

Calthorpe had delegated the inspection of the ships and their condition to his officers; he himself had been greeted at Sevastopol by a succession of delegations and authorities, who appear to have arrived serially. There was a Russian rear admiral, Klochkovski, though it is not clear what authority he had, or which Russian government he answered to; possibly he hoped to secure the return of the confiscated ex-Russian ships. It seems that no attention was paid to him, and he is not mentioned again. There was General de Bode, a representative of General Denikin, in command of the counter-revolutionary Volunteer Army. There was a representative from the government of Ukraine, presumably the puppet government set up by the Germans, now bereft of that support, one from the Crimean government, which had seceded from both the Russian and Ukrainian republics, one from the city of Sevastopol, and one from the Poles of the city.

Calthorpe does not report what his interviews with any of these groups consisted of, if anything. It must have been clear that none of them exercised any real authority or armed force – except perhaps Denikin's representative, de Bode. Calthorpe does, however, report on his talks with two German officers who had also arrived. Vice-Admiral Hopman had command of the German naval forces in the Black Sea, which included the formerly Russian ships for the last couple of months, and which the Allies had now acquired. With him, Calthorpe argued out the issue of the merchant ships. Also there was Lieutenant General Count von Waldersee, who had commanded the garrisons of Odessa and Sevastopol, the major German forces that still existed in the southern Russian territories. There were 11,000 German troops in the Crimean region alone, another 4,000 in Odessa, and more elsewhere in Ukraine and coming in from the Caucasus region. It was from these two commanders that Calthorpe might be able to get the best information as to the situation in the interior. The two Allied admirals, Calthorpe and Rear Admiral Lejay, met the two German commanders, excluding any Russians, a symbolic indication of the actual location of military power in Crimea.

It quickly became clear to Calthorpe that neither Denikin's Volunteer Army nor the Crimean government had any real authority or power in Crimea, but that the German forces did. There were large quantities of munitions in Sevastopol being kept under fairly loose guard, if at all, and he must assume there was more elsewhere, and that some had probably been acquired by the local Bolsheviks. Committees of naval officers were set up to investigate the ships, the munitions, the inland part of Crimea, the other Crimean cities, and Sevastopol, and anything else of military or naval interest.

The Russian ships that had gone to Novorossiisk, in the territory controlled by Denikin's Volunteer Army, had, of course, been mainly sunk or scuttled. The cruiser *Liverpool*, accompanied by a French cruiser and two Australian destroyers, took the British Military Mission to liaise with Denikin; this would enable the officers to see the state of any surviving Russian ships in that port. This was another part of the Anglo-French competition, since the French cruiser also carried a French Military Mission to Denikin. In fact, the British mission had been sent off by General Sir George Milne from Constantinople (on instructions from London) only when it was discovered that the French were about to do so.

Calthorpe spread his naval forces throughout the sea, intending that they should show the Allied flags as widely as possible, and locate any unaccounted-for enemy warships. Novorossiisk would be investigated by *Liverpool*. The destroyer *Beaver* collected the head of the British Mission to Romania, Major General Christopher Ballard, at the Danube and took him to investigate the situation at Odessa; the destroyer *Nereide* followed on, coming from Varna in Bulgaria, and these two were joined by the scout cruiser *Skirmisher* from Sevastopol.

Tribune and *Shark* and a French destroyer were sent to Nikolayev, the major Russian shipbuilding centre. Several Russian warships were seen to be partly built, including a dreadnought and some submarines. None of these, particularly the submarines, were to be allowed to fall into Bolshevik hands. (Calthorpe, having been in command of the anti-submarine campaign in the Mediterranean, was particularly sensitive to the submarine threat.) This was also the port where the German and Austrian soldiers and sailors would begin their inland journey to repatriation, so long as its rail connection to the interior was still usable. They had to travel through Ukraine and Poland – not a pleasant prospect for any German soldiers by this time.

Three more Allied destroyers went into the Sea of Azov, one to visit Berdiansk and Ghenichesk at the Perekop peninsula, which links Crimea with the continent; two destroyers, one British and one French, were to visit Kertch at the entry to the Azov, and then Mariupol and Taganrog in the sea's north-east corner; from there, officers went ashore to visit Rostov and Novocherkassk. In Crimea, other destroyers visited Yalta, the old imperial holiday resort, and Theodosia. And, a little out of the sequence, the scout cruiser *Forward*, fifteen years old by now, visited Trebizond on the North Anatolian coast, which had been under Russian occupation, but was now being retaken by the Turks.

This was a reminder that Calthorpe's responsibilities were much wider than simply the Russian fleet and its bases. This was in addition to *Liverpool* and a destroyer at Batumi in the Caucasus region; these were to be replaced by the heavy cruiser *Theseus* when it arrived. This was spreading Calthorpe's force out very thinly, and the appearance of a single destroyer might not have made a great impression on a hostile group determined to resist. But Calthorpe shuffled his ships about to investigate or control affairs in all the cities around the sea, no doubt giving the impression that he had more, or more powerful, ships than he actually commanded. The smaller ships in the British force were sent to search for and sweep mines, but this was such a major task that Calthorpe concentrated his efforts at first on the Bulgarian ports, Varna, Constanza, and Burgas, which he could use as bases and where he could land and store supplies.

Calthorpe took his flagship, the battleship *Superb*, to Odessa to assess the situation in the city, to follow up reports by *Nereide* and *Skirmisher*, and probably by General Ballard, the British representative on the Danube. Odessa was a major port, and he found there at least seventy merchant ships, which were unable to move due to a lack of crews or fuel. He arrived at the city on 4 December, and the next day the French began to land officers to scout out the situation in the city. Several French vessels had already arrived, as well as the earlier British ships.

The city was being kept in order by 4,000 German soldiers whom it had been impossible yet to repatriate. In addition to the Germans and the French, there was a Ukrainian governor; some of the forces of Simon Petliura, who had gained control of much of Ukraine, were approaching from the north. As these came closer a small force of the Volunteer Army, and any forces of the Ukrainian government, both left; the same thing happened at Nikolayev. Calthorpe expressed some confusion over the situation, but he was at least able to ask for ten German transports to be sent to repatriate the German troops, though their removal would take away the only organised force able to control the city.

It took some time for Calthorpe to get a handle on the situation in his area, because, as he said, it changed rapidly. When he sailed in *Superb* to Odessa early in December before the French force arrived, he had found the city quiet, because of the presence of German soldiers. They obeyed the local Ukrainian governor, who had been appointed by the German-dominated Ukrainian government. This was repudiated by Petliura, who was anti-German and also defying the Ukrainian government. His approach to Nikolayev had induced Calthorpe to send the cruisers *Grafton* and *Canterbury* to exert their forceful influence in that port, and in order to supplement the earlier presence of the two destroyers *Tribune* and *Shark*; he did not want any of the warships there to fall into German or Russian control until matters had been sorted out.

Nikolayev, as an industrial city with a major shipbuilding yard producing warships, was likely to have a fairly strong pro-Bolshevik party, though in all likelihood without a Bolshevik majority. A Royal Navy presence might just be enough to deter the Bolsheviks from attempting anything decisive. On investigation in detail later, the ships in the yards were assessed as being a long way from completion, four destroyers which were '60 per cent' completed, and five new gunboats at various stages of completion or commission. But what worried Calthorpe most were the six to eight submarines, which were '60 per cent' completed. He did not wish to have to face, or hunt, these boats. No work was currently being done on the part-built ships, but the dock installations were undamaged, and he thought that two or three of the submarines could be completed for sea within about three months.

The French General Staff's ambitious plans, made before the armistices, for the occupation of Crimea and even of a large part of Ukraine, were produced on the assumption that the German forces that occupied those regions would surrender to them, and that the French would have the use of a large French army for the purpose. However, these plans had turned out to be vastly over-ambitious when the fighting ended. Ukraine had declared its independence, partly under German prompting or insistence, but also with a good deal of popular support; it was now being invaded by Denikin's Volunteer Army, which came from the east, and by the Bolshevik forces – the Red Army – from the north; both of these were aiming at gaining control of the imperial territories. The French soldiers, like the soldiers conscripted for the war everywhere, were only interested in being demobilised and then going home. Having identified the enemy only as Germany and its allies, they were not keen on fighting any other enemies, and certainly not an army of Russian revolutionaries. The manpower that the French staff required for their eager plans, and which had existed earlier in 1918, when the fighting was taking place inside France, had quickly evaporated as the various armistices took hold and units were demobilised; at the same time, the Socialists in France were hostile to any military intervention against the Bolsheviks.

Odessa had been one of the main targets of the French from the start, since it was the main commercial centre of the Black Sea. The many immobilised merchant ships in the harbour, noted by Calthorpe, were testimony to the city's commercial activity in peacetime. The French occupiers found, just as elsewhere in South Russia, a conflict of authorities. The Bolsheviks were lying low, as their fellows in Crimea were; the German-nominated Ukrainian prefect had little authority; the Ukrainian leader, Simon Petliura, a brutal commander and anti-Semite, had seized part of the city on 11 December. The French officers investigated, then troops were landed with the aim of also seizing parts of the city, but they had to fight to do so.[8]

From Nikolayev, Captain George Chetwode, commanding the two destroyers *Tribune* and *Shark*, expressed concern to Calthorpe at the approach of Petliura's Ukrainians, so Calthorpe added the cruisers *Grafton* and *Canterbury* to Chetwode's command. These had rather greater firepower than the two destroyers had, and could bolster the defence, or pose a threat, whichever was necessary. Meanwhile, Admiral Amet had brought the French battleships *Mirabeau* and *Justice*, which had been part of Calthorpe's Allied force in the Aegean under Lejay, to Odessa.

At Sevastopol, Calthorpe put 500 marines on shore to keep order; they had been collected from the garrisons of the forts in the Dardanelles and the Bosporos. The several authorities in the city he had met were much divided and none had any real power, except the Germans, who, as at Odessa, were urged to stay and keep order. The Sevastopol city council was described as composed of 'men of little influence', and it had no effective forces, civil or military, at its command. The Volunteer Army detachment in the city was only about 1,000 men. Of the munitions in the city, some were being guarded by the Germans, some by the Volunteers, but much was in unlocked stores and some had been looted already.

It was claimed that if the German troops were removed from Sevastopol the local Bolsheviks would assert themselves, seize power, and 'all its attended horrors' would follow. In fact, the Bolsheviks had earlier had considerable trouble 'asserting' themselves in the region, the majority of the population being indifferent to them, though they had made some progress by persuasion. The Bolsheviks had quickly vanished from view when the Germans arrived, which behaviour rather reduced their local influence. The rumours of their strength that circulated were based partly on their reputation; their present invisibility tended to mask their threat, but the rumours exaggerated their supposed strength. They were widely perceived as a threat and they certainly induced fear amongst the rest of the population.

The French armed forces' slow arrival at Odessa left Calthorpe concerned at the situation at Sevastopol, which was also theoretically in the French zone. The German occupying troops would be leaving as soon as they could go, and the several competing Russian factions would then be able to get at each other's throats. This was the main reason he had landed the marines in the city. He could thus, along with his ships, make an attempt to control the city (and its port, where his men were landed), though the rest of Crimea would have to look after itself until the French arrived.

Even as he was reporting these developments in his monthly 'letter of proceedings' to the Admiralty on 12 December, however, he heard that Petliura's forces were moving into Odessa and Nikolayev, and that the local representatives of the Ukrainian government and of the Volunteer Army had swiftly moved out. The French then began landing their major forces at Odessa on 17 December.[9]

Back at Sevastopol, the German and Russian warships that had been confiscated were being prepared to sail to the British base in the Gulf of Ismid. Two of the German U-boats, in better condition than the Russian ships, had already been sent to the British anchorage in the Gulf; *Volya* and the two Russian destroyers taken by the British were undergoing test runs. This produced complaints – 'considerable feeling', as Calthorpe put it, in his naval-cum-British understated way – from the Russian sailors and the population at the intended removal of these originally Russian ships by an originally Russian ally, but Calthorpe put on a stone face and insisted that they would go, crewed by minimal crews from the British battleships when they sailed.

Calthorpe's post as high commissioner at Constantinople and the Ottoman Empire was essentially a diplomatic post, aimed at keeping some sort of co-ordination between the Allies. As high commissioner he was subject to instruction from the Foreign Office, while in his original post as commander-in-chief in the Mediterranean, and for naval activities in the Black Sea and the Aegean, he was responsible to the Admiralty. In the aftermath of the various armistices, and in the face of the complications in Russia and its fragments and its conflicts, not to mention the problems of the Ottoman Empire and Constantinople, the majority of the Mediterranean Fleet had been brought into the Aegean and the Black Seas. Beyond these seas and these affairs, he was also, in some vague way, responsible for events in the Caspian (where Norris commanded the Royal Naval presence) and in Central Asia, though he could hardly affect matters in either of these areas.

Calthorpe therefore put his subordinate, Rear Admiral Sir Michael Culme-Seymour, in charge of the fleet in the Black Sea. Meanwhile, General Milne had command of 'the Army of the Black Sea'. Both men took up their posts in December, and both at once set out on tours of inspection of their commands. In the Caucasus, perhaps partly because Milne could now give the attention to the region that Calthorpe had been unable to do earlier, the 27th Division was sent to establish British authority and enforce the armistice.

Two thousand British and Indian troops of the division, commanded by Major General Sir George Forestier-Walker, were landed at Batumi, and a battalion had moved along the Batumi–Baku railway as far as Tbilisi in Georgia. The political situation was, as usual, confused, but Georgia, Armenia, and Azerbaijan were now more or less independent of Russia and of each other, but each of them now had a contingent of British troops present, mainly to ensure that German and Turkish forces were excluded, or evicted. Their presence, and the independence of the republics, conflicted with the policy of General Denikin, who was fighting for 'Russia, One and Indivisible'. Allied policy had tended to favour the independence of these territories. The quarrel over this divergence, such as it was, did not produce a serious rift, for Denikin needed British arms and support, and the Allies were not really very interested in the Caucasian states' independence, despite their policy.

In the Black Sea, Seymour surveyed the situation, just as Calthorpe had on his arrival not long before, visiting the usual trouble spots and thereby being kept constantly on the move in the battleship *Lord Nelson*. Any solution to a problem he devised, however, could be no more than purely temporary, given the volatile situation involved. He made an early tour of the eastern part of the sea, visiting Batumi and Novorossiisk in particular. He could report little activity, this being the winter season, with the Russian rivers and the northern part of the sea frozen. The Georgians, where General Kress von Kressenstein and a numerous group of German settlers were influential, were said in one paragraph of his report to be 'awkward and difficult', and in another to be 'amenable', which may be taken as a fair indication of his and Calthorpe's difficulties. General Denikin was said to be preparing an offensive against the Bolsheviks and had moved his headquarters from Ekaterinodar, inland from Novorossiisk, to Sevastopol, a sign of his increasing geographical range, but also of his need to keep in contact with the Allies.[10]

Other senior officers, mainly British, passed through on various missions. These included Milne's survey of his responsibilities, travelling from Constantinople on a month-long tour to visit British forces all the way to the Caspian and Central Asia; this was his tour of inspection, after which his recommendations had a major effect in Central Asia in particular, as noted in the last chapter. Minesweeping had been organised and started in the Black Sea, but was then suspended when a message came from London that only volunteers should man the minesweepers; the crews had to be interviewed individually, and then each ship's crew had to be reorganised. The sweeping was thus significantly delayed.[11]

On 18 January 1919, Calthorpe, in a detailed letter to the Admiralty, described the tasks he had to accomplish, and laid out the dispositions of his ships. He was responsible for shipping in both the Aegean and the Black Sea (as was Seymour, until he appointed Commodore Maurice Fitzmaurice as his subordinate in the Aegean). Calthorpe listed the detailed tasks as the 'supervision of merchant shipping; blockade; government transport; supervision of men-of-war; transport of British, German, and Turkish troops'. To this, he could have added support for, and liaison with, the French in the Black Sea – a matter that became more important as time passed – and the supply of stores to them as well. All this was in addition to his wider naval command in the Mediterranean.

In connection with his office as high commissioner, he noted that there were no British diplomatic personnel in the whole region, and only one vice-consul – at Novorossiisk – 'and he a Swede'. This meant that he and his officers had to do the diplomatic work as well as command their ships – he noted several issues, including when a French officer decided that he was a high commissioner, while his equivalent British colleague was a British sub-lieutenant, who was not overawed. The French were relying on him for support, naval and logistical, and yet at times he had to confer with and defer to them. Then there were the messages from London: 'the numerous and extremely varied requests for information or action which I receive from the Admiralty and the Foreign Office' were clearly time-consuming and vexatious, though that was why he had a staff. He had been compelled to pull back from active involvement in the maritime affairs of his command and leave the detailed sea command to his immediate subordinates such as Seymour and Fitzmaurice – and yet, of course, he was in command, and was responsible.

The ships in the Black Sea were distributed to Odessa (*Grafton*), Nikolayev (*Sentinel*), Sevastopol (*Temeraire*), Batumi (*Theseus*), and Constantinople (*Superb*); three other ships were refitting, and one was returning home. Seymour used *Lord Nelson* as his mobile headquarters. Five other ships, three of them monitors, were retained to be used on the Russian rivers when they unfroze. He also listed the ships in the Aegean, which was part of his command: *Adventure*, a scout cruiser, was at Smyrna, and the old third class cruiser *Pelorus* was at Cape Helles 'until the Dardanelles minefield is cleared'. He noted that four of his ships had been paid off or sent home, as had some of his monitors. 'Sloops and old fleet messengers are doing essential ferry services,' he reported, and that included moving stores, mails, and 'important' officers, which in fact was the usual use of many of his destroyers. The report is supplementary to his monthly letter of proceedings, and is clearly intended to emphasise his difficulties, and the serious effects of the reduction of his ships on his numerous tasks. He was being tasked with numerous jobs while at the same time his resources were being repeatedly reduced in number.[12]

By the end of January 1919, when Calthorpe sent off the letter to the Admiralty from which this information is taken, and Seymour sent off his own report a week later, the navy had clearly successfully established itself in the Aegean, the Straits, at Constantinople, and in the Black Sea. Yet the fleet was unable to do much to affect the conditions on land, where great armies of Russians swirled back and forth. The scout cruiser *Sentinel*, the only ship left at Nikolayev, would hardly deter a determined army such as Petliura's as it closed in towards the dockyard and perhaps began to complete the half-built ships there. The British Marines based at Sevastopol were withdrawn and replaced by French and Greek troops in late December.

The Black Sea commanders thus had much wider responsibilities than the sea and its coasts. Already the Turks were becoming resentful at the British for serially breaking the terms of the armistice, above all by occupying Constantinople in strength. Mustafa Kemal had been testing the air in the city for some time, and exercising his formidable persuasive powers on the sultan to acquire an official post as Inspector of the forces in Anatolia. He then headed off into the Anatolian hinterland, just ahead of an Allied arrest order. And there was also the volatile condition of the Caucasus, the problem of the Caspian Sea, and as an extension of these, a developing difficulty in Central Asia. Calthorpe was right to emphasise his problems.

Chapter 7

British Control

In his first report, the newly appointed commander-in-chief in the Black Sea, Rear Admiral Sir Michael Culme-Seymour, who took up the command in December 1918 – his first report was dated 25 January 1919 – had in effect detailed the tasks he saw he had to perform. He had indirect responsibility for naval operations in the Caspian, but this was being left largely to Commodore Norris; he received Norris's reports and either included them or summarised them in his own. Similarly, Seymour had appointed Commodore Fitzmaurice as his subordinate in the Aegean. As a result, he was in direct command only in the Black Sea, the Sea of Marmara, and the Straits. A hierarchy of authority had therefore rapidly evolved, with Calthorpe in overall charge as Mediterranean commander-in-chief.[1]

French forces were to take command of the western half of the Black Sea, from Crimea to Odessa, as Seymour did for the eastern half; this region included the Caucasus coast, Batumi, the northern Anatolian coast, the Sea of Azov, and the eastern coast of Crimea – and the Caspian. This British section included, therefore, relations with the Turks, with the Georgians, and with the White Russians, above all, the Volunteer Army commanded by General Denikin, which was currently located and based east of the Sea of Azov and south of the Don River, the Russian Don province. Seymour was also largely responsible for Sevastopol, the inevitable naval base, though it was occupied by a small French and Greek force. Admiral Calthorpe had withdrawn his marines when the French finally landed their own garrison troops; they were accompanied by contingents of the Greek army. There appear to have been no Italians outside Constantinople, other than the occasional ship; they were mainly concentrating on their ambitions in Anatolia.

There were parties of German soldiers scattered all across this northern area of the Black Sea, from Odessa to Georgia, and none of these were at all friendly to their ex-enemies. In Georgia, for example, 1,500 Germans were living on ships in Poti harbour and were free to visit the town nightly, where getting drunk was their main occupation. When they met British officers they were openly insulting; the drunker they became, the more insulting they were. It could have been a dangerous mixture if the British had bothered to respond. As victors in the Great War, they scarcely needed to.

Seymour took a train journey to Ekaterinodar, 140 or so kilometres from Novorossiisk, to meet General Denikin, with whom he seems to have got along well enough, though the general was usually a fairly prickly person. The Russian officers were able to pelt Seymour with many questions about Britain's attitude and policy and when military support would be provided – tanks and aircraft were mentioned – none of which he was able to answer. He took refuge in non-committal and vague replies. No doubt the Russians understood perfectly well – British support would not be provided just yet, if ever.[2]

In a leisurely way, Calthorpe asked the Admiralty, three weeks after receiving Seymour's report, 'whether active assistance may be given to the Volunteer Army'; a fortnight later, and so equally non-urgently, the Admiralty replied. The War Cabinet had agreed that 'active assistance' could be given, so long as no naval forces, which would include sailors and marines, were landed. This at least would allow material supplies, including guns and ammunition, to be delivered, and ships used to support Volunteer operations along the coast.[3] It is evident that at this period – January and February 1919 – no serious problem was apprehended, in part because the northern Black Sea would be blocked by ice until about April.

Later, in March, Calthorpe was becoming concerned again at the number of issues he had to deal with. By this time his area was the most active militarily, and was complex as well, so he received the full attention of the British government's ministries who were interested – Admiralty, War Office, Foreign Office, Air Ministry, at least – not to mention the Prime Minister's Office. He replied to the Admiralty's permission message on 22 March, reporting that Bolshevik forces were advancing from the north, and that they had gained control of the naval base of Nikolayev. He was worried about Smyrna, and Egypt (where a rising against British control was developing), the Caucasus, and the north coast of Anatolia, and he pointed out that his forces were being so reduced in number that he would not have enough ships to cope with all these issues. He also made a point of reporting on the 'uncertain and feeble' French actions.[4]

Seymour, in charge while Calthorpe was at Port Said, also expressed concern at the Bolshevik advance. He sent a monitor (*M.17*) to the Perekop peninsula, which connects Crimea with the mainland, to support the Volunteer Army units which guarded that passage, and which was subject to Bolshevik attacks. The monitor would work with the seaplane carrier *Empress* and its two seaplanes, which would be used to spot the fall of shot. He wanted more monitors for a similar project further along the Azov coast.

In the French section of the sea, the Bolsheviks attacked at Kherson, which fell. Seymour's report on this expresses suspicions. The Bolshevik forces are said to have been 'superior' to the French; there was 'heavy fighting'. And yet, all Allied subjects were successfully evacuated, Allied casualties were slight, while Bolshevik casualties were 'severe', and they lost 'over 2,000 men'. The exaggeration and distortion that is evident in all this suggests that Seymour was relying on a French report which was concocted to justify their immediate evacuation of the city – and which was rapidly followed by the abandonment of Nikolayev. A contingent of German infantry was in the Nikolayev area and they were ordered to cover the evacuation, and were then themselves also evacuated – except for those who joined the Bolsheviks. In the city, Seymour decided that the French commander, General Philippe d'Anselme, had 'lost his head', and had precipitately ordered an evacuation, after having made an agreement with the Bolshevik commander that he would withdraw, leaving all the equipment and material in the dockyard undamaged, so long as the Bolsheviks held their fire. Seymour was scathing in his comments on this, and reported that the yards at Nikolayev had over twenty warships under construction, though the only one that was likely to be completed within the next three months was a submarine – if, that is, anyone was actually working in the construction yards. He conjured up visions of a Bolshevik submarine roaming about the Black Sea to the perennial danger to Allied – that is, mainly British – ships. This was something that Calthorpe was particularly sensitive to, as Seymour must have known.

This affair at Kherson and Nikolayev was reflected also at Odessa, where, by the end of March, that city had also come under threat from Bolshevik forces. Seymour reported that General Franchet d'Espèrey had arrived to put grit into the defence, but he (Seymour) was not suggesting that any improvement would actually take place.

There was, as it turned out, rather more to the situation than Seymour could see, since his comments were based only on what he had been told, and so at second or third hand. The city of Odessa was starving (except for the rich), had no electricity, was short of coal, and was even short of wood (trees and telegraph poles had mainly disappeared), and was overflowing with refugees. That is, the situation was not simply a matter of the failure of naval or military command. Politically, the French had been attempting to co-ordinate, under their own command, all the anti-Bolshevik forces in South Russia, but had come up against the complete contradiction between, on the one hand, the Ukrainians, who wanted independence and had been able to construct a rudimentary government, originally under German sponsorship but now largely in the hands of Petliura, and, on the other, Denikin's Volunteer Army, whose policy was of 'Russia, one and indivisible', which was as much anti-Ukrainian as anti-Bolshevik.

Nor were the French generals pursuing a single national policy. For example, General d'Anselme at Kherson and Nikolayev had been personally opposed to French intervention in Russian affairs from the start, and had, like his men, become very weary of war after four years of fighting, which for him had included a long spell in the Balkans. He could not tolerate Denikin's intransigence and unwillingness to compromise. He was also at odds with the more violent anti-Bolshevik officers in the French army, who included General Berthelot at Odessa. (Note also that there is repeated evidence throughout the British reports that the French were held in contempt, particularly by naval officers such as Seymour; they perhaps did not voice such sentiments in public, but they certainly did so in the privacy of the official messages they sent up the chain of command.)

The ordinary French troops, the *poilus*, were very largely unwilling to fight anyone by this stage in the war. There was a good deal of sympathy for the Bolsheviks in the ranks – the Socialist Party was strong in French politics, and if not pro-Bolshevik, it was certainly anti-interventionist. The French policy for Russia had included not just sending five divisions to support the anti-Bolshevik forces, but recruiting as many local Russians into French-officered units as possible. This policy failed. The refusal of many Russians to join the Allied forces was obvious in Odessa, where the French reckoned that there were more than 100,000 men of military age in the city; the vast majority were unwilling to be recruited into the anti-Bolshevik cause. In

Nikolayev, it was noted that civilians, particularly women, had stoned the French as they withdrew, while a section of the German garrison joined the Bolsheviks. The failure of the recruiting policy meant that all of the fighting fell to the unwilling French soldiers.

At Kherson, the Bolshevik attack that captured the city came from a local brigand, the 'Ataman' Gregoriev, who had collected a large force and had then decided, when the Bolsheviks were seeming to be successful, that he was a Bolshevik – but he had earlier fought for Petliura, and later was to fight purely for himself. In the fighting at the city, at least one French unit had refused to take part, and the civil population had joined the Bolshevik forces in the attack, probably because of the earlier unpleasant behaviour of the Franco-Greek garrison. The '2,000' casualties which the French reported as having been suffered by the Bolsheviks, and which Seymour repeated in his report, were mainly civilians killed and wounded when the French pulled out; it was more a French massacre than civilians becoming involved in the fighting.

General d'Anselme found the same set of problems at Nikolayev. He complained that the repatriation of soldiers from his forces had reduced his two divisions to only 1,200 soldiers and that the men who were still in Russia were in a very low state of morale, no doubt in part because they had not yet been promised a date for their own discharge. (Once they received a date, they were, of course, even less willing to fight.) In mid-March, he claimed that his men were 'unemployable', and that on that day four separate units of his forces had refused to fight. This attitude, of course, was reflected in the bad behaviour of the French troops towards the local population, which is partly the reason the men in Odessa had refused to be recruited, and why the civilians at Kherson had risen against the French as the 'Bolshevik' forces of Gregoriev attacked the city.[5]

By the last week in March, the pressure on the French to evacuate Odessa was becoming much stronger. In Paris, the Council of Four – President Wilson, British Prime Minister Lloyd George, Italian Prime Minister Orlando, and French Premier Clemenceau – discussed the issue for two days, while at the same time in the French Chamber of Deputies a prolonged attack led by the Socialists was mounted against the government's – that is, Clemenceau's – intervention policy. On 29 March, Clemenceau at last gave the order to evacuate Odessa, perhaps more to defuse opposition in

Parliament than for any specific military reasons. This would certainly now reduce the French presence in South Russia to Sevastopol alone.[6]

The order reached General d'Anselme on 2 April and he began the process of withdrawal next day. (General Franchet d'Espèrey assured Seymour at about the same time that the French would stay in Odessa, but it was d'Anselme's decision, not his, or rather d'Anselme and Franchet d'Espèrey were obeying orders from Paris, and the latter was probably merely a little behind the time.) That the French were about to leave was publicly announced, and panic and chaos erupted throughout the city. This rather implied that it was the French presence that had maintained order so far, and that the Bolshevik approach was no more welcome than the French occupation had been.

The local Soviet decided that the Volunteer Army members should not be allowed to leave, nor any members of the local middle class; it seems likely the intention was to murder all these people. The French had developed a considerable amount of antipathy towards the Volunteer Army and Denikin in the past few months, so perhaps the Soviet's members anticipated having a free hand. But d'Anselme stood firm and the Soviet gave way the next day. Amid constant disorder, the evacuees moved out, partly going by sea, and partly by land west to Bessarabia (Romanian territory). It was reckoned that the total to be moved amounted to 30,000 French and Allied (mainly Greek) troops, 12,000 Allied civilians, and 50,000 Russian civilians, including the Volunteer Army people. D'Anselme in the result was efficient and did not discriminate against anyone; and he succeeded in moving them within his self-imposed time limit of five days – a considerable achievement amid the disorder. By 6 April, the evacuation was completed.[7]

Admiral Seymour was told on 2 April by the captain of the Greek cruiser *Averoff* that he thought the evacuation of Odessa was imminent. Next morning, this was confirmed by a telegram from the captain of the scout cruiser *Skirmisher*, which was at Odessa, who reported that the evacuation had been officially announced.

Seymour claimed that the given reason for the evacuation was that the city was short of food, but he did not believe it; indeed, he had reached a state where he instinctively disbelieved anything the French said. Nevertheless, whatever he professed to believe, the city really was on the point of mass starvation – unless you were rich enough to pay the sky-high prices that were being charged for food by the profiteers. Seymour felt that the real reason for the French pulling out was actually 'political'. He did not spell this suspicion out, but, of course, he was correct, if by 'political' was meant French Metropolitan politics, which were revealed as strongly anti-interventionist in the Chamber of Deputies' debate. The attitude of the French soldiers and sailors, who were also citizens of a democracy, professing liberty, equality, and fraternity, was also heavily in favour of leaving.

Even if he was unimpressed by the stated reasons, Seymour did try to help. He sent several ships to assist the removal of the refugees. He had already sent the fleet messenger *Princess Ena* (formerly a Q-ship) to bring out a small group of British subjects who had expressed a desire to get away from the dangerous chaos of the city, a traditional Royal Navy task. Now he sent the light cruiser *Caradoc* from Constantinople to Odessa, and the sloop *Heliotrope* from Sevastopol. In another consultation with Franchet d'Espèrey, Seymour gained the clear impression that Sevastopol might well be the next place for evacuation, so he ordered up the battleship *Marlborough* from Ismid. Its actual destination was Yalta, where the Dowager Empress Marie and other members of the Russian royal family were waiting to be evacuated. He took on board as many of the royal family as he could; the dowager empress was the sister of Queen Alexandra, and so King George V's aunt. Using a battleship to rescue an empress was perhaps extravagant – Countess Tolstoy and her children only merited evacuation in the destroyer *Tobago*, and were then sent onward from Constantinople to Malta in *Forward*, a scout cruiser – but Seymour's career undoubtedly rested in achieving the empress's rescue. She brought a suite of eighty staff with her, but insisted that the captain must wait at Yalta until the evacuation of the other refugees from the place was completed.[8]

In addition to these warships, Seymour had sent five requisitioned transports to Odessa from Sevastopol, and had requisitioned the Cunarder *Phrygia*, which was lying empty at Constantinople, for the same purpose. Both the French and the Greeks had asked him to help in evacuating their subjects from the city. The refugees began to arrive at Constantinople on 5 April. When he heard that *Marlborough* was remaining at Yalta for some time, he sent two destroyers (*Stuart* and *Speedy*) and two sloops (*Dianthus* and *Hibiscus*) to escort the battleship, and presumably to collect more refugees, and brought the first class cruiser *Grafton* across from Novorossiisk to Yalta as well. This was in addition to a smaller contingent of ships sent to lift the 4,000 refugees who had gathered at Yalta. Eventually, after Calthorpe arrived at Constantinople, Seymour in *Lord Nelson* also visited Yalta. The refugee royals and most of the other refugees were disembarked at Novorossiisk, which was by then overflowing with them; others went to Batumi, but they were not welcomed there, and still less at Constantinople.[9]

The main naval problem was thus removed to Sevastopol. The Allied garrison in the city consisted of French and Greek soldiers, commanded by Colonel Eugène Trousson. He had been nominated 'Senior Officer in Command of the Allied Forces', and as such he outranked the admirals and generals who were present, and who certainly looked askance at his office and his conduct. It scarcely mattered. All the admirals and generals in the world would not prevail against the new Bolshevik attacks. The Red Army attacked the Volunteer Army forces at the Perekop peninsula, and broke through without difficulty. Orders to repair the fortifications of the 'Turkish Wall' (an ancient fortification in bad condition) had been ignored, and the monitor *M.17* had been moved to Yalta, so the defences were thin. Control of the peninsula gave the Bolsheviks access to all of Crimea, though Sevastopol was held by its Allied garrison. Bolshevik and opportunist supporting groups among the population emerged from the shadows to welcome the Red Army soldiers. Some of the White forces withdrew eastwards into the Kertch peninsula and set up a defensive line there, under the command of General Nikolai Schilling.

The only other place where any serious resistance was made was at Sevastopol itself. The Allied garrison was quickly reinforced by the arrival of several battalions of French colonial troops, Algerians and Senegalese, but Trousson was unwilling to listen to local opinion and, in accordance with French policy, he completely ignored the Volunteer Army troops in the city. Probably he had good reason for this, for that army was generally lazy and undisciplined, recruited as they were from former Imperial Army officers; they withdrew into the Kertch peninsula to join Schilling's forces.[10]

The Red Army came into the city on 15 April, but the first arrivals were held off in two days of fighting. By this time there were British and French ships outside, forming a maritime blockade, and able to provide bombardment support as requested. Admiral Seymour arrived, this time in the battleship *Emperor of India*. He had transferred from *Lord Nelson*, which was to take the

Empress Marie to Britain, along with a cargo of grand dukes.[11] On his arrival he found that a naval bombardment by the light cruiser *Calypso* was about to take place, but this was prevented by the sudden appearance of Red Army negotiators waving white flags from the shore. Their demands, essentially surrender, were predictably unacceptable to the Allies, but both sides agreed to observe a truce until the 25th. Seymour discussed the attacks with the senior British officer in the area, Captain Richard Thesiger of *Calypso*. He also saw Admiral Amet, who was in command of the French ships that were present. Amet was supervising the recovery of the old battleship *Mirabeau*, which had struck a rock and been badly damaged. (Amet, like Seymour, had carefully kept away from the Odessa evacuation and debacle, using the need to supervise the recovery of *Mirabeau* as his excuse.) He also had the battleship *Jean Bart* on hand.

There was a brief fight between Bolshevik cavalry and the French ships, which, despite Allied assumptions of large Bolshevik casualties, probably did little damage to either side. The French received a supply of barbed wire and proceeded to string it out to fortify part of the city, more or less along the line that had been defended by the Russians during the Crimean War siege in 1855; the Mamelon was, as before, the central point. It was captured by the Bolsheviks on 15 April, and then retaken by the French – the very reverse of the events of 1855. With the truce in force, both sides began reinforcing and fortifying themselves in preparation for a new struggle. The Bolsheviks' demand for surrender had largely been a bluff since they had very few troops at Sevastopol at that time. It seems probable that the French soldiers, who soon, along with the Greeks, numbered about 7,000, supported by the artillery from the ships, would be able to hold off the Bolsheviks, and Admiral Amet seemed determined to fight on.[12]

The British naval commanders, Calthorpe and Seymour, were deeply sceptical of Bolshevik good faith and certainly doubted that the French had the will to continue resisting their attacks. (Admiral Amet had been in negotiation with the Bolsheviks, and had forwarded a draft of an agreement to the British, which would let the French leave.)[13] They appreciated that, just as the French were preparing new defences, so the Bolsheviks would be bringing up reinforcements during the truce, and felt that the defences would not be sufficient. They were very concerned that the city and harbour still held large quantities of ammunition and other munitions, which they did not wish to allow to fall into Red Army hands. There was also a large number of Russian warships present, the largest surviving part of the Russian Black Sea Fleet. Most of the ships were more or less in working, or near-working, order, though needing better maintenance and a good deal of cleaning. It was these ships, above all, that the Royal Navy now targeted during the truce, aiming to render them useless, at least temporarily. Seymour gathered together four lighters, towed by a tug, to remove 500 mines from a store and away from the land – an interesting priority for a sailor. It does not appear to have occurred to Seymour that by agitating to destroy these munitions and sabotaging the ships, he was exhibiting the same defeatist attitude that he had detected and complained about in the French command.

Seymour understood that Admiral Amet hoped to use some of the smaller ships, submarines and destroyers as a lure in treating with the Bolsheviks. He would offer to leave the ships available, in exchange for allowing the Allied forces to get away in peace; this was the procedure used at Kherson and Nikolayev, but this was a course neither Calthorpe nor Seymour felt they could approve.

Amet refused to allow a large munitions store holding grenades and torpedoes to be blown up, as it would probably destroy a large part of the city, but British naval artificers did set about defusing as many of the munitions as possible, and preparing other means of destruction, particularly of the Russian ships. Some of these were sunk outside the harbour, particularly the submarines; the four submarines in good condition were carried off to Novorossiisk for Denikin's forces, and the destroyers, cruisers, and battleships were to be rendered unusable by internal destruction and explosions. All this was prepared during the truce, and the destruction actually began to take place on the morning of the 15th, the last day of the truce.[14]

Seymour had set out on the 20th to go to Novorossiisk, where General Sir George Milne had arrived for consultations and to deliver decisions. Milne had already overseen the British withdrawals from Central Asia and from the Caucasus region, and it is very likely he was considering a similar withdrawal from the Caspian Sea and even the Black Sea. As with all such tentative plans, however, events intervened. On the way to the meeting, Seymour was recalled by a message from Captain Thesiger in *Calypso*, informing him that 'a Bolshevik outbreak' had taken place in the French fleet at Sevastopol. Thesiger also reported that as a result, the French had decided to evacuate Sevastopol forthwith. Seymour turned about and returned to the scene. His arrival in *Emperor of India*, with its ten 13.5-inch guns, gave him a powerful authority.

Thesiger's terminology had been needlessly alarmist, though the situation had become difficult enough. As these things do, it was a minor incident that had sparked the mutiny (the 'Bolshevik outbreak'), but underlying the response that this provoked was a more substantial background of continuing discontent, which had not been addressed by the French officers. The sailors complained of the bad food they were served – they were French, after all; they complained of boredom; it is also evident that many of them held socialist convictions, and had considerable sympathy for the Bolsheviks. The spark for the mutiny – which was more akin to a strike in most ships than an active opposition to authority – was the arrest of two men, an engineering officer and a sailor, on the destroyer *Protet*, on a charge of plotting to seize control of the ship and take it to join the Bolsheviks. That was on the 16th. Three days later, there was a 'disturbance' in the battleship *France* and then also on the *Jean Bart*, the flagship of Admiral Amet.

Demands were made for an end to the war in Russia, for a return to France, and for improved conditions on board, and these protests were repeated by the crews of the other French battleships present – *Justice*, *Vergniaud*, and the damaged *Mirabeau* – as they became aware of the original complaint. One of the origins of all this was newspaper reports of the debate in the Chamber of Deputies about the intervention, which had taken place at the end of March. The newspapers reporting the debate had finally reached the ships, by way of ships that had been stationed at Corfu. They had received the newspapers more quickly and easily than the vessels in the Black Sea, and copies had then been sent on to Sevastopol. Admiral Amet reported to Paris that he could not rely on any of the ships in his fleet, and summed up the sailors' demands by saying that they did not want to fight the Red Army.

The men of the two mutinous ships, *France* and *Jean Bart* (as opposed to those voicing support for them), were given shore leave in an attempt to defuse the mutiny. About 500 men went on shore, where they were quickly contacted by some local Bolsheviks in the city, and the two groups marched about waving red flags. A patrol from *Jean Bart* fired over their heads in an attempt to break up the demonstration, which seems to have been more than just a peaceful mutiny. This did not work. It is doubtful that the patrol would have fired on their own fellow shipmates, and it is equally doubtful that their fellow sailors believed that they would do so. Instead, another patrol, composed of French marines and Greek soldiers, fired into the crowd, causing about forty casualties. This, of course, increased the sailors' anger and expanded support for the mutineers in the fleet. The danger of a much wider mutiny emerged.

But then the mutineers themselves went too far. Some of the sailors began secretly forming soviets on board *France*, and this alienated those who were simply complaining about the food and conditions, or did not want to fight the Russians, or anyone else, or who simply wanted to go home. Some will have wanted all of these, of course. That is, most of the sailors had these everyday demands and complaints, but were not political in the sense of being Bolshevik. Captain Thesiger's wording had been extravagant.

In the same way, the rest of the fleet was also less than interested in revolution. Admiral Amet intended that the battleship *France* should set sail for France, partly to remove it from contact with the rest of the fleet, and so prevent the spread of the 'infection'. The French officers on board persuaded those in control in *France* to set sail, pointing out that their destination was home; this removed the most committed of the mutineers, and scuppered the wider support the extremists had been relying on. The ship was then ordered to Toulon for the sailors to be discharged. Since to go home was a common denominator of the complaints of the entire crew, this imputation that the whole fleet was destined for an early return to France quelled support for the mutiny. Admiral Amet, despite the initial mistake of sending patrols after the men on shore leave – if it was his decision – had handled the mutiny quite successfully; he was able to regain some control of the remaining ships, but it was now obvious that the sailors in the French fleet could not be used to fight the Bolsheviks in Sevastopol.[15]

Seymour had also been busy. He appears to have had no doubts as to the 'loyalty', as he would have put it, of his own crews. He made a round of visits to the other commanders, to Admiral Amet, who was now determined to evacuate the French forces, to Admiral Kokoloudis, the Greek naval commander, and to Colonel Smyth, who was on the staff of General Tom Bridges, the head of the British mission attached to the French land forces. The Greek admiral was against any evacuation, and Smyth reported that the French and Greek soldiers in the city felt the same. There was thus already an obvious division between the French soldiers and their sailor *confrères*; the main reason for this was that the largest element among the French soldiers were colonial recruits, mainly Senegalese, who were probably not too unhappy at being able to fire on white French sailors, or Russians. These colonial regiments, however, scarcely represented French metropolitan opinion, which, as the Chamber of Deputies' debate had shown, was now strongly against the intervention in Russia. The Greek soldiers were involved in large part because the Greek government of Eleftherios Venizelos wanted to earn points with the French, and with the Allies generally, for his own political and expansionist purposes.[16]

Four British sailors who had been on board the battleships *Jean Bart* and *Justice* to help with signals were now taken off. Three of them were also due to be discharged and were sent off to Constantinople. The fourth was a French-speaking chief yeoman of signals called Dowling, and he was able to provide Seymour with plenty of information about conditions on the French ships.

On 24 April, the day after the mutinous battleship *France* had sailed, Amet told Seymour that he had orders from Paris to evacuate Sevastopol. Amet had met a Bolshevik delegation the day before to discuss the removal of the French forces from the city. He asked Seymour to attend, but Seymour had refused. (Amet was, just possibly, using his courteous invitation as a contrast with the way he had been excluded by Calthorpe from the Turkish armistice talks seven months before.) Seymour also refused to accept or accede to the terms that had been concluded between Amet and the Bolshevik delegation. In fact, Admiral Amet himself did not sign the document, and the terms of the agreement were held only in his own memory.

The French evacuation meant that both the ships and the soldiers in the garrison would leave, and it would not be possible to hold the city with only the Greeks (who were anyway only there to please the French) and the sailors from the British ships (who were not supposed to be used on shore, according to the Admiralty's orders). So the removal of the French would require that all Allied forces must leave.

It was then that the demolition of the Russian ships at last took place. Calthorpe arrived in the battleship *Iron Duke* to give support. The demolition was helped by an extension of the truce for four more days; presumably, the Red Army was not yet ready for an assault on the city, and the French evacuation was clearly known to them. This would probably result in the removal of the French and therefore of the British as well; there would be no point in fighting. The Bolsheviks held to their word – they were getting what they wanted without fighting, after all – and had not breached the truce agreement in the days before (other than the Bolshevik intrigues with the mutineers). Calthorpe organised the seizure of a workable minelayer, though Amet successfully objected to his order that 'everything floating in the harbour' should be removed. By the end of the truce, the French had left, and the Royal Navy artificers had done their destructive work. The Red Army's 4th Regiment of the Zadnoprovskaya Division marched into the city to popular rejoicing – at least according to later Soviet accounts; Bolshevik methods in dealing with open dissent were known to be drastic; such enthusiasm was sensible self-defence.[17]

The Volunteer Army soldiers in Crimea, who had retreated into the Kertch peninsula under Schilling's command, provided White forces with a continuing foothold in Crimea. They were supported by British ships, which bombarded Red Army positions from positions to north and south of the peninsula. When Seymour brought the *Emperor of India* to the area, its guns were able to reach well inland and could destroy the crucial railway junction at the village of Vladislovoka, which was also the local Red Army headquarters. The shells of the British ships boosted the sketchy morale of the Volunteer Army soldiers, and they were able to recover some lost positions with this naval help.

The peninsula was not particularly narrow – it was 25 kilometres wide at its root – but it extended for almost 90 kilometres eastwards from the site of the Red Army's headquarters, with Arabat Bay on the north and Kaffa Bay on the south. The narrow section at the root of the peninsula rendered British naval gunfire all the more effective. There were several ships already present at the scene; in Arabat Bay were the destroyer *Fury*, two monitors, *M.17* and *M.18*, and a French destroyer; in Kaffa Bay were the light cruiser *Caradoc*, the seaplane carrier *Empress* – whose aircraft were to be used as artillery spotters and for reconnaissance – the destroyer *Parthian*, a French destroyer, which was changed frequently, and the Greek destroyer *Lemnos*. It is evident that the French, despite disliking the Volunteer Army, were not proposing to see them totally destroyed.

To these forces Seymour now added several more ships. He sent the destroyer *Montrose* to Arabat Bay, added the monitor *M.29* and a hired trawler; and later he sent the cruiser *Centaur* as well. His flagship, the battleship *Emperor of India*, also operated from Kaffa Bay. It was claimed that the naval gunfire was very demoralising for the Red Army soldiers, and that its infantrymen were observed being driven into the attack by a whip-wielding Cossack. However, this report is second-hand, and may only be a Volunteer Army officer's romantic imagination – after all, this army was recruited largely from former imperial officers (which accounts for their lack of discipline and general laziness), and they had certainly used such methods in the Great War and even before, but they would hardly tolerate the use of these methods on each other.

The Red Army clung on, forming a blockade by land, but making no real progress against the entrenched White Army and the British ships' guns. The fighting was reduced to shelling from the ships; a balloon, flown from the destroyer *Coreopsis*, and aircraft were used to spot for the gunners. The Red Army flew at least one aircraft, a Henri Farman, presumably a remnant of the French military supplies provided during the Great War, and this compelled the British to add antiquated Volunteer Army fighter planes as protection for their seaplane spotters. Then still more ships arrived. The cruiser *Calypso* came up from Sevastopol, as did the battleship *Marlborough* from Constantinople, having unloaded its royal refugees. Escalation was in progress.[18]

A report that ships in the Sea of Azov were ferrying supplies and men to the Red Army called for action. Two destroyers, *Forester* and *Parthian*, were sent to cruise along the north Azov coast looking for enemy ships to destroy. They found a group at Ghenichesk and began shelling the harbour, only to be subjected to counter-fire from a battery on land, clearly to their surprise. Both ships were hit but replied with fire that they thought had compelled the battery to desist. The battery's fire had distracted them from the ships in the harbour, and forced both destroyers to withdraw out of range of the shore. Guns on the ships in the harbour had also replied (so they were not just civilian ferries and fishing craft as might have been expected), but the two destroyers' guns' longer ranges eventually allowed them, even at their greater distance, to reach and bombard the harbour at their leisure. They destroyed an icebreaker, which had been a particular target, and in the report they submitted, claimed to have destroyed, or badly damaged, all the ships in the harbour – a claim that was possibly accurate.[19]

The situation at Kertch calmed down, partly because neither side could make any progress in the fighting, or perhaps could not be bothered to, and partly because the main military action was suddenly elsewhere. In May, General Denikin's army began to advance north and west from its camping grounds south of the Don River. In the next month, it took over all Ukraine. This included Crimea, where the White armies to the north of it more or less sucked the Bolshevik armies out of the peninsula northwards – Crimea was a useful fortress, but it also could become a trap. The brigand who had led his guerilla army into Nikolayev, 'Ataman' Gregoriev, changed sides again opportunely, as did other Cossack hordes, largely due to the propensity of the Bolsheviks for violence and cruelty, and to their persecution of the Church, which activities collectively alienated the uncommitted, pushing them to be explicitly opposed. 'Uncommitted' would best describe all of these groups who accepted the authority of whoever was most powerful at the moment; their allegiance could not be taken for granted by anyone. The advance was substantial on the map, but did not have much substance, since too often it was these 'uncommitted' who succumbed with no enthusiasm.[20]

Calthorpe had been in charge of anti-submarine operations and convoys in the Mediterranean during the last year of the war, and was clearly extra sensitive to the problems of submarine warfare. He repeatedly referred in his reports to the submarine danger that he apprehended in the Black Sea. He had approved, indeed urged, the destruction of the captured Russian submarines in Sevastopol, some of which were sunk at sea, though most were simply disabled and put out of use, while four that were operational were handed over to the White forces at Novorossiisk. But he felt that the real danger would come from Nikolayev, where a number of incomplete warships had fallen into the hands of Gregoriev, who was at the time pro-Bolshevik. These included 'six to eight' submarines, described as '60 per cent complete'; a later account suggested that at least one could be made ready for sea in six months or so. However, it hardly seemed that the slapdash Ataman Gregoriev would be interested in setting out on a naval campaign, or in promoting the hard and careful work of shipbuilding – but then he did not have the time to do either of these.

Soon after the evacuation of Sevastopol, Calthorpe composed a message to the Admiralty surveying the 'naval situation in the Black Sea', in which he drew attention to the ships that were still part-built in the yard at Nikolayev. Admiral Amet had received assurances from the Bolsheviks that Allied officers would be able to visit the Nikolayev yards to check that work was not being done on the ships, but Calthorpe was less than pleased at the idea, nor was he convinced that the work would not be restarted. Meanwhile, a small French patrol operated off Odessa, Ochakov (at the estuary of the Bug and the Dnestr rivers, where Nikolayev was), and Sevastopol, but this was only a watching patrol, not an active blockade, and employed only a single ship. Calthorpe did not expect any serious inspection to take place. Nikolayev was some distance upriver, and there were powerful batteries at the estuary and it was generally difficult to monitor what was happening. The small French patrol was scarcely an effective deterrent. Calthorpe did, however, allocate several Royal Navy ships to provide support for the French ships.

Calthorpe had felt that at least one submarine at Nikolayev might be commissioned in the next three months – or possibly six – but he pointed to the difficulties the Russians would be facing in getting efficient work done in the yards, and that there would then be the need for training and operational practice, which would take a considerable time. He noted that any submarine must sail out of Nikolayev along the river estuary (the city was 40 kilometres upriver) and past Ochakov, on the surface all the way, and then must sail for several miles out to sea, again on the surface, before finding a sufficient depth of water in which to submerge. During this time, it could be detected by any Allied patrol (and, by implication, sunk). As yet, with none of the unfinished ships near completion, there was no immediate danger, but he felt that such danger was sufficiently great that, on 1 May, he provided a long list of naval requirements that he would need to institute an 'Ochakov Barrage', which would block access (and egress) to Nikolayev, and to Kherson. He included two or three aircraft carriers and their aircraft, and hydrophone 'P' boats (twelve required), a drifter, eighteen motor boats (already there), a minelayer, two ships to set out nets, a repair ship, and a depot ship, as well as the four destroyers he already had. To this, he added a suggested system for convoys: one route between Constantinople and Odessa, and a second on a circular route from Constantinople to Novorossiisk, to Batumi, and back to Constantinople. The list of requirements for a hypothetical blockade is reminiscent of the list composed in Central Asia of the manpower required if the Central Asian Railway was to be held – that is, it was a means of scaring the government at home into making some sort of a decision, with the assumption that the stated requirements would compel a decision to abandon the present activities.

Several days later, Calthorpe was informed that the French patrol was to be placed under his command.[21] In the aftermath of the unrest in the French ships came signs that all was not well with the British ships. There had been some unrest among the sailors who were due for demobilisation when this was delayed in order to keep a near-full complement in the ships. The ships that were active and busy seem to have had no personnel problems; the difficulties came with ships that remained largely inactive. In May, the stokers of the depot ship *Europa* 'refused duty'. The ship was old, having been built in 1897, and was parked at Mudros as a depot ship, so probably one of the factors in the situation was boredom and lack of leave, and lack of facilities for recreation. Stokers, of course, had by far the worst job on board. All fifty-seven men were placed under arrest, but almost at once, seventy-six seamen also refused duty. (In civilian life, these actions would have been called a strike, and, as 'hostilities only' men, these were essentially civilians.) All the men involved were due for demobilisation, even overdue, but this had apparently not yet been promised – there were, no doubt, detailed calculations among the men as to when they should be demobilised, and as the anticipated date was reached and passed, discontent would increase. It was the same problem as on the French ships where no date for release had been agreed.

Calthorpe was not surprised. He had told the Admiralty several days earlier that the situation was approaching a crisis. He had ordered crews, particularly of the battleships, to be reduced in order to relieve men for demobilisation, though this had not been done yet. But this would mean, among the stokers particularly, that the remainder would have to work harder. It is probable that the action of men on the French ships a month earlier was being taken as an example. Calthorpe sent Commodore Fitzmaurice to the *Europa*, and he spoke to a meeting of the 'refused duty' men (now numbering 178) and, though he does not explain what he said, they returned to work, apparently without suffering punishment.[22]

The mutiny, if that is what this was, apparently had its effect. A committee had already been set up to discuss and recommend how reduction in crews could take place. In June, seamen on another old cruiser converted to a depot ship, *St George*, refused duty because the captain could not give them a date for their demobilisation. Fitzmaurice commented that 200 men had been sent home for demobilisation recently.[23] Evidently, matters were speeding up. Fitzmaurice, in his next report on 14 July, claimed that all men eligible for release had been dispatched – with just nineteen exceptions. Three hundred men had just sailed for Malta on their way home.[24] No doubt, relief was felt not only by the men who were on their way to demobilisation but also among the officers who had had to cope with the problem. They could now rely on professional sailors. At the same time, it is clear that, as with the 'disaffection' on *France* earlier, the 'mutinies' were effective. The men were soon released.

Early in June, Calthorpe reported that no blockade of Ochakov existed, other than the French watching and cruising patrol by a single ship. Nor had he received any of the reinforcements and extra equipment that he had asked for. He now listed the submarines at Nikolayev, identifying them by name and number, eight of which were in various stages of completion. His letter made it clear that, despite his fears, it was going to be very difficult to get any of these boats to sea, manned, armed, and efficient, even if they could be completed soon.[25] On the Kertch peninsula, a Volunteer Army unit had raided and destroyed the Whitehead Torpedo Factory at Theodosia late in May; since none of the Bolshevik forces had ships or submarines that could use the torpedoes, one wonders if it was not Calthorpe who had urged them to make this pre-emptive raid.[26]

The situation in Crimea finally began to change when General Denikin began his advance, pulling the Volunteer detachment in the peninsula into the campaign, and enticing the Red Army to move out of the rest of Crimea, though it withdrew rather than was driven out, for it was ordered to move out to help defend Moscow.[27] For the next three months, this put the whole north coast of the Black Sea in Denikin's hands, and so the theoretical submarine threat was less of a danger to Allied ships. By then, the French had largely withdrawn from participation in the Russian intervention (as had been signalled at Sevastopol and by their ceding control of the patrol to Calthorpe). Some of their ships did remain, and their presence at Constantinople continued. Their forces had now been evacuated from the last foothold in Crimea, and their ships were no longer reliable for such work as a blockade; however, they did continue to intrigue amongst the various forces in Ukraine, and to maintain that they had exclusive rights of Allied operations in the western part of the sea. But the success of Denikin and the Volunteer Army in recovering the whole Ukraine had foiled them on this activity, and they and Denikin were still at enmity. The Black Sea was therefore largely left to the British, who themselves had now withdrawn from Central Asia and the Caucasus, and were in the process of withdrawing from the Caspian. The only French participation in the region now was at Constantinople, but there again, the British were dominant.

Denikin's advance along the north Black Sea coast was supported by two of Calthorpe's destroyers, *Seraph* and *Speedy*. In the advance westwards along the north coast of the Sea of Azov, these ships shelled three of the coastal towns. It was rumoured that the Bolsheviks had a set of submarine parts stored in railway trucks at Simferopol in Crimea. The cruiser *Calypso* went to investigate at Ghenichesk, but the train had moved on, or did not exist. When the local Bolshevik authorities refused permission for an inspection of the town, *Calypso*'s commander, Captain Thesiger, threatened to bombard it. The tone of his report is such that the captain clearly acted as though he had a right to conduct such an inspection in someone else's country; the Bolsheviks reacted as one would expect those who felt that they were the rightful government to react: affronted, refusing, and threatening. Similarly, the destroyer *Montrose* went to Theodosia, and was refused permission to 'inspect the town'. (The recent Volunteer Army raid had perhaps rasped nerves there.) Bombardments of both Ghenichesk and Theodosia were threatened, but not apparently carried out; the navy's bluff was being called.[28]

The Volunteer Army in the Kertch peninsula advanced out of its shelter on 18 June, as Denikin's main army cleared the way for it in Crimea. The Kertch force met only minimal resistance, but it relied on naval gunfire to open the way where a clash did occur. This was certainly efficient, but it would hardly harden the army to future combat, when any difficulty was handed over to the Royal Navy to solve. By the end of the month it was clear that the Bolshevik forces were withdrawing from all Crimea. Calthorpe sent the monitor *M.22* and the seaplane carrier *Engadine* to the Perekop peninsula to help the Volunteers, but refused to send any ships to Sevastopol. (A White Russian destroyer was sent there, and the captain put his officers in charge of the government offices in the town, very much as General Thomson had done at Baku). HMS *Sportive* visited and found the town 'perfectly quiet', a condition that might in fact have been more a sign of the fear of White vengeance rather than peacefulness. The whole force had behaved very badly in their previous occupation of the area.

The destroyer *Martin* and the monitor *M.18* assisted Volunteer forces who were held up along the Arabat Spit. Calthorpe otherwise avoided Sevastopol and Crimea; if the Volunteer Army was in the city he did not need to send a ship there, and if the Volunteers, as they had elsewhere, indulged in reprisals on the local population, he wanted not to be involved. He may not have liked the Bolsheviks, but nor did he regard the Whites as any better, a sentiment shared by almost every naval officer: it was also an attitude held by General Malleson in Central Asia, not to mention General Milne, whose description had been 'loathsome'. By early July, Crimea had been completely retaken by the White Army, though the Red Army had withdrawn rather than being driven out. Seymour then reshuffled his ships, with six ships and two monitors based at ports on the south coast of Crimea, and with patrols in the Sea of Azov, but calling occasionally at Sevastopol. He hoped for 'a relaxation from war conditions'. The steady advance of the White forces across southern Russia and then northwards seemed to be destroying the Bolshevik menace, though, as in Crimea, it was mainly occupying territory abandoned by the Bolsheviks.[29]

At sea, the minimal presences of the White fleet, the French, and the other Allies, meant that the Royal Navy, even reduced in men and ships, was supreme. It had achieved this with the minimum of fighting, its only hostile actions having been bombardments in favour of the White forces. Hostile Russian ships had been systematically destroyed in their base, and the four surviving operational submarines and other ships were in friendly hands. Admiral Calthorpe, who was succeeded as high commissioner by Admiral John de Robeck in July 1919, more or less at the height of the White successes, might have congratulated himself.

Chapter 8
British Withdrawal

By late July 1919, when Admiral John de Robeck took on the post of Mediterranean commander-in-chief and British high commissioner at Constantinople, the British involvement in the southern regions of Russia had lasted a little over six months, and it was becoming clear that without a serious increase in the investment of British land forces, its efforts were going to be less than decisive. Given the large area of Russia, the Royal Navy could not affect matters on land more than, literally, marginally. Trans-Caspia was not the navy's problem in any way. General Sir George Milne's overview of the whole matter – he was the only officer on the spot with the sufficient range of authority to be able to do this – had already concluded that only in the Black Sea was the navy of much use, and, as an army man, he was properly sceptical of its effectiveness even there. There were, however, certain areas where the navy was still able to operate with some purpose – on the intricate coasts of the Black Sea, around Anatolia, in Constantinople, in the Aegean, and in every port on all these areas and coasts, interrupting or enabling voyages. Here, therefore, in a sense following in Milne's tracks, it is time to trace the progress, or perhaps regress, of the British withdrawal.

The Caspian Sea Flotilla was technically under Seymour's command, and Commodore Norris reported to him, but there is only one report, dated 25 May, on record.[1] Occasional notices were reported and summarised in the admiral's letters of proceedings, but it is clear that neither Seymour, nor Calthorpe, nor de Robeck were really much concerned over events to the east. On the other hand, as Caspian issues began to fade, and the problems of Central Asia were diverted into Afghanistan, new areas of concern developed in the Aegean Sea and Anatolia. This will be discussed in future chapters, but it is worth noting them here as examples of the new concerns. Calthorpe and his successors were quite liable to be distracted from Black Sea affairs by events elsewhere – Calthorpe had been concerned over Malta and Egypt, Smyrna and the Caspian, and while some of these had faded from his immediate view, there was always the Aegean to concern him. Calthorpe produced a lengthy report on the Greek landing at Smyrna in May 1919, but it was not something he was to be actively involved with during his last couple of months in the Mediterranean command. But it did mean that, for the time from April 1919 to early 1920, the Black Sea, the Aegean, Crimea, Russia, the Caucasus, and Central Asia (and Afghanistan, where war began in April) were all regions of concern to the commander-in-chief in the Black Sea, and areas of active involvement for the Royal Navy and its commanders insofar as their influence could extend to such a distance. For the moment, having dealt with Central Asia and the Caspian in previous chapters and to look at the Aegean affairs later, the story will concentrate on the declining British presence in the Black Sea, but also its continuation in Constantinople.

The new commander-in-chief, de Robeck, arrived just as the last of the men who were entitled to be relieved because their enlistments had expired had left. Admiral Calthorpe had speeded up the process after the minor mutinies in depot ships at Mudros in May and June. Commodore Fitzmaurice had reported on 14 July that all but a few of these men had gone home, and de Robeck was in office a fortnight later. The fleet de Robeck now commanded, therefore, was manned by 'active service ratings' – professional sailors.

De Robeck, as usual with a new commander, set off on a tour of his new command, particularly seeking to discover the situation in the Black Sea – the Caspian command was by then being wound down. De Robeck was, of course, the admiral who had commanded at the Dardanelles operation, so, to put it mildly, he was familiar with the area and at least some of its problems.

The Volunteer Army had by now produced a navy, using the ships they already had and those that had been sent from Sevastopol; they had another flotilla in the Caspian, using the ships handed on from the British Caspian Flotilla. Admiral de Robeck was quite impressed by the conditions of the 'new Russian fleet', as he called it, and thought he could see that work on improving the relations between officers and men was having an effect. In the circumstances of an effective alliance between Denikin and Britain, it was scarcely possible to do anything about suppressing the Nikolayev ships, which the White forces acquired. The city become a naval base for the Volunteer forces and the unfinished ships had become Volunteer ships. The battleship *Volya*, taken by the British from Sevastopol a year before, was also to be returned into White hands.

Through 1919, the British involvement in Central Asia and in the Caspian had been diminishing. By the time of de Robeck's appointment, the main British attention in the Middle East had switched from Central Asia to the Afghan War, and General Malleson had moved his command back to Meshed. The withdrawal from the Caspian had taken a little longer, but by September, it was effectively completed. There remained, therefore, only the naval presence in the Black Sea, and a residual army involvement in part of the Caucasus, where the 27th Division was being gradually withdrawn westward from the Caucasus, leaving the local republics to fend for themselves. The last units left Baku on 24 August, and the last British forces were taken out through Batumi early in September. Batumi itself continued to be occupied, and the Black Sea remained an area of British naval interest for the present.

During this extended period of withdrawal, however, the Aegean and continental Turkey became steadily more important. Any hopes of disengaging completely were disappointed. On 15 May, the Greek army began landing to take control of the city of Smyrna and the area around it. Calthorpe had a week's notice of this move, during which he and other Allies gathered ships to lie off the city to supervise. This was all in accordance with the peace conference's decision that this area was to be awarded to Greece, not as a mandate, as other areas carved off the Ottoman Empire such as Syria and Mesopotamia, but in full possession.[2]

The matter at Smyrna was made extra complicated by Italian ambitions and actions to the south of Smyrna. Italy had withdrawn from the peace conference three weeks before the Greek landing, and was now going it alone in the very area the Greeks were also claiming.[3] The Italian aim was to secure control of south-western Anatolia, from the Antalya area to close to Smyrna – classical Karia, Lykia and Pamphylia. Their proximity to the Greek operations was to cause problems.

There were powerful and predictable objections from the Turks to these land-grabs, and it was at this point that Mustafa Kemal slipped out of Constantinople. He had a commission from the sultan as inspector of the army, and sailed to eastern Anatolia.[4] That was the region where the surrender of Turkish arms had been especially slow, and it abruptly stopped as a result of the Greek move. One reason for this reluctance was that a war between an Ottoman army and the Armenians was being fought in the east, and the Ottoman commander reasonably refused to disarm while he was under threat; this refusal extended to the civilian population as well, fearful of Armenian possible successes. From this moment, there was a likelihood of a violent Turkish reaction – Mustafa Kemal later insisted that it was the Greek landing at Smyrna that awoke the Turkish resistance, and this was clearly a problem for an army to deal with, but it would take some time before the Turks were able to field an effective one. Meanwhile, Mustafa Kemal spent the summer of 1919 investigating the Turkish situation in the Anatolian interior and formulating his political plans.

For the moment, at the change of the British commander, the situation in the Black Sea was generally calm, in accordance with Seymour's hopes for a 'relaxation from war conditions'. In Ukraine, the Volunteer Army continued its advance westward along the Black Sea coast, capturing Kherson on 18 August. Denikin proposed to push on even further westwards and his forces expanded their campaign northwards as far as Orel, also in August.

Denikin did not get on well with the French but they were foremost in repatriating Russians from captivity or exile in the west, no doubt seeking to boost the anti-Bolshevik strength in the south (and also as an antidote, and perhaps as an alternative force to Denikin's). The British and Denikin were not directly concerned in this repatriation, but it was suspected that the returnees would very possibly be Bolshevik supporters, or at least hostile to Denikin. One transport, the *Buenos Aires*, carrying 1,200 Russian returnees, was blocked from reaching Odessa by the White cruiser *General Kornilov*, and another vessel, a Turkish ship carrying 700 returnees, was diverted to Novorossiisk, Denikin country.[5] Earlier contingents, amounting to 3,000 people, had been landed at Odessa port successfully. This would indicate that they had generally not joined the Bolsheviks.

In May, the Volunteer Army was about to attack Kherson. The army brought up its naval forces, using Sevastopol and Tendra Bay, a little north of Sevastopol, as its bases. The next step on from Kherson would be Nikolayev, and the sensitive nature of that city induced Seymour to send the cruiser *Caradoc* to Sevastopol to find out the Volunteers' plans from Admiral Sablin there. Sablin, who clearly had information from the front line, reported that the Bolsheviks were evacuating Kherson and going to Nikolayev in local boats. The French patrol ship, *Bambara*, which was at Tendra Bay, was informed, as were the British warships in the area. *Bambara* was fired on from Ochakov, but the forts on the south bank of the channel were said to be unmanned.

The Volunteer plan was to capture Ochakov, then send armed barges (the type of vehicle that Commodore Norris had met in the Caspian), manned and armed, against Kherson. Once these barges got up the Dniepr River, there was a joint attack on the city from the river and by land. A British squadron including *Caradoc*, three destroyers, two monitors, and the seaplane carrier *Engadine* were collected to back up the attack on the city. They assisted the seaborne attack, and the ships were involved in an artillery duel with Ochakov, which was regarded as a success. The city of Kherson was taken the next day (14 August).[6]

Both Nikolayev and Odessa were next on Denikin's list, with another seaborne landing to be made in order to assist in the taking of the latter. The French, having evacuated the city, were maintaining a blockade of the place, and were landing repatriated Russians, so the Volunteer plan presented some unpleasant diplomatic complications. Captain Kerr, the former British consul general in Odessa, who was in *Caradoc*, the senior British ship, visited Admiral Margerie of the French navy to alert him to what was planned; Margerie was clearly scared of his own government's reaction if he co-operated with either the British or the Volunteers, but Kerr told him that the Volunteers would go ahead whatever either of them wished, so he reluctantly approved. A further complication was that this was the moment when the two ships carrying Russian returnees from France were intercepted at sea, the first by a Volunteer ship, the cruiser *General Kornilov*, and compelled to return to Constantinople; the second was diverted to Novorossiisk. Seymour referred to the returnees as 'a potential reinforcement for the Bolsheviks', though this was not accurate.[7]

Denikin's forces' forward momentum brought a wide but only superficial success. At Odessa, the army carried out a successful landing from the sea near the city on 22 August, supported by gunfire from the British ships there. The landing was a surprise, even though less than half the force intended actually took part. Nevertheless, the surprise magnified their strength, and they captured the batteries at Fontana, close to their landing place. The Bolshevik counter-attack, with field guns, was bombarded and dispersed by the British ships. Next day, the ships targeted a railway bridge, and attacked the Bolshevik armoured trains using the line. Meanwhile, Ochakov was taken by Volunteer sailors landing from Russian ships, so the estuary leading to Kherson and Nikolayev was opened. The city of Odessa was captured on the

24th. Nikolayev was also taken, and with it came the return of the question of the future of the incomplete ships in the yards. De Robeck gave specific instructions: that the submarines at the yards were to be put 'definitely out of action', and if possible, 'scrapped'. Denikin was to be told he could not be allowed to use any submarines under any circumstances. This fierce instruction was modified a little later but de Robeck was as adamantly opposed to any Russians having any submarines as Calthorpe had been.[8]

At the same time, Denikin was sending a force against Astrakhan, and others of his troops were campaigning against the independence of the Caucasians. Both of these were slow campaigns over very long distances, and eventually were unsuccessful. Denikin's strategy was evidently to attack everywhere, but as a result, he had to spread his forces very thinly.

This was in fact the height of Denikin's successes, his furthest advance having reached Orel in October, about 300 kilometres short of Moscow. Then in November, his forces were compelled to retreat, and it was a retreat that continued throughout the autumn and into the winter; at the end of December, the territory he controlled was reduced to only three separate areas: part of the south-west, including Odessa, Crimea, and his original base south of the Don River, east of the Black Sea. It was clear that the end of his campaign was approaching. The Red Army was a much more effective military instrument than the Volunteer Army.

The British ships were deployed once again to assist Denikin's defence, but with their commander's eyes fixed principally on the future of the Russian naval bases and the warships. In several messages despatched in January 1920, Admiral de Robeck was clear that there was little hope of Denikin's force surviving. He did suggest landing troops, a battalion here, a battalion there, to assist in the defence of Crimea and at Novorossiisk, and he thought, perhaps very optimistically, that this would halt the defeat. He also suggested that at least 50,000 Russian refugees could be expected, and he reported on his measures to reinforce the British position in the sea.[9]

De Robeck's ships at the end of January were spread from Constantinople and Ismid to Odessa and from Odessa to Batumi, quite apart from those in the rest of the Mediterranean. The Admiralty issued orders to cope. De Robeck had been ordered to go into the Black Sea 'with all available ships' – he was at Malta at the time (15 January). This message crossed with a report from the admiral explaining that it seemed that no more than Crimea could be held by the White forces. He advocated holding the peninsula 'at all costs'. If it fell to the Bolsheviks, he anticipated setting up blockades of Sevastopol, the Bug estuary (the river of Nikolayev) and the Sea of Azov. *Iron Duke*, *Ajax*, and the destroyers were ordered into the Black Sea; six ships with oil and coal supplies were ordered to the Constantinople base; and extensive medical arrangements were made in Constantinople, Malta, and Egypt in preparation for casualties and for caring for the refugees.[10]

The Admiralty also returned to the question of the Caspian. De Robeck was to send a party of sailors to recover control of the ships handed to Denikin earlier, and suggested that the crew of the battleship *Ajax* be the source of the party, plus contributions from other ships, leaving only enough men on *Ajax* to navigate the ship back to Malta. A joint reply from de Robeck and General Milne on 25 January 1920 envisaged putting troops into Odessa and Novorossiisk, maintaining the existing troops at Batumi; the navy was to man the Caspian Flotilla again, and the army to take back control of Baku. An indefinite number of troops would be needed in Crimea if it was decided that it should be held.[11]

The retreat of the Volunteer Army reacted, again, on the issue of refugees. Professor Halford Mackinder had been appointed high commissioner for South Russia, and had given guarantees that the refugees would be protected by the British. How this was to be delivered, whether by concentrating them in a defended part of Russia (perhaps in Crimea) or removing them out of Russia altogether and so delivering them elsewhere, was not clear, and would only become clear as events unfolded.

The Cabinet in London, faced with another detailed list of requirements needed to carry out its policy from the man on the spot, declined to commit troops to assist the defence of Crimea. De Robeck, though not reminded by the Admiralty, did not forget the ships in the construction yards at Nikolayev. As the city came under threat of Bolshevik recapture, all those ships that could be removed – 'one cruiser, two destroyers, two submarines, one transport, one seaplane carrier, and one icebreaker' – were taken away. These were not the ones that earlier admirals had been bothered about, but were the vessels of the 'new Russian fleet', that is, the ships of the White forces that had been operational all along, and had been collected at Nikolayev from Mariupol and Sevastopol. De Robeck thought that the incomplete ships would not be of use to the Bolsheviks 'for some considerable time, if at all'.[12] This was one way of ignoring them as a threat, though Calthorpe had been rather more certain of their potential value, especially the almost completed submarines; in the event, Calthorpe was right.

In fact, three of the viable submarines at Nikolayev were removed from the port, and two of them were scuttled in January 1920: the third went first to Sevastopol and then to Constantinople, and finally, with the rest of the White Russian 'Black Sea Fleet', to internment at Bizerta in Tunisia. Five part-built boats remained in the Nikolayev yards, and were then completed by the Bolshevik government, one as early as September 1920, and the rest by 1923. The assumptions of the British officers were correct, and all their recommendations for destruction came to naught.[13]

The Red Army covered much ground from the beginning of its advance at the start of November, pushing the White forces back relentlessly. As a result, the main work of the navy in the Black Sea during 1920 was the evacuation of enemies of the Bolsheviks to safety, as in Mackinder's guarantee. Odessa fell to the Bolsheviks in January, once again amid wild scenes of looting and disorder.[14] As before, another combined contingent of anti-Bolshevik troops and refugees marched west into Romania, a distance of about 40 kilometres, ignored by the Bolshevik victors, who were presumably only too glad to see them go. At Crimea, it was intended that the defensive position at the Perekop peninsula was to be held. The Volunteer Army units stationed along the Don River erected fortifications, but Novorossiisk fell to the Bolsheviks late in March. Those in Crimea also built up their defensive fortifications, using the old Turkish Wall at the Perekop peninsula as the basis for their defence once again, though more deliberately and carefully this time. Denikin finally resigned his command in April and was succeeded by the more effective Wrangel, but it was all too late.[15]

Meanwhile, the Mediterranean Fleet was mobilised to render assistance both to the beleaguered White forces and, above all, to the refugees. As much of Malta's medical supplies as could be spared were to be loaded into the battleships, and six ambulance and hospital ships were to be sent to the Black Sea; supplies of warm clothing were also collected. The operation was a great deal more than simply sending ships, or collecting refugees. Three destroyers were ordered to the Black Sea; the battleship *Ajax* had already been ordered there; the depot ship *Blenheim* was to make good its defects and then come to twenty-four-hours' notice for sailing; the battleship

Benbow was ordered to go from Constantinople to Novorossiisk; six oilers and colliers were to go to Constantinople, mostly from Malta. The military in Egypt was to prepare to receive wounded and sick Russians, perhaps up to 3,000 cases.

De Robeck had been ordered to send personnel to reclaim those ships handed over to Denikin that were in the Caspian. When he was ordered to revive the Caspian Flotilla, he expressed great doubts about the revival of this exiguous force, and at the need to send an expedition to man the ships. It would be necessary, he pointed out, to occupy the Batumi–Baku railway, and take over Baku yet again; unless this was done, he did not think the expedition – for which arrangements had been made – should go ahead. Of course, by refusing to allow military expeditions on land, the Cabinet had not made an exception of the Caspian.[16]

The reports to and by the admirals in February are mainly concerned with collecting refugees, at Odessa, at Nikolayev, at Ochakov, and at Novorossiisk.[17] Large numbers of transports were used, and the whole process was made more difficult by ice in the harbours. The ships involved had more than once to act as icebreakers to extract other ships trapped by the ice. A thousand British troops were landed at Novorossiisk to maintain order at the port while the refugees embarked – the only use made of British troops in this operation. A former merchant ship, SS *Overton*, now a Royal Fleet Auxiliary, was sent to Odessa with a cargo of rifles and machine guns, and a million rounds of ammunition; the ship was then used to evacuate Allied personnel and civilians.[18]

At the end of January, de Robeck tabulated the spread of his ships throughout the sea. His battleships were at Constantinople (*Iron Duke*), Sevastopol (*Marlborough*) and Novorossiisk (*Benbow*). Also at Constantinople were the light cruiser *Cardiff* and five destroyers; at Odessa was the light cruiser *Ceres* and one destroyer; other light cruisers and destroyers were at Ismid, Sevastopol, Theodosia, Ghenichesk, and Batumi. This was clearly a temporary distribution of the navy in an area that it was obvious would soon be abandoned; there were also a few ships, usually destroyers, in the Aegean.

The Admiralty had taken up the French practice of delivering arms to 'colonists'. The 7,000 rifles and accompanying ammunition sent to Odessa on the *Overton* were for the captain of *Ceres* to distribute. The recipients were now both Russians and Germans, the latter described as 'colonists'; the captain reported that 4,000 to 5,000 of these men had recently been under arms, but that, once they received the rifles, they had 'apparently dwindled away'. This had been the experience also of the French earlier, but they took comfort from the fact that the population was now well armed and if they rose against their oppressors they could well be effective. Some assistance was to be given to the Volunteer Army in Crimea, with the destroyer *Tribune* stationed in Karkinit Bay, north of Sevastopol, and the French destroyer *Casque* and Russian armed motor boats also on that (western) side of the peninsula. On the eastern side, assistance was concentrated again at Ghenichesk to defend the Perekop position – the destroyer *Tomahawk*, the French destroyer *Capitaine Mehl*, and two Russian gunboats.[19]

This was, of course, just the start of a long and complex operation, which stretched through most of 1920. The intermittent Bolshevik attacks on Crimea lasted until November. General Wrangel did effective work in arming and training the men he commanded – necessary elements Denikin had tended to ignore – and by the time of the final Red Army assault, the White Army was a much more useful fighting force – but it was less than 30,000 men in the face of an attack by more than 100,000 sent into the assault by the Bolsheviks. It is doubtful that a reinforcement of British troops would have been of any real use, though de Robeck had suggested that this could save the situation. In the event, a major army would be needed – to reach parity of numbers would require at least five British divisions, and if other cases of British troops 'helping out' in the region are anything to go by, it would be the British forces that did most of the fighting. The fate of the White Russian warships was noted by de Robeck as Novorossiisk was coming under siege. A Russian battleship at Sevastopol, the *General Alexiev*, was planned to be moved to Ismid. All the ships at Nikolayev that could be sailed were removed. He found that they had apparently all gone to Crimea. He noted that 'all naval and military guns and stores' were removed.[20]

From January until November, the navy's work in the Black Sea was concerned mainly with the removal of refugees and watching as the area under White control was gradually reduced to Crimea alone. Novorossiisk was evacuated in March; other refugees were collected from small ports, while the main White forces held on in Crimea. By June, there was one light cruiser off Sevastopol, and the battleship *Ajax* (which had not had to surrender its personnel to re-man the Caspian Flotilla, after all) was supervising the ending of British presence in Batumi.[21] Otherwise the British ships were mainly at Constantinople (four battleships), or at Ismid and Chanak. That is, the navy's attention was now on events in Turkey, while a major naval demonstration in March had supervised the military occupation of Constantinople (see Chapter 9).

One of the continuing difficulties, amid all the involvement with the Russian Civil War and its production of refugees, and now Turkey, was the issue of Batumi. This small city in the far eastern corner of the Black Sea was claimed by both Georgia and the Ottoman Empire (and vainly by Armenia). It was important as a useful port, and as a starting point of the railway that led eventually by way of Tbilisi (or Tiflis), the Georgian capital, and to Baku, which, as before, was the object of much manoeuvring and fighting in the last months of the war.

Batumi had been one of the places to which Admiral Calthorpe had sent a ship as soon as he had entered the Black Sea, and when the 27th Division arrived, it landed in part at Batumi; a garrison remained there when other parts of the division moved further on into the Caucasus lands. This occupation lasted until September 1919, at which time two of the division's brigades, the 81st and the 82nd, were disbanded for demobilisation; the 80th Brigade remained in Batumi as the garrison, commanded by Brigadier General J.M. Cooke-Collis (who claimed to be a sort of viceroy of the area). The brigade included three battalions, the 2nd King's Shropshire Light Infantry, the 3rd King's Royal Rifle Corps, and the 4th Rifle Brigade.

The garrison appears to have survived several serious incidents during 1919. Admiral de Robeck visited the place at least twice, but in neither case did he do more than mention the fact in his reports.[22] The garrison was of little use where it was but its continuation was regarded as important politically, and it was a port through which stray refugees could be evacuated. It was alternately menaced and caressed by the Georgians as their policies shifted.[23] The White defeat brought their forces fleeing into Georgia, with the risk of conflict again. In March 1920, the British force in the city, still under Cooke-Collis, was renamed the Inter-Allied Force of Batumi, but remained mainly British in personnel, and Cooke-Collis was now referred to as the military governor. The Bolshevik army's advances brought conflict closer again. In April, Admiral Fremantle, Seymour's replacement officer in command in the Black Sea, visited the town in the battleship *Revenge*, finding in the harbour two (White) Russian torpedo boats (*Jivoi* and *Derski*); he supplied *Jivoi* with enough fuel to get it to Sevastopol, and saw them on their way.[24]

The Bolshevik advance along the Black Sea coast seemed menacing. Lord Curzon sent a message pointing out that holding the town was important, but that defeat by the Red Army would be a disaster. He claimed to be in agreement that a White battalion could be sent from Thrace if needed. De Robeck replied that the danger was not so imminent as Curzon seemed to believe. General Milne also recommended holding on to the town, but not necessarily the province around it; he also pointed out that the ships could be of only limited support.[25] (He was also concerned the Turks might attack.)

A month later, the Cabinet had decided to negotiate the garrison's withdrawal, though it took another month to arrange matters with the Georgians, and to get transports to Batumi to remove the soldiers. Rear Admiral Seymour was on the spot in the battleship *Emperor of India* when the withdrawal took place, and this probably helped to keep everything calm. Finally, on 7 July 1920, the garrison was embarked in the transports. A parade was held to hand over to the Georgians, and at a formal dinner for the senior officers, the Georgian foreign minister made a pro-British speech 'to the disgust of the French and Italians present', as Seymour reported. The Allies, having been jointly in the garrison for a year, were as happy a family as ever.[26]

French, Greek, and American warships came to assist in the various evacuations, but inevitably it was the British ships that were the most active, simply because there were more of them. By early March, the Red Army was in control of the Black Sea coast from Odessa to Kherson, and the main refugee crisis had shifted to Novorossiisk. The will to continue the intervention was failing, just as was the will of the defeated Volunteer Army to resist the Red Army. When General Wrangel was about to take up his command at the beginning of April – he was in exile in Constantinople at the time – he was shown a message from the British government that Britain would no longer lend him its support.[27] Even earlier, de Robeck had been instructed by the Admiralty to tell Denikin that support would be limited to ships acting at sea, and several of his requests for naval bombardment had been refused; the Russian soldiers had exaggerated ideas of their effectiveness, possibly a result of boasts by British officers. Denikin was informed that he might have to 'come to terms with the Soviet government'. This idea, of course, with his forces confined to Crimea and unable to operate outside it, was wishful thinking in London, of which there had been plenty in the previous months, and there would be more later.

The notion of reactivating the Caspian Flotilla seems to have been abandoned when de Robeck's determined objections sent to the Admiralty and the Cabinet sank in, though there was a momentary suggestion that the ships might be attached to the government of Azerbaijan; again nothing came of this. Azerbaijan was threatened by every Russian force in the region (its oil being the attraction once more), and chose to submit to the Bolsheviks rather than to Denikin, whose forces were clearly failing by that point. By autumn 1920, this republic was allied to Moscow, which had promised it a degree of autonomy, unlike Denikin. (The autonomy promise vanished, of course, once the Bolsheviks took power in the new republic.) The ships that had been in the Caspian Flotilla, and were then Denikin's for a time, eventually went to Enzeli, where some of them, in their civilian guise, had been based before the fighting; there they were interned by the Persians.[28] Georgia was persuaded to accept Russian suzerainty once more; by 1921, all three republics had lost any autonomy they had bargained for in their submissions.

Crimea, with the rest of Russian territory recovered by the Red Army, was now of little importance, except to the followers of General Wrangel. It took time, but eventually the Red Army gathered a large enough force to break through the Perekop position once more and again invade Crimea, but it took until October 1920 to get properly organised. Wrangel spent the time imposing discipline on his troops and turning them into a proper army, which Denikin had not managed to do. Wrangel had been warned by the British government that he must not move his forces out of Crimea. He did so, and the British regarded this as Wrangel forfeiting Allied support, not that he had received very much.[29] De Robeck, who was on the spot and who was clearly angry at the government's varying and cynical policy (the warning was clearly designed as a future excuse for abandoning Wrangel and his forces), pointed out that Wrangel's extra-Crimea expedition had been mounted to gather food supplies, and so to avoid starvation in his territory. The decision does not seem to have had any serious effect; such British support as had been tendered simply continued; there was not much of it; de Robeck kept his ships on the spot and they gave assistance where they could.

The end came with the attack by the Red Army in October, which succeeded in conquering Crimea in a fortnight. The Red Army was using a force of 133,000 men against Wrangel's 23,000. Wrangel, a sensible and competent commander whom the Whites should have employed much sooner if they had really wanted to win in the civil war, had already prepared shipping at Sevastopol for the evacuation of refugees. The cruiser *Centaur*, and the destroyers *Seraph*, *Dianthus*, and *Shamrock*, evacuated refugees from several of the smaller Crimean ports. The largest number was lifted from Sevastopol, of course. De Robeck reported that 40,000 people had been evacuated to Constantinople, and 'all effective Russian men-of-war, including submarines' had been removed; they sailed to Constantinople 'with Russian flags and French at the main'. Wrangel hoisted the French flag on the ships to indicate that they were under French protection, which was understandable given the British public refusal to assist, but rather ungrateful since they had in fact done by far the most. But the removal of the ships out of the reach of the Bolsheviks was what really counted for the British; the ships were taken to North Africa, where they rotted away over the next fifteen years.[30] The real problem now shifted first to Constantinople, and then to Turkey.

The Royal Navy had thus effectively withdrawn from the Black Sea, but only from proximity to the Russian coast. The Turkish crisis called for a new patrol, called the North Anatolian Patrol, along the coast of republican Turkish territory. This was a minor matter, and the ships would finally be removed by the Turkish peace treaty, by which any later naval entry into the Black Sea would require Turkish permission.

In estimating the overall result of the navy's activities in the Black Sea it is first necessary to work out what it was supposed to be doing there. If it was to dominate the failing Ottoman Empire this ended with the final peace treaty and the expulsion of the navy, but in this it had been largely ineffective once Mustafa Kemal roused the Anatolian Turks to fight; if it was to support the anti-Bolshevik case then that was a failure also, except in rescuing the refugees. But neither of these purposes were at all feasible from the start: no navy could, until the advent of long-distance aircraft and guided missiles, hope to dominate a continental area. It must be accepted therefore that the presence of the Royal Navy in the Black Sea was always intended to be temporary, and still more so the naval presence in the Caspian. It was not actually a matter of success or failure, just temporary necessity.

Part IV

Controlling the City

Throughout the events of 1918–22, in Central Asia, in the Caspian, in the Caucasus, and in the Black Sea, the city of Constantinople remained the essential nerve centre. It was the headquarters of all the Allies, and it continued to be the official government centre of the battered Ottoman Empire. However, by 1921 it was becoming clear to those who could see what was going on that the centre of gravity of the surviving fragment of the Ottoman Empire has shifted into Anatolia, where Mustafa Kemal was gathering his Republican forces. Even then, his Turkish Republic would be incomplete without control of the Great City, which was also desired by other contenders. For the moment, it seemed as though the Allies would keep the city, detaching it from the empire, and from the Republican Turks altogether.

This chapter concerns the whole period from the arrival of the Allies' fleets off the city as a result of the armistice of 30 October to the arrival of the threat of assault by the Turkish forces in 1922.

Chapter 9

Constantinople Occupied

The conquest of southern Russia by the Red Army, completed in discrete and relatively slow stages, propelled a series of waves of refugees out of the country, from Odessa, from Nikolayev and Kherson, from Crimea, from Novorossiisk, as well as any other place around the Black Sea where boats or ships were available to carry them away. The most popular target – popular in the sense that it was the inevitable destination for most of those who were fleeing – was invariably Constantinople, though on two occasions those leaving Odessa made the short march to Romania, and others went into the Caucasus republics or eastern Anatolia, usually only temporarily. Constantinople, besides being the biggest urban centre in the Black Sea area, was a place Russians had yearned to visit, or trade with, or to possess, for over a thousand years. They had never achieved actual possession by war, though they had come close in the previous fifty years more than once, but now a large number of them used it as a refuge in their distress; in a sense, they might claim that at last the Russians had occupied the city; most of them, however, did not stay.

For the refugees, of course, the move to Constantinople could only be, at first, no more than temporary. Most arrived hoping to return to Russia. If they were of the White persuasion, this would be by reconquest, if Red (and there were a number of Bolsheviks amongst the refugees), they would return voluntarily. There were also plenty of involuntary refugees who would return to Russia if they could, whatever group ended up in power there. Most of those reaching the city, used it only as a point from which to go elsewhere, hopefully to return to Russia in some way; others would head on to other Mediterranean or Western European cities, or even further away. In other words, the city was both an end and a means for most refugees, a refuge first, but then a new start, whichever way they went.

Those who stayed in the city, of course, were in a community, or a set of communities, probably as mixed and cosmopolitan as any in the world, but generally, each group had differing religious or ethnic allegiances. There were always fellow Russians to take up with. This is an interpretation that was also available for all the other regions in this story, for at this period every country and place had been rattled and shaken by the events of the end of the Great War, and they had to make their own choices of the available future.

Above all other changes, the successful Bolshevik conquest of mainland Russia put an end to Imperial Russia; this was symbolised, perhaps, by the murder of almost the whole Romanov royal family by their imperial successors, the Bolsheviks, and by the exile of the remainder – a few of the survivors were evacuated in British ships. There was no real wish in Russia to revive that regime, especially once the White officers' army (Denikin's Volunteer Army) had been defeated. The intention of the commanders, such as Denikin and Admiral Kolchak, to return to the imperial system had been a major part of the failure of White campaigns. At the same time, it was also obviously the start of a new regime, and not only in Russia itself, but in Central Asia and the Caucasus also.[1]

In the Ottoman Empire, the old Russian enemy – the two empires had fought each other every generation for centuries – another change was taking place at the same time, and one that was as great as that in Russia. The sultanate-caliphate of the Ottoman sultans gave way to the Republic which was about to be conjured up by Mustafa Kemal. The change, as in Russia, involved a Civil War, the repulse of a foreign invasion, and an Allied intervention, and was almost as violent as the Russian version. And one of the central places that was involved was, inevitably, Constantinople.

The Ottoman Empire had been at war continuously ever since 1911, first the Italian War in which Libya and the Dodecanese Islands were taken, then the Balkan Wars in 1912 and 1913, in which the remaining Balkan territories of the sultan, except Thrace, were taken; the city had then been under siege for a time, with enemy artillery firing within the hearing of the citizenry, though the defence against the Bulgars at the Chatalja Lines west of the city had been successful, and those fortifications remained to be used again. There had not been many refugees from Libya, but the Balkans were a complex mixture of peoples and religions, of whom Muslims now became the objects of Christian war and persecution (just as Christians had been persecuted in earlier wars). So there had been large numbers of destitute refugees, mainly, but not entirely, Muslims, in the city even before 1914.[2]

During the Great War, the massacres perpetrated on the Armenians drove hundreds of thousands of them from their homes. In addition, the fact that the Armenian-populated areas in eastern Anatolia and the Caucasus were the scenes of fighting between Russians and Turks produced even more refugees. Many of these, fleeing whatever threat, perhaps up to 400,000 people, ended up, of course, in Constantinople. In a way it was an Armenian city as much as it was a Greek or Turkish one; an Armenian patriarch governed the Armenian Church there.

Thousands of Turkish peasants had also arrived in the city from the agrarian crisis in Anatolia, which developed during the war, and now the Russians had come, fewer in number than the Armenians or the Turks, but perhaps more numerous than the Balkan refugees; but they were not subject to the same degree of threat of massacre and tyranny as were their refugee relations, at least not yet.

The final and largest contingent of Russian refugees arrived from the Bolshevik conquest of Crimea in October and November 1920, travelling in over a hundred ships, mainly transports, but including Allied warships, and the last remnants of the Russian Black Sea Fleet, or the 'new Russian fleet' as de Robeck had termed it for a short time. This included the battleship *Volya*, which had been passed from hand to hand in the past two years, from the Russians to the Germans to the British to the Whites and finally to the French. The ship's experience constituted a sort of metaphor for the varied fortunes, up and down, of Russians and of the Allied interveners in the Civil War. The French were welcoming of some of the refugees, and especially of the warships, but put all of them on shore or at anchor at Bizerta in North Africa. No one knew what to do with any of them, people or ships; the people gradually leaked away, to metropolitan France, where Paris became a White Russian headquarters, to America, North and South, to South Africa, to China, to other parts of Europe, to the many cities in the Mediterranean, or back to Russia. The ships themselves decayed.[3]

The French inspected the Russian ships and incorporated four patrol boats into the French navy, but the larger vessels they had acquired were irremediable. (So much for the constant concern of the British over the fate of those ships.) As with all other belligerents, the French were, in these first days of the new peace, overstocked with warships, having built frantically in the last year of the war, and an extra battleship, or the other larger ships, were of no use. Eventually, much the worse for their stay at anchor in North Africa, the ships were broken up, and the proceeds of the sale of the scraps were donated to White Russian charities. This at least was a sort of victory for the Allies, who had feared the possible use of the Black Sea Fleet by their Bolshevik enemies.

But this was a decade and more later. In Constantinople, the refugees were less easy to dispose of than in Western Europe, where they could be absorbed into the host populations (or, in a different sense of disposable, returned to Russia, where the Bolsheviks had a more brutal solution). For a start, a large number of them, perhaps 30,000, were from the Volunteer Army, and had arrived with their arms. This was too much for the Allied occupiers of the city. They turned the refugees out to live in camps, some in the Gallipoli peninsula, others in Thrace – where they were put under guard behind barbed wire fences. Again, the accumulation of these refugees, when they were not allowed to resume their war, gradually dissipated to other regions, as did those who went to North Africa.

The Russians' arrival, as noted, took place in stages during 1919 and 1920, as the armies in Russia swirled back and forth. In a way, the necessary concentration on the humanitarian process of accepting the refugees to a degree hid from the sight of the Allies the developments in Anatolia. The significant moves for the future were, in retrospect, in May 1919, when Mustafa Kemal, after six months living in Constantinople, received his commission from Sultan Mehmed VI as Inspector General of the Ottoman armies in Anatolia, and sailed from Constantinople to land at Samsun.[4] The terms of the armistice permitted the Ottomans to retain an army of 50,000 men, though surplus weaponry was to be surrendered. From Samsun, he travelled into the interior, where his position as 'inspector' allowed him to travel widely and make contacts with the surviving soldiers, in and out of the permitted army.[5]

As it happened, Kemal's journeys also coincided – to the very day – with another major development, which again distracted Allied attention from events in central and eastern Anatolia during the next months, and deeply affected the conduct of the Allies and the ambition and progress of Mustafa Kemal. This was the Greek attempt to expand their control into Asia Minor and Thrace, and possibly Constantinople, for which they had been given permission, within strict limits, by the peace conference in Paris. The Greeks and Turks therefore collided. (The Greek landing at Smyrna and Mustafa Kemal's move to Samsun took place almost simultaneously; there is hardly any event that could not have played more directly into his aims but that Greek invasion.) Admiral Calthorpe kept an eye on the situation in Smyrna, but interfered only when he felt justified.[6] He was informed in detail of the events at Smyrna within two days of the landing.[7]

These affairs will be considered, above all from the British naval and military standpoint, in the next chapters. Here the subject is the city of Constantinople and its occupation by the Allies between 1919 and 1923, following on from the initial Allied arrival in November 1918. It is worth emphasising that the long-enduring crisis in the Black Sea and the progressive Greek moves into Anatolia were happening at the same time as the events discussed in this chapter – and those in previous chapters on the Caucasus, though the Central Asian involvement came to an end during 1919.

Increasingly, the city had been stealthily occupied by the Allies over the three months or so after the armistice, first as the site of the Allies' headquarters – which required the presence of over 2,000 Allied soldiers – then in stages as units of British, French, and Italian military arrived and stayed. In the surrounding neighbourhoods of the city there were also Allied forces occupying the strongpoints along the Dardanelles and the Bosporos, as well as a rising number of officers and their guards occupying buildings, supposedly as other headquarters. Beyond the immediate environs, there were camps of Allied soldiers overseeing the refugees or the local inhabitants.

Perhaps the two decisive events cementing the occupation in place were the order, in the sultan's name, for the disarmament of the Turkish population and soldiers, issued early in December 1918, and, a month later, the instruction to General Sir George Milne to take charge of the policing of the city, with General Sir Henry Maitland Wilson as his deputy, the latter in effect the police commander.[8] The Turkish policing system was inefficient and in disarray, and individual policemen could be actively obstructive of the Allies, but the occupiers' method was to disregard a local system and install their own, and better efficiency was always a good excuse, justified or not. The usual justification was to claim that the occupiers were bringing in Western values and practices and administration for the benighted natives – not an attitude likely to commend itself to those 'natives'. It also involved discarding the experienced administrators who knew the Ottoman system and administration – a thoroughly wasteful policy.

In all these cases there were more or less adequate excuses for the measures – the need to maintain order in the city, the dangers of guns in the hands of so many civilians, particularly the Greeks, the need to control the working of the Straits, while attention had to be given to cleaning up the city to reduce disease. And yet, in total, this amounted to a constantly expanding Allied military occupation, which the Allied truce negotiator, Admiral Calthorpe, had promised Rauf Bey would not happen.

The sultan meanwhile turned on the surviving members of the old Committee of Union and Progress (the Young Turks), arrested those he could find, and arranged for their trial on various war crimes charges.[9] (He missed Mustafa Kemal, the only one of these men who was now an active opponent.) The real purpose, of course, as Calthorpe explained to the Foreign Office, was to intimidate the remaining Young Turks into keeping quiet.[10] The Turkish courts were, however, in Calthorpe's view, useless and inefficient. Perhaps this was a deliberately obstructive tactic by judges and officials since the judges were quite probably reluctant to convict the accused, either because they sympathised with them, or because they feared assassination if they convicted them. Calthorpe therefore removed the accused men and took them and the process to Malta, and reconstituted the trial as an 'international' court. But this was just as unsatisfactory, since the court manipulated the evidence, disregarding much of that already gathered by the Turkish courts, and left the process wide open to criticism. When de Robeck became high commissioner, the trials were abandoned and the accused were set free.[11]

Lesser cases were now the responsibility of consuls, by the terms of the capitulations (though these had been abolished by the Turkish government at the beginning of the war, but this abolition was not recognised by the Allies, and the Capitulation regime was now restored). The Turkish courts were now only to try cases between Turks; those between Turks and non-Turks went to the consuls (with predictably distorted results). It became all very complex, and in addition, there were a series of problems with Greeks, who were not covered by the capitulations, but could hardly be tried by a Turkish court. Yet the Greeks were the most disorderly group of all; a few Greek troops were allowed into the city, to guard their embassy, but otherwise were excluded – about the only one of Calthorpe's promises that was kept.

It was the new police organisation, however, which was the detail that stamped Allied control most certainly on the city. The city was divided into three parts, each allocated for policing to one of the occupying powers – Galata for the British, Scutari for the Italians, and the main city (Stambul) for the French; these were then each divided into two sections, each with a patrolling force of up to sixty officers. But this was not all. Military guards were placed on every public building, and military patrols were instituted to deter attempts at interfering with the railways. Military courts dealt with 'serious' cases.[12] Gradually, other public functions were taken over – a Sanitary Commission, a Prisons Commission, a captain for the port, and these officials often displaced Turks in similar offices who had previous responsibility (and experience).

There was, as always, a certain friction between the Allies, above all between the French and the British. This was epitomised in February 1919, when on the 8th, General Franchet d'Espèrey, the designated commander-in-chief of the *Armées Alliées de l'Orient* (but not including the British forces), made a ceremonial entry into the city, riding on a white horse, as if as a conqueror. The effect of this was somewhat spoiled when he realised that General Sir Edmund Allenby, who had commanded in the conquest of Palestine and Syria, had done the same the day before.[13] Whether this was a deliberate snub by the British is not clear, but it would not be surprising if it was, and even if it was not so intended, Franchet d'Espèrey might very well have taken it so. He moved into the palace of Enver Pasha as his quarters, and the French headquarters, and, clearly to the surprise of the British, made no fuss about being subordinated to the overwhelmingly British administration in the city. General Milne (his former subordinate in the Salonika campaign) had arrived two months earlier and had set up the new administration before the French turned up. Franchet d'Espèrey found that he was largely excluded from both command and the administration. It was suggested that it had been hinted by Marshal Foch that he should co-operate; presumably with the peace conference really at last under way in Paris it would be best not to rock the boat. Eventually, in October 1919, the French 122nd Division was removed by Franchet d'Espèrey from the Allied command and replaced by four Senegalese battalions and two French; the removed division was then designated as a reserve force.

A small United States naval continent had also arrived in the city, commanded by Rear Admiral Mark Bristol. The United States had not been at war with the Ottoman Empire, so its naval presence at Constantinople was something of an anomaly; in addition, Admiral Bristol was not designated by his state department as a high commissioner, as the heads of the belligerent Allies in the city were. This meant that even when Bristol's status was raised to that of a high commissioner, after he had been in post for six months, the United States contingent was generally ignored by its allies; Bristol himself was a calm, diplomatic type and made a generally good impression. He directed United States' diplomatic efforts towards increasing trade with Turkey, something many Royal Naval admirals felt was beneath them. He used his men to help out with the refugee crisis, and to generally assist in relieving distress. His ships were also to be prominent in the Smyrna crisis. But the United States' non-belligerent status meant that Bristol was not involved in the political side of events.[14]

Two areas had been chosen by the Allies to be occupied by their forces under the armistice – the city of Constantinople and the Gallipoli peninsula. The domination of Allied ships, however, also in effect included the Straits and the Sea of Marmara in the occupied areas – the British fleet, for example, used the Gulf of Ismid as its base, and Allied ships were constantly moving through the Bosporos. Eventually, the whole area came to be called the 'Zone of the Straits', and in the discussions over the Turkish peace treaty, this became a formal description, a region that was to become subject to an international commission, in which, as set out in the final version of the first peace treaty, there was to be just one Turkish member amid sixteen commissioners. It was a conversion of the military/naval occupation into a permanent international one.[15] Needless to say, the Turks objected strongly, but then they objected strongly to the whole treaty, and succeeded in rejecting it.

It was an indication that the affairs of the city were not isolated from those in the rest of Turkey, and, indeed, of Europe. Above all, the inhabitants reacted to the events close at hand. The constant arrival of Russian refugees, and the presence of Armenian and Turkish and Greek inhabitants and refugees in the city, provided plenty of combustible material when events elsewhere affected any of these national groups. The Greeks had already reacted with wild displays of enthusiasm to the arrival of a Greek warship as part of the Allied armada when it came to enforce the armistice, but their troops were given no part in the city's occupation – an early indication that the Turks were able to enforce certain conditions on the Allies. The news of the Greek landing at Smyrna brought a great demonstration of Turkish annoyance in the city, a display that the Allied occupiers did not oppose. The Italians, however, who were equally disliked by the Turks, did take part in the control of the Asian suburb of Scutari.

It was the arrival of refugees from the Russian Civil War that dominated the conditions in the city throughout 1919 and 1920, culminating in the arrival of more than 100,000 people late in 1920 after the Bolshevik conquest of Crimea. As noted already, many of the refugees moved on as soon as they could, and the city administration was very ready to assist them to leave. Other refugees, Armenians and Turks, could not so easily be disposed of, however, since these were already Ottoman citizens, and the latter in particular reacted strongly to news of the events unfolding in Anatolia.

All through the second half of 1919, Mustafa Kemal was reviving Turkish spirits in Anatolia, employing his commission from the sultan to do so. (He had left the city just before being arrested by the British, so they had gained some idea of the danger he posed.) He travelled on foot, on horseback, in cars, on trains, by whatever means was available, to visit groups of Turks, large and small, particularly demobilised Turkish soldiers, wherever he could find them, all over eastern Anatolia. After the Greek invasion of Ionia in May 1919, he had a new and all-too-visible grievance to articulate, and by August, he was sufficiently confident to call a congress of his supporters in the eastern provinces at Erzurum, where there was proclaimed the intention to preserve the integrity and independence of 'the Ottoman motherland'. He was joined by a similar, but less obvious, movement from the south of Anatolia, led by Jemal Pasha, another Great War general. They joined in a second congress, held at Sivas, which ordered, amongst other measures, the occupation of all telegraph offices within their reach.[16] This isolated Constantinople to a large extent from the news of events in Anatolia – the dissemination of which could therefore be controlled by Kemal – though Kemal was also careful not to interrupt Allied, and in particular British, messages (to which, of course, he could listen). The Anatolian Railway had been occupied by the Allies as part of the armistice terms, but in the face of widespread Turkish hostility, the troops were gradually being withdrawn.

The Royal Navy, as everyone else, was largely preoccupied with events in Russia and the Black Sea during 1919 and 1920, and this allowed the Turkish Nationalists to operate without much interference, or indeed without much notice being taken of them, largely hidden in the depths of Anatolia as they were. Nevertheless, by October 1919, General Milne was able to point out that the peace terms being worked out at Paris had already inflamed Turkish opinion – one of the terms was the supposedly definitive transfer of Ionia to Greece – so that the Allies were being pushed into a difficult military posture.[17] The lack of current intelligence from the Anatolian interior, and the realisation that there were plenty of arms still available there, was unnerving.

The victory of the Bolsheviks in Russia, and the fact that the Turkish Nationalists and the Bolsheviks faced the same enemy in the Allied intervention forces, brought the two dissidents together, warily. They made an agreement concerning trade and their interests in the Caucasus. This evidence of diplomatic recognition, even if it was by two regimes equally seeking such recognition, and was concerning an essentially minor issue, was gratifying and encouraging to both, and a clear warning to the Allies.[18]

The Nationalists were at some enmity with the sultan's government, but both took part in elections for the Chamber of Deputies in December 1919. This resulted in a parliament, which met in January 1920 and had a clear majority of Nationalist members.[19] The members declared the Allied occupation to be illegal (which it possibly was, being largely based by this time on the catch-all 'emergency' clause in the armistice), but such a statement would not endear the parliament to the Allies' military authorities. The feeling was mutual. The more militant Nationalists began raiding depots for munitions, which were sent into the interior to equip a new Turkish army. One particular raid, at the end of January, seized the fort of Akbash in the Gallipoli peninsula. It was guarded only by seven hapless Senegalese soldiers, who were overwhelmed. The booty, consisting of 30 machine guns, 8,500 rifles, and 500,000 rounds of small arms ammunition, was transported to Panderma on the Asian side of the Strait, and handed over to a Nationalist force. General Maitland Wilson reacted by sending a force of Punjabis to disable the remaining munitions in the Gallipoli peninsula, and gave orders that French troops were not to be used again to guard depots along the Dardanelles. The Turkish government – that is, the sultan – offered to send a force to deal with the Nationalist bands in Anatolia, understanding that they were all fairly small in numbers, but this was rejected.[20]

These events in other parts of the Ottoman Empire fuelled resistance in Constantinople, whose inhabitants felt most directly the unpleasantness of occupation and government by foreign armies. There had been sporadic instances of resistance in the city, fairly easily crushed, and bureaucrats who proved to be particularly awkward were removed to Malta and internment. The resisters became therefore an underground force, stealing weapons, spreading the word, communicating with the Anatolian resistance. The Allies perceived this at first as little more than a nuisance, but the Greek War in Ionia and the rising importance of the Republican movement in Anatolia enthused and angered the city's resisters. Then came the peace terms.

On 5 March 1920, de Robeck was warned by the Admiralty that the peace terms with Turkey being produced at Paris were 'severe'. He was asked to submit what measures he would employ to cope with expected trouble.[21] The Allies decided that the city should be formally occupied, and that took place on 15/16 March, so quickly that it seems obvious that a plan for the occupation already existed. (It was not wholly a surprise, for some French officers told Ottoman officials what was coming, allowing them to leave the city; it had been the gossip for a few days in the Pera Palace bar also.) The Allied fleet was gathered at Constantinople for the occasion, which involved landing a large party of armed sailors and marines, all British, in support of the army units, which, again, were almost entirely British by this time. Ten British ships (eight battleships, a seaplane carrier, and a torpedo gunboat) made up the main naval force, along with two French ships (one battleship, one cruiser), one Italian (a cruiser), one of the United States (which had no business being involved), and one Greek battleship, plus a number of destroyers. Other destroyers were sent to lie off Mudania, Rodosto, and Therapia to act threateningly in case of trouble.[22]

The purpose of this enormous display of naval power was to pre-empt any resistance that the Turks might make to the terms of the peace treaty. The Allies had decided that the pre-war agreements made between them to divide up the Ottoman Empire would be institutionalised as part of the treaty, involving Italian and French annexations as well as British. Opposition was expected, and Admiral de Robeck drew attention to the development of opposition amongst the Anatolian Turks under Kemal.

The landings took place on 16 March, when 2,600 sailors and marines were put ashore in Galata and Stambul from the battleships, with another 490 put into Haidar Pasha, the site of the Asian railway terminus in Scutari. They were supported by seaplane patrols over the city launched from *Ark Royal*, and three of the battleships took up menacing positions, with their guns trained on the city, ready to bombard if necessary. In the city, there were some reactions from the Turkish 10th Division, and by the students at the military music school, where ten of them were shot. There were other signs of trouble at Rodosto (where Greeks were landed), at Rumeli Hissar, the Ottoman fortress on the Bosporos, and at Adrianople, the old mediaeval Ottoman capital. None of these manifestations of resistance lasted very long, thanks to the Allied forces menacing in sufficient strength, but that they had occurred at all in the face of such a massive threat was clearly ominous. The sailors and marines who had performed the original landings were soon relieved by soldiers and returned to their ships, but they remained organised as landing parties for another couple of days. The armies were left to continue the expanded occupation, so providing more targets for the internal resistance, the *Karakol*, who were active in the city, and who had been partly inspired to organize by Mustafa Kemal while he was in the city.

The operation was thus very successful in that the condition of the city was regarded as 'normal' only two days after the landings, which was hardly the case. The operation was a classic military *coup d'état*, one worthy to be studied by plotters. It helped that the occupiers had a force of battleships where the preparations could be made out of sight of the victims. The various Turkish ministries, particularly the War Ministry, were taken over by (mainly) British officers. The Turkish gendarmerie were disarmed and the communications (post, telegraph, telephone) were seized. The leading journal *Yeni Gun* was closed down. The parliament was, in effect, closed down by the arrest of a large squad of Turkish politicians who then were exiled to Malta. It was a successful military operation, but one that extinguished any Allied pretence to be bringing civilisation to the benighted Turks.[23]

The Admiralty had prodded de Robeck to answer their message of 5 March, with a more pointed question: 'What naval steps would you propose to enforce Peace Terms on Turkey?' A blockade was suggested.[24] De Robeck's answer, a week after the occupation of the city, came ten days later. He pointed out that a blockade would have only a very limited effect since the Turks did not rely much on trade and imports. Interruption of internal trade in food would only make the situation worse, particularly in Constantinople. It would also require a very large fleet to enforce it. Turkish retaliation would probably be directed at the local Christians, not the Allied forces. He suggested the occupation of Turkish islands and of a series of Turkish coastal cities.[25] The admiral's lack of enthusiasm for all this is patent in his telegrams, and the growing crisis of Denikin's confinement to Crimea by the Red Army drove the Turkish problem out of sight for the present. The occupation of the city had also reduced the immediate threat of Turkish trouble.

The occupation of the city caused some rifts among the Allies. It had been carried out by British forces, on the orders of General Milne and on the instruction of the British War Office, but with no more than some minimal naval participation by the other Allies. No doubt there were good reasons, and de Robeck, who was always prepared to dispute orders he did not like, had apparently no objection to his men taking part; on the other hand, it had partly been the report by him on the Nationalist attitudes that had provoked the move. Yet none of the other Allies took part in the landings, and none of them joined the British in colonising the Turkish government offices. Milne ignored this abstention and simply went on until, eventually, the other Allies did reluctantly join in and took up the offices he had assigned to them.

The result among the Turks had been, as seen, largely passive at the time of the landings and in the face of massive Allied (that is, British) force, but the news acted as yet another grievance to increase the annoyance of the Nationalists in Anatolia, and the Turks generally. In effect, the coup had left the sultan almost alone as the legal government of the empire. He reacted by pointing out that 'there would be no one left to blame'; the British were setting up the sultan as a fall guy, and he knew he would not survive for very long once he had obeyed the Allies' instructions, as he had to do in allowing his representatives to sign the treaty. Kemal called for new elections, and from then on the divide between the sultan and the Nationalists steadily widened.

In the city, the Allied show of force compelled the resistance to quieten down. In the neighbourhood of the city, however, they developed clear threats in the months following the occupation. These threats came from both west and east, from the Greeks in Thrace, and from the Anatolian Turks. As a result, the occupation force came to be seen also as a defence force, since the Greeks seemed to be the most potent threat, and any Turk in the city naturally feared a Greek occupation far more than one by the British.

On 11 May, the draft of the peace treaty (the Treaty of Sèvres) was delivered to the sultan's government. The Turks could not bring themselves to sign it. Not only were the conquered territories removed into foreign possession (Syria to the French, Palestine and Mesopotamia to the British), but the unconquered regions, notably Smyrna and several Aegean islands, and the Zone of the Straits, were to cease to be under Ottoman control – the zone to be under an international commission, and Smyrna and the islands to go to Greece, which had already occupied Smyrna and its region. Another treaty between Britain, France, and Italy laid out their several spheres of influence in Anatolia: for the French in the south-east of Cilicia, neighbouring on Syria, and for Italy along the south coast; some of Armenia was allocated to the United States, which eventually refused it. Only north-central Anatolia was unallocated, but this was exactly the area where the Nationalists were particularly strong.[26]

The sultan's government understood clearly enough that to sign this document would hand the political initiative to the Nationalists, who rejected it entirely. Under Allied compulsion, however, it was finally signed at Sèvres, a Parisian suburb, on 11 August, by reluctant representatives of the sultan. Anger and derision by the Nationalists was instant.[27] It was another nail in the coffin of the sultanate.

Anti-Nationalist guerilla groups operating in the interior of Anatolia had been armed and encouraged by the British, but they had little effect on the Nationalists. Armed Nationalist groups – it was hardly possible to call them an army yet – emerged into activity in the Ismid area. Parts of the Anatolian Railway had now been abandoned to Nationalist control. In June, advanced British positions came under pressure and shortly some began to be withdrawn. General Milne had asked for a British force of twenty-seven divisions to suppress the Nationalists in Anatolia. This, as he will have known, was out of the question. This was the same tactic as that used by him and Malleson in Central Asia, and by de Robeck in the Black Sea, a method of forcing the coalition government, assumed to be seriously out of touch of the reality of the events on the ground, to face that reality. The 'loyalist' guerilla movements were scaled down and some were suppressed. In Constantinople, the Turkish garrison had now been disarmed, and prominent Turks were already leaving the city to join the Nationalists, who had now located their headquarters at Ankara, a display of confidence.

In mid-June, de Robeck had already expressed concern that Ismid was under serious threat, that the Allied hold on the Bosporos was also threatened; he had few serviceable seaplanes.[28] At the same time, the Admiralty said that the 1st Battle Squadron was to return to Britain for refit in a month's time.[29] A few days later, de Robeck reported that all the south coast of the Sea of Marmara (i.e. the Asian coast) was in the control of the Nationalists, as was all the Asian side of the Dardanelles except the fort and town of Chanak. He reported that all the guns in the forts on the Asian side of the Bosporos had now been blown up, and that the same was to be done along the Dardanelles. In other words, the Allies' defence line was almost back to the Straits and the Sea of Marmara.[30]

De Robeck offered 2,700 men from the battleships to the army to assist in the defence of the Constantinople area and the Dardanelles; French forces were guarding the Gallipoli peninsula and manning part of the Chatalja Lines (just west of Constantinople). The British ships were now largely concentrated in the Straits and the Sea of Marmara, and de Robeck ordered up more destroyers from Malta.[31]

At Ismid there had been fighting between the Nationalists and the sultan's forces, in which the Nationalists had driven their opponents back to the 'British lines'. When they retreated to those lines the sultan's army had to be disarmed before being allowed through, in accordance with the earlier decision to disarm the Ottoman forces in the city, so destroying the usefulness and morale of the sultan's forces. And yet, despite this enmity to troops who were fighting their own enemies, the navy was using its firepower against the Nationalists. During the day, the battleship *Ramillies* fired on various targets at the request of the army commander.

The Gulf of Ismid was also where the interned enemy ships were held. The threat was such that the *Yavuz Sultan Selim* (ex-*Goeben*) and a Russian destroyer were towed away to Tuzla, near Scutari, to prevent their capture by the Nationalists. Seaplanes carried out bombing raids and reconnaissance, and the battleships fired to drive out the Nationalist forces that had seized the 'drapery factory' in Ismid, a large building that was said to house the Nationalists' headquarters. *Ramillies* fired 36 15-inch and 140 6-inch shells at the building, much of which was ruined as a result – hardly surprisingly, but it was an extravagant method of destroying the rumoured enemy headquarters. Meanwhile, two Turkish motor launches and three British destroyers patrolled the Gulf to intercept unauthorised local traffic, a measure thought to have been successful in preventing the passage of men and supplies, and information.[32]

The fighting did not resume after the destruction of the factory (on 18 June). The Greek army began to advance from Smyrna into the interior at much the same time, and the reconnoitring seaplanes could see no Nationalist troops in the Ismid area on the 25th or the 28th. It was evident that the Nationalist strength had been diverted to resisting the Greek invasion.

Greek advances into European Thrace clearly affected the British position in Constantinople. The British had assisted the Greeks, already established in Smyrna and its surroundings, to expand their Asian conquest by a landing at Panderma to the north, and from there the Greeks aimed to send a force across the Sea of Marmara into Thrace.[33] To an objective view, it was clear that the main Greek target was not so much Thrace as Constantinople; by assisting, the British were building a problem for themselves.

The British commander reported on this Greek plan; they wanted naval help in conducting a landing at Rodosto. De Robeck described the whole plan as 'rash and ill-advised'. He conjectured that it was provoked by the French, quite possibly General Franchet d'Espèrey, who was in Paris on 'leave' to prevent him irritating the British at Constantinople. The object, de Robeck thought, would ultimately be to broker a Franco-Greek connection in Thrace 'to detract from our present predominant position' – further evidence of Franco-British mutual dislike.[34] The Greeks pushed forward into Thrace, capturing Adrianople, the ancient Ottoman capital, on 25 July; they had already taken Brusa in Anatolia on the 8th, and had advanced north from their positions in the Smyrna area; these were presumably other reasons why the Turkish Nationalist fighters pulled back from Ismid.

These events almost constituted a new siege of Constantinople, or perhaps, more accurately, the frustration of an attempt at such a siege. The Nationalist advance against Ismid, and their control of much of the Asian shore of the Marmara, would permit them to cross to the European shore almost with impunity, as the Greeks had, since the Royal Navy could not properly patrol that lengthy stretch of coast; it was taking them three destroyers and two Turkish motor launches to patrol the Gulf of Ismid alone. The threat to the

Bosporos from Nationalist armed bands infiltrating along the peninsula had led to the prohibition of traffic through the Bosporos for a fortnight, leading to privation, if not starvation, in Constantinople; de Robeck derided the effectiveness of such a prohibition as creating more trouble than it solved.[35]

The peace treaty (of Sèvres) was eventually signed on the sultan's behalf on 11 August, but was not yet ratified. Theoretically, the sultan personally could do that, but he was not foolish enough to present his Turkish enemies with such a stick with which to beat him. So he called a Senate meeting (not the Chamber of Deputies, which was prorogued, and anyway had a Nationalist majority). Assembling the Senate would spread the blame, whether it ratified or refused to ratify. The Nationalists, of course, refused to participate, or even to consider ratification, and denounced the sultan for even considering doing so. The Turkish opposition was clear, voluble and convincing. The sultan's government therefore replied to the Allies that ratification was impossible.

The British government meanwhile had made some decisions of its own. On 13 August, two days after the sultan's representatives in Paris signed the treaty, and apparently assuming that ratification would necessarily follow, the British Army in the Zone of the Straits was ordered to be reduced. Four of its infantry battalions and a cavalry regiment were to be withdrawn, and the air force contingent reduced by a squadron. Six weeks later, at the end of September, a further reduction was ordered. A Greek division now took over the Ismid defence position.[36]

In October 1920, there was a general change of command amongst the British: Admiral de Robeck was replaced as high commissioner by a diplomat, Sir Horace Rumbold; General Milne was replaced as commander-in-chief of the (much reduced) Army of the Black Sea by General Sir Charles Harington; de Robeck remained as commander-in-chief of the Mediterranean Fleet. The two positions, high commissioner and commander-in-chief, had always been incompatible, of course, and much of the high commissioner's work had gone on with only minimal involvement by the admiral, who was frequently at sea in other parts of the Mediterranean.[37] With the assumption of the approaching end of the need to attend to the Black Sea, de Robeck's work could be simplified. Also, it had now become clear that the Ottoman Empire was replacing the Russian Civil War as the new problem. The Greek–Turkish War continued, and while the ending of the Russian fighting in Crimea did not come until November, attention shifted decisively to the Turks and Constantinople.

Another change in command occurred also in Greece. King Alexander, who had become king after the Allies ousted his father Constantine in 1917, died in October 1920 (of an infected monkey bite), and his father returned as king in December after a referendum, with, as a result, a much enhanced position of power. Elections resulted in the defeat of Prime Minister Venizelos's party, and the king made wholesale changes to the command of the armed forces, replacing competent and experienced commanders with inexperienced men, and at the same time urging a new offensive in Asia. It took a while to arrange matters, but this new attack was clearly going to take place during 1921.[38]

De Robeck's first report as commander-in-chief alone in 1921 was not sent until the end of February, and he suggested that there had been little change in the city for several months. He had developed a certain antipathy towards the Greeks and their adventure; in fact, the return of King Constantine was deeply annoying to the Allies, and de Robeck was reflecting that attitude (Constantine had favoured the German side in the Great War). This had led to a freezing of relations. With all the Russian refugees and the ambitions of the Greeks, de Robeck felt that the city might suffer from 'mischief' from Greeks and/or Bolsheviks. The Greeks were said to be planning a *coup d'état* to seize the city, but the Bolsheviks were less active, willing, he thought, to wait on events. Neither he nor General Harington was seriously bothered by the Greek rumours.[39]

By June 1921, however, de Robeck was concerned that the Straits were coming under threat from the Turkish Nationalists, and feared that they could exert strong pressure on the passageway in the event of the Greeks in Asia Minor pulling back. He detailed the force he would require in that case, and, as was a typical practice by now in this command, he fixed his requirements high (as Calthorpe had done in the face of the submarine threat in the Black Sea, and as Milne had done for a campaign in Anatolia); that is, he wished to compel the government in London to pay full attention and to give his situation its full consideration. If his report was accepted, his command would be boosted; if rejected, he could retire his forces gracefully with full governmental approval. He already commanded a force that included five battleships, five light cruisers, ten destroyers, and a seaplane carrier with five seaplanes. In the event of a threat to the Straits, he claimed that he would need a reinforcement of a further division of battleships (to be taken from the Atlantic Fleet), thirty-two torpedo boat destroyers, a destroyer depot ship, an aircraft carrier, and two ammunition ships. (He did not list the logistical support that this enlarged naval force would also need; that would be detailed later; its absence rather suggests he knew his 'requirements' would not be met.) He had worked out how these ships would be deployed: he would institute a blockade of the North Anatolian coast to prevent raids by sea, and to intercept reinforcements and resupplies from outside (meaning the Soviet forces, presumably); patrols would take place in the Bosporos, the Gulf of Ismid, the Sea of Marmara, the Dardanelles, and the Gulf of Edremit; the whole scheme would isolate western Asia Minor, but presumably would not prevent Greek forces from arriving, nor stop supplies reaching eastern Anatolia from Russia or from French and Italian sources through southern ports under their control. As a scheme, it was leaky in the extreme, but it was clearly directed at suppressing the war effort of the Turkish Nationalists.

He warned that if these precautions were not taken, it was likely that the Nationalists would be able to close the Straits. He claimed that the opening of the Straits and of the Black Sea was 'the principal benefit resulting from our defeat of Turkey': seeing the Straits closed would allow Russia to build a fleet in the Black Sea that 'could issue without warning and retire without fear of pursuit'. (It is not clear if he knew that the new Russian government had completed at least one submarine at Nikolayev, and was working to complete four more; he was clearly assuming that the Bolshevik government in Moscow and the Nationalist government in Ankara would continue in alliance.)[40]

The atmosphere in Constantinople was less than relaxing. Both the French and the Italians were known to be conducting talks with the Nationalists, and there were rumours that the Nationalists were receiving military supplies from both countries. General Harington had inherited a very slimmed-down garrison. The threat to the Ismid peninsula remained and a defence line across that peninsula was fortified. De Robeck, however, was not convinced that the French, who were assigned to hold the northern part of the line, would fight. The threat here diminished as the Greeks in Asia Minor restarted their advance from Smyrna, aiming first of all to move north and north-east into Anatolia, which would shield Ismid. De Robeck gathered his ships and conducted a large-scale exercise in the Sea of Marmara, not only to sharpen up his sailors, but in a visible display of power as a reminder to the Nationalists. At the end of the exercise, the whole fleet sailed up and down the Bosporos in another display of power.

This was part of a pre-emptive demonstration to block an apparent plot by Nationalists in the city, who were, it was believed, aiming to launch a coup, or perhaps an uprising – the underground *Karakol*, a Nationalist organisation, remained in existence. The parade through the Bosporos was followed by the sailors' and marine battalions from the ships mounting a parade through the city, and a formal inspection parade by General Harington, watched by a collection of Allied generals and admirals. There is something compelling and persuasive about such a determined march, bands playing, boots tramping, shouted commands obeyed in unison, especially one that so obviously ignored the onlookers, as though they were destined to be victims. At the end, the men marched back through the city in a further display of power. The plot had been detected by the garrison before the display and had been thwarted, and the subsequent display was therefore an affirmation and reminder of the Allied garrison's power, and its success in thwarting the plot. A large crowd witnessed the events, to 'a good effect', de Robeck thought. Such were the methods of a military government.[41]

There was a distraction for the light cruiser *Cardiff*, which was detached to collect the former Habsburg Emperor Karl and Empress Zita at the Romanian port of Salina, and then transport them to their final exile at Madeira; they had failed to persuade the Hungarians to accept them as restored king and queen, and had no other recourse than to appeal for rescue to the Royal Navy. The diarist on *Cardiff* who recorded the whole transaction thought the empress was 'distinctly pretty', but Madeira did not 'look inviting'.[42]

Constantinople was not affected directly by the Greek–Turkish War, at least by outside events as opposed to the possible uprising, until the summer of 1922. Then in July of that year, the Greeks brought a large army into European Thrace and began to menace the city. This was at a time when the overstretched Greek army in Anatolia was about to come under attack from the Turkish forces there, and its morale was very low. The Allied commanders in the city regarded it as extraordinary that the Greek command should be so clumsy as to detach a major force away from the main battlefront at such a crisis, but, even so, serious plans had to be made to defend the city, and perhaps to retaliate. Quite probably, the Greek aim was to gain control of Constantinople as an alternative to holding a slice of Anatolia, if the latter was lost or severely reduced.

The new commander-in-chief in the Mediterranean, Admiral Sir Osmond Brock (who took up the command from de Robeck in May 1922), reported the problem to the Admiralty on 26 July, and received a bloodthirsty reply from the Deputy Chief of Naval Staff, Vice-Admiral Sir Roger Keyes (who had, of course, been similarly gung-ho during the Dardanelles campaign). He suggested that possible actions could include bombarding Piraeus, interning all Greek merchant ships found at sea, and warning all Greek warships not to put to sea on pain of being sunk. This advice was replaced two days later by a much milder instruction that Brock should meet General Harington and co-operate with the army to defend the city. Keyes had clearly been brought to heel.[43]

The Greeks did make a hostile move on the 31st, whereupon a meeting of Allied admirals directed that the Greek warships were to be expelled from the Bosporos, and Greek merchant ships were to stay where they were, though not quite interned. The Greek government had suggested to the Allies that it should occupy the city, but this was rejected completely. Such a reply was no doubt fully expected, and the exchange was probably initiated by the Greeks to provide an 'excuse' for their attempt to seize the city by force. But the reaction on the ground will have convinced them that to move against the city would involve fighting the Allies, British and French, together with the Turkish defence contingent which the Allies had now embodied in Constantinople, and so the distinct prospect of being defeated. (The Turkish force in Constantinople – the sultan's army – might not fight well against the Nationalists in Asia Minor, but it was quite certain it would fight hard against Greeks anywhere and in defence of Constantinople.) As General Harington commented, the Greek plan was 'a mad project'.[44]

Earl Balfour, acting foreign secretary in London, was not quite as assertive as the admirals, though he insisted that the Greeks must pull back; diplomatically (he was writing to the high commissioner, Sir Horace Rumbold) he said that 'it must be a request, and not a command'. General Harington, more practically, brought British and French forces to occupy the Chatalja Lines, and recruited the force of Turkish soldiers to defend the city, which was his version of a 'request'; no doubt, his Turkish soldiers were keen to defend the city, and at the same time to fight the Greeks, just as the Greeks were keen to fight the Turks. Harington also had the advantage of advice from Turkish generals who had commanded at the lines back in the Bulgar war of 1912; they were perfectly happy to provide advice that would thwart the Greeks just as they had been happy to defeat the Bulgars.[45]

The Greeks' advance halted in the face of all this and a conference to settle this particular issue was convened at Venice, though it went nowhere. It was overtaken by the Turkish attack in Anatolia, which broke the Greek army, and led to the sack of Smyrna and to the Chanak crisis.

Part V

The New Turkey

The Royal Navy, the dominant British agency in the Eastern Mediterranean once the Great War ceased to be active, had been operating since the armistice essentially to limit the damage resulting from that war. The threat of the Russian civil conflict spilling over into other countries had been stemmed, the revolt in Egypt was crushed, and concessions on internal autonomy agreed. But the problem of Turkey was less easily dealt with. For a time, there were two Turkish governments; that of the sultan, which was recognised by the Allies, was the weaker, while the Republican uprising in Anatolia was an unknown quantity. The weakened and divided Ottoman Empire was seen to be available for slicing into new colonies for the Allies, and the lands to be seized would leave only a small part to the Turks. But this provision, based on wartime partition agreements, had allowed Greece to launch a serious invasion of Anatolia, and, while Britain held Palestine and Mesopotamia, France took control of Syria, and France and Italy were intent on carving out territories in Anatolia for themselves.

None of this was acceptable to either of the Turkish governments, so the Allies were faced with the necessity of enforcing the 'severe' peace terms they had produced, just at the time when they were all were turning away from the region to deal with new problems at home. The result was that the solution to the 'Turkish problem' would be reached by violence.

Chapter 10

Smyrna, Greeks, and Turks

The war between the Greeks and the Turks that developed during 1902 and 1922 involved the Royal Navy in difficult choices and decisions. In the first place, Greece had been an ally in the last year of the Great War while the Turks were still technically at war with Britain, France, and Italy after 1918, despite the existence of the armistice. But in the second place, there was a lengthy and compelling backstory to this ultimate clash of these several states: the Greeks had been lionised and idolised among Western Europeans as freedom fighters for the previous century, and had been admired as the supposed successors of 'the Glory that was Greece', though closer acquaintance with modern Greeks tended to modify that impression decisively in a downward direction. On the other hand, the Turks had been vilified for centuries as the great enemy of Christianity, then as the 'sick man' of Europe, the oppressor of Christians, effete, cruel, Muslim, and alien.

Nevertheless, these inherited attitudes were changed somewhat during the war. The abiding impression for many Allied soldiers who fought against the Turks in Syria and in Gallipoli was a reluctant admiration for their fortitude and fighting ability – 'Johnny Turk'. In both regions the Turks were usually outnumbered, poorly equipped, hungry, often sick, and had to fight with worse and fewer weapons, yet they had proved to be extremely difficult to defeat. They had won decisively at Gallipoli; in Mesopotamia, they had forced the surrender of a whole British army; in Syria, they held the British forces at bay for over a year in three battles at Gaza, and it was only in the last months of the war that they were finally defeated soundly in Palestine.[1] As for the Greeks, the long neutrality enforced by the kingdom's fractured internal politics, and by a pro-German king, steadily reduced the old admiration until the Allies had forced King Constantine out in order to bring Greece into the war on their side.[2] After the main fighting of the Great War was over, the Greeks were avid to go on fighting, kicking the Turks when they were down, though their greed for Turkish – that is, Ottoman – territory was shared by the other Allies. The general Allied attitude, however, was that to go on fighting after the armistice which had brought an end to the killing during the greatest of wars was perverse. Neither the Greeks nor the Turks agreed with that attitude.

The burden of moderating the behaviour of the Greeks and the Turks and imposing the armistice terms had fallen mainly on the British, and particularly on the Royal Navy. There were British troops in the region, in Constantinople and the Zone of the Straits; others occupied the railway in Anatolia for a time, and control officers attempted, ineffectually, to enforce the armistice terms (while serially breaking those terms themselves). Those forces who occupied sections of the Caucasus, such as Baku, or the 27th Division in Batumi and Tiflis, were relatively few and left quickly. But the French and Italians were as much interested in securing Ottoman territories as the Greeks, though marginally less violent about it. (The British, of course, had already gained control of the parts of the Ottoman Empire they had wanted, Palestine and Mesopotamia, seeing them in part as forward defences for Egypt and India.)

The area for naval activity therefore shifted from the Black Sea, where the navy was busy until the end of 1920, into the Straits, the Sea of Marmara, and the west coast of Asia Minor, where activity had already begun in mid-1919, and there were other maritime regions – the southern Anatolian coast in particular – where navies were active. Politics and geography, however, dictated that the coast from Constantinople south to Ionia was the region where maritime action was predominant.

Whereas the British were generally content with their spoils from the war with the Ottoman Empire – Egypt and Cyprus in full sovereignty, Palestine, Mesopotamia as mandates, by far the largest share of the old empire acquired by any European state (but then the British had done the fighting in those areas) – the Italians were keen to seize territory in the south-east of Anatolia, and the French to expand their area of Syria (another mandate) that they had occupied. The Italian forces were landed at Antalya in March, and at Bodrum, opposite Rhodes; further deployments by Italian troops took place to Scala Nuova (modern Kusadasi), which was very close to the area the Greeks had marked down for their own. The Italians then worked their way inland along the Maiander valley.

Both the French and the Italians were assuming that their moves would be validated by the peace treaty, probably as mandates; the Greeks, who were operating outside the magic circle of the Big Four, needed validation in advance. They received this early in May 1919, being allocated the region around the city of Smyrna, and at once prepared a military expedition to take control of that city, but defining the city's bounds very widely.[3]

Admiral Calthorpe and Commodore Maurice Fitzmaurice, the British naval commander in the Aegean, were told of this on 7 May; the Greeks were well enough organised to be able to move a division of troops to Smyrna by 15 May.[4] The justification for this allocation was that the majority of the population were Greek-speaking, and there was a considerable Greek-speaking population also in the surrounding rural areas. There was some anxiety that the Italians, who had been eyeing territory in the Smyrna area, might oppose the Greek expedition, but in the end did not.[5]

The Admiralty pointed out that the withdrawal of Greek ships from the Black Sea might have an effect on the fighting at Kertch in Crimea. Calthorpe – or rather Fitzmaurice, in all likelihood – was to assist in the transfer of the Greek division, which was to come from Kavalla in Thrace, by providing transport if the Greeks did not have enough ships of their own, and he should also provide escorts for the troop transports from Kavalla to Smyrna; at Kertch the officer in charge there, Captain C.T.M. Fuller, was to seek French help if necessary, to replace the withdrawn Greek ships. Three days later (11 May), Calthorpe was ordered to Smyrna to oversee the landing, which now also included British, French, Italian, and Greek landing parties (all of which must be the same size); a United States battleship was also under way to the scene.

There are plenty of accounts of the eventual fate of Smyrna three years later, and there are some by senior Royal Navy officers who witnessed these events. But there are also detailed reports of the Greek landing in May 1919, written within two or three days of the event, also by senior naval officers. It does not seem that either of these sources is normally used by historians, so the events will be related here from the naval point of view.

There are two reports of the landing in the British archives, one by Captain H.L. Boyle, captain of the scout cruiser *Adventure*, dated 17 May, two days into the landing, and the other by Calthorpe, dated 20 May.[6] (The cruiser *Centaur* was already off Smyrna, and was one of the ships that had been involved in the operation at Kertch until called away to Smyrna.) Calthorpe sailed from Constantinople in the battleship *Iron Duke*, but he was reluctant to leave that city without it facing the intimidatory effect of a battleship, so he called in the *Emperor of India* with Rear Admiral Seymour to replace *Iron Duke* – the ship and the admiral also came from the operations at Kertch. The Admiralty's apprehensions that the Greek adventure would have wider repercussions on other naval operations had been correct.

Calthorpe arrived at Smyrna on 13 May, and at once called a meeting of the senior Allied officers. Fitzmaurice, who had taken up quarters in *Centaur*, having arrived in a destroyer, was there, as were the French Admiral Sagot-Duvauroux in the battleship *Paris*, Captain Magliano in the Italian battleship *Duilio*, Captain Dayton of the battleship USS *Arizona*, and Captain Mavroudis of the Greek cruiser *Averoff*. There were thus four battleships, from four separate navies, present off the city. All these were accompanied by their escorting destroyers – Calthorpe had brought five, *Arizona* had two, and *Averoff* was shadowed by one. Other ships appeared every now and again; there was thus a formidable fleet present, though the commanders responded to differing instructions.

The French Admiral Sagot-Duvauroux had arrived before Calthorpe, and as a senior officer present he had called his own meeting of Fitzmaurice, Colonel Smith (the British military representative in the city), the representative of the high commissioner, James Morgan, and Captain Boyle. They decided to land small, armed detachments to seize control of the approaches to the harbour. The British would take over Long Island, the French would take Foujes and its neighbourhood; Kara Burun would be for the Italians, and the Greeks would occupy Sanjak fort. These deployments were confirmed by Calthorpe's meeting in *Iron Duke* later in the day, with the stipulation that the forces would all be equal to each other in size – in each case, 120 men. Squads of soldiers, again equal in size, twenty men each, were also put ashore to act as consulate guards. Colonel Smith notified the Turkish military commander of these moves, and Morgan was sent to the vali, the city governor, to deliver the same message.

These messages went ashore at the same time as the preliminary landing parties – there was no pretence of asking permission. The vali, Izzet Bey, who had answered Calthorpe's message with a note saying that he had been told what was happening by the Ottoman government, had apparently accepted the situation. But he later arrived to see Calthorpe; apparently, he had only later realised that a full occupation of the city was to take place (by the Greeks), and not just a few forts. Furthermore, he had also come to understand that this occupation would be by Greeks alone, rather than a force or forces of the Allies. He feared that trouble would result, but he was given no reassurance by Calthorpe other than he was expected to keep order in the city. Calthorpe at best was complacent about the Greek occupation; he clearly did not have the imagination to appreciate what the response would be to a Greek army landing in force in a Turkish city, though he will have known that the majority of the Greek population would welcome the Greek army boisterously, as had happened at Constantinople when the cruiser *Averoff* anchored opposite the imperial palace. On the other hand, Calthorpe had come across the Greek–Turkish antipathy when negotiating the armistice, and at Constantinople, and he should have understood the problem. The vali was officially notified at 10 p.m. that night, and both he and the Turkish commandant were 'very bitter'. The vali sent a formal protest, which had no effect.

Apprehensions and protests did nothing to delay the Greek landing, nor did the veiled threats voiced by a group of Turks who had been waiting outside the vali's office when the messages were delivered. The first set of Greek transports arrived at nine o'clock next morning (15 May). Detachments from the Greek ships cleared the quay, and the troops landed as soon as the ships arrived. A second set of transports arrived later. To put this in context, it was two months since the city of Constantinople had been occupied by a large, mainly British, force, and four days since the sultan's government had learned of the 'severe' peace terms intended to be imposed by the Allies. Now a major city of the empire was being occupied by a sworn enemy – the blows were falling all too frequently.

It must have been obvious that there would be trouble, as the vali and the crowd outside his office had proclaimed. There were enough Turks in the city, including the Turkish garrison, to cause difficulties for the Greeks, added to which the city government was exclusively Turkish. The news of the Greeks' imminent arrival had spread through the Greek population – who were perhaps half to three-quarters of the total in the city, and a crowd had gathered at the quay in welcome. Calthorpe calls them 'large and excited crowds', Captain Boyle reports that they were 'in good humour' and 'cheered them wildly'. The Greek troops who had taken over the landing quay had difficulty in holding them back – if they had really tried. The welcoming crowds were numerous enough and excited enough to slow down the troops' march into the city. The Greek archbishop of the city, Metropolitan Chrysostom, blessed the troops as they passed, which increased everyone's excitement; the archbishop in the Turkish system was in effect the head of the Greek community; his approval was crucial to the local Greek reaction, but it was fully expected, since he was a vocal Greek nationalist.

The Turkish garrison had been confined to barracks. This appears to have been a decision by the Turkish commandant, together possibly with the vali, both of whom had expressed their apprehensions at the arrival of the Greeks to take over a city with several minority populations. They were thus doing their best to keep control and the peace by removing any possibility of armed military resistance to the Greeks, but they were unable to exercise the same control over the Turkish part of the civilian population; this, of course, could only have been done by the Turkish troops, who were locked into their barracks. The Greek excitement was clearly enough to bring about the trouble the Greeks had expected, and about which the Turks had warned.[7]

When a Greek detachment came marching past the Turkish barracks, shots were fired 'by a number of Turkish soldiers and armed civilians', or by a single soldier shooting from the barracks, or by a Greek, or by an Italian – sources differ, probably in some cases intending to veil or disguise the truth. In fact, the Greek battalion was there by mistake: there had been a misunderstanding – the Greek staff work was not very good – and they had been landed at the main quay when they should have landed elsewhere, further north. So to get to their allotted positions they had to march along the road in front of the barracks. It is said that the shot that was fired killed the Greek officer who was the standard-bearer, though this is possibly a Greek gilding of the lily. It was clearly a very confusing situation, though it was certainly established that the first shot was not fired by a Greek.

The Greeks did, however, return fire when fired on, as one would expect from troops who had been fighting in the Balkans. Three hundred Turks were taken prisoner, many of them wounded; the Greeks suffered just one killed and four wounded in this particular incident. Many civilians, both Greek and Turkish, were involved in the subsequent firing and suffered casualties, though the Turks suffered much more than the Greeks. It is evident that even if the Greeks did not start the firing, they were fully prepared to fire indiscriminately into the crowd. The Greeks arrested many Turks, including the vali, all of whom were treated badly, some with extreme cruelty. The wounded were not cared for; those taken prisoner were confined in the liner that had brought the Greek troops.

It is clear that the Greek troops were worried, before they arrived, that they would be opposed, but also that they were keen to drive out the Turkish population and to dismantle the Turkish administration. The vali's office, for example, was trashed, and all his records were destroyed, so that when he was rescued and returned to his office, he remained helpless. The Greek population of the city was certain that they were seeing the annexation of the city and its region into the Greek kingdom, and they welcomed this and participated in the hostile activity of the troops. Captain Boyle records several incidents of brutality, all by the Greeks, including the murder of wounded captives, and that Greek civilians had been busy pointing out Turkish houses and shops to the soldiers, who then fired into them. He also noted that the Greek sailors behaved much more humanely than the soldiers. On the other hand, he also claimed that after the firing started, the 'mob' attacked Turks in the streets, and that the principal assassins were 'women armed with knives'.[8]

The British acted as neutrals, but in the situation when they intervened it was usually necessary to assist the Turks, who were the victims. A Turkish customs caique was fired on by numerous Greeks, who believed that it was the source of a single shot; Captain Boyle intervened and arranged to rescue the crew. The British chaplain in the city was able to assist the wounded and was described as being 'tireless in his efforts'. Boyle also sent the Royal Navy trawler *Thomas Evison* to rescue the Turkish gunboat *Hizir Reis* – the crew was taken off, the ship towed out of the harbour, and the crew restored. Nevertheless, there was little the sailors could do outside the harbour area.

The United States' presence – the battleship *Arizona* and two destroyers – was also in effect neutral, partly because the United States had an ambiguous position in the area, but also because, as Admiral Bristol complained, he had ambiguous instructions as well, and he was eventually ordered back to Constantinople, leaving the captain of *Arizona*, Captain John H. Dayton, in charge. Dayton could also do nothing, despite making attempts to persuade the Allied contingents to intervene.[9]

The violence in the city spread out into the surrounding countryside almost at once, and both Greeks and Turks gathered into groups and armed themselves. The arrival of the Greek battleship *Kilkis* with Rear Admiral Kakoulides gave Calthorpe hope of an improvement in the Greek command situation, which he saw was unstable and ineffective, but it was, even on the first day, probably too late to establish any easy control. Both sides were now seeking vengeance and loot. Calthorpe complained to Kakoulides, who promised to get a grip on the situation, and later did detail the series of measures he was taking. His efforts were certainly eventually successful, at least in lowering the level of the violence, if not in ending it, but he had even less effect on events outside the city.

A Greek governor was appointed, Aristeidis Stergiadis, with the title of high commissioner. He had earlier governed Epeiros, gaining a good reputation for a careful and just, if stern, administration, and at the same time, he had operated successfully against the local bandits. It must have seemed like a good recipe for success in Smyrna – except that the 'bandits' were swarms of Turks and their families who had been persecuted and driven from their homes and were now fired up with nationalist feelings – and were Muslims, not dissident Christians as in Epeiros. But Stergiadis did not arrive until 21 May, by which time the violence in and out of the city was endemic.[10] He was also faced with a quarrel with the Italians, who were attempting to gain control of the Maiander valley to the south, which was also claimed by the Greeks. This was a problem for diplomacy, however, and Greek Prime Minister Eleftherios Venizelos reached an agreement on the issue with his Italian counterpart, Tommaso Tittoni, in July.[11]

The Turkish guerrillas were less easy to deal with. For a start, they were convinced that they were in the right, and they certainly had a legitimate grievance, having been driven out of their homes. In an area to the south, at Vourlah, all the villages around the town had been burnt. Further, the area that the Greeks controlled was undefined, and so the frontier, such as it was, was porous. The Italian agreement helped, since the Italians had been helping the guerrillas, and that help was now reduced, if not wholly ended. But Stergiadis's dictatorial methods, though usually just, were unpleasant; he also tended to foster a certain antipathy between Ionian (that is, Smyrnan) Greeks and those of Greece proper, the 'mainland', or the 'kingdom'.

In sum, the Greek expedition to seize Smyrna was a disaster from the start. There was plenty of blame to go around. The peace conference's decision to let the Greeks take over the city had been fairly casual, the Greeks themselves were poorly organised – the late arrival of Admiral Kakoulides and High Commissioner Stergiadis left the command system without direction for up to a week, during which the massacres began – the complacence of Admiral Calthorpe in the face of clear warnings from the Turkish officials that trouble was expected, and the apparent lack of control by their commanders of both the Greek and the Turkish troops, all contributed to the mess.

From the navy's point of view, however, when some sort of order had been imposed by the Greek commissioner, there was little further to concern the Royal Navy, despite the continuing tension in the area. From the navy's point of view, this was fortunate, given the continued fighting in Russia, which brought the White forces to be confined to Crimea by January 1920.

General Milne was brought in to sort out the causes of the fighting in the interior beyond Smyrna. He and a commission of high-ranking generals were organised by the peace conference to discover what was happening. His report, produced in October 1919, was quite clear that there was a war on between the Greek occupiers and Turkish 'bands of brigands'. These last were, in fact, official Nationalist forces of irregular organisation, a traditional Turkish resource – sometimes in the past called 'bashi-bazouks'. Milne laid out a line that would be more or less defensible by the Greeks, and the peace conference accepted it as the Greek boundary, without paying much attention either to the line itself or to the caveats that Milne included, and without indicating whether it was to be permanent.[12]

General indifference in the Paris Conference to the whole scheme was obvious. On the ground, the Greeks were only permitted to counter-attack, and then only allowed to pursue for 3 kilometres beyond their line. In effect, Milne had arranged a frontier zone separating the two sides, but it was actually a recipe for continued fighting. The report of a Commission of Enquiry, produced alongside Milne's decisions, recommended the withdrawal of the Greek forces and their temporary replacement by British troops, until a Turkish gendarmerie force could be organised; needless to say, this was rejected wholly by the Greek government, and ignored by the British. The commission had taken evidence about the events in and about the city, and its report laid much of the blame for the trouble on the Greeks – a finding inevitably at once rejected by them. The British government repeatedly refused to allow the report to be published, which was a clear sign that they had realised that their encouragement of the Greeks to go ahead with their landing made them complicit in the violence and murders.

The navy was only marginally involved in Greek and Turkish affairs in Anatolia for the next year. Instead, it was much involved in the Whites' disaster in Crimea, and only distantly in the military revival of the Turks in Anatolia. The navy certainly had the excuse that there were a number of difficulties and preoccupations to distract it from the events in central Anatolia, and these were barely known for much of 1919 and into 1920, and anyway, that area was unreachable by the navy. There was, for instance, the continuing problem with mines in the Black Sea, and as late as October 1921, the appearance of floating mines at the northern entrance to the Bosporos provoked the assumption that Turkish or Russian caiques were being used as minelayers, but it was also considered that the mines might be those which were breaking away from the minefields that had been laid by various of the Great War combatants in the northern part of the sea, those off Constanza and Odessa being especially likely.[13]

A further worry, one that predated the navy's arrival in the Black Sea, and had continued all through the Russian Civil War, was the problem of submarines. The navy had a well-founded fear of submarine attacks and knew that here and there in the Black Sea there were several of these boats, some of which were viable. Major efforts had been directed at Sevastopol to sink or seriously disable the submarines of the former Russian Black Sea Fleet, but some of them had been handed on to the Whites at Novorossiisk, and these had later returned to Sevastopol when the White forces were forced to take refuge in Crimea. Wherever the boats were, by November they had either been wrecked or, more seriously from the navy's point of view, they could have fallen into Bolshevik control. The fear of them had faded when the Whites had held those boats; it revived after the Red victory. And there were the half-completed submarines in the yards at Nikolayev, now being completed – one was at sea by September 1920, the rest were being worked on.

The threat of Soviet submarines was something that had been entertained more than once in earlier years. There had been some viable naval ships at Sevastopol when the Red Army originally took the port, and some of these – destroyers and submarines – were then still in working order, or could quickly be made so. This was despite the extensive sabotaging done by the navy's artificers more than once in the past. Most ships still capable of hostile action were taken by the refugees in their escapes in late 1920, and were handed on to the French, but some still remained for the Bolsheviks to use if they wished.

The withdrawal of most of the Mediterranean Fleet from the Black Sea did calm its fears somewhat. An experiment was conducted in June 1919 by which the British submarine *E.46* made the passage from north to south through the Bosporos, to see both if the voyage was possible, and if it could be done in secret. (There had been several voyages in both directions through the Dardanelles during the war, though the usefulness of reaching the Sea of Marmara had been very limited, partly due to the lack of targets, and it had proved to be expensive, seven boats having been lost in the process.)

Lieutenant H.L. Rendel made the Bosporos passage in *E.46* on 24 June 1919. He showed that the obstacles were very difficult to overcome, even without facing hostile fire. It was necessary to use the periscope all the time, which would render him visible to those on shore. He travelled at one point with his conning tower above water, so that he could see where he was going. The number of boats and ships in the passageway rendered his discovery all but certain even if he had been invisible and permanently underwater. The 'speed of passage' – that is, the strength of the current forcing the boat onwards, plus the power of his engines – made accuracy of navigation a constant problem. He does not mention it, but the passage is narrow and twisting, requiring constant changes in direction; it must have been hair-raising to pass through the double bend at Büyükdere, and again at Kandelli, while being driven onwards by that current, which could reach up to 8 knots. Rendel did suggest ways of making the passage – the boat could be disguised, or could make the passage in the night-time – but he added that in neither case would the boat be able to return against the current, and if it carried only one or two torpedoes, the loss of the boat would be pure waste. (The supposition was that he was playing the part of a Soviet boat, of course.)

Calthorpe passed Rendel's report on to the Admiralty, and in effect endorsed everything he said. He described the risks involved as 'prohibitive'. All that would be needed to make the voyage a failure was sufficient lookouts at the northern entrance to the Bosporos and at three or four places along the passage; these would almost inevitably discover the boat, even if it was not already spotted by the enormous number of small craft constantly sailing along or crossing the Strait, or by people on the banks – fishing was a widespread occupation. The report will have calmed the fears and apprehensions of those British naval officers who knew of Rendel's experiment.[14]

The Greek adventure into Smyrna, which had begun a month earlier, had roused opinion in Constantinople, particularly Turkish opinion. There had been large demonstrations with much waving of Islamic black flags.[15] This was one of the reasons that Calthorpe, despite much activity in the Kertch area of Crimea and in Smyrna, had insisted on bringing the battleship *Emperor of India* to lie off Constantinople during the initial period of the crisis. This was only two months since the full British military occupation had been imposed on the city, to the annoyance of the Turks, whose capital it was, and of the Greeks, who wished to possess it, and the sultan's annoyance had no doubt been made public. So Calthorpe had to be concerned with three areas of varied activity, in each of which it must have been difficult to decide just what his task was – not to mention the rest of the Mediterranean. No doubt he was pleased enough to be succeeded in July by Admiral de Robeck.

By this time, the primary naval concern had returned to the Black Sea and Constantinople. The Greek–Italian agreement of July calmed one aspect of the Smyrnan problem, though Captain Boyle in that same month reported a growing friction between the two groups of Greeks – 'Hellenic' and 'Ottoman'. They were, however, unlikely to fall into a fight with each other, with Italian and Turkish enemies on all sides. Nevertheless, a division in the Greek ranks was to be welcomed in the circumstances. Milne's drawing of a line of division between Greeks and Turks was a further reassurance of sorts.

And yet, the real enemy, of the Greeks, of the occupation, of the treaty, were the Nationalist Turks, who were becoming organised, and were fuelled up with great resentments. They were so menacing, not only towards the Greeks of Smyrna but also to any Allied forces in the Anatolian interior, that General Milne issued a clear warning to the Foreign Office, that the peace conference should avoid imposing hard terms on the Turks, which would only inflame the situation. He pointed out that the Anatolian Turks were armed (the disarmament process had clearly failed), and he could not calculate what strength they could display 'in the event of a national rising'. He was also preparing for whatever the Nationalists might do, particularly in the Constantinople region.[16] The Nationalists' forces were at that time

(October 1919) comprised mainly of the guerrilla bands which had become familiar at Smyrna, but Milne went further and sent out officers to locate the best lines at which to defend Constantinople, both in northern Anatolia and in Thrace; the guns in the forts along the Bosporos and the Dardanelles were either removed, or rendered unserviceable.

The increase in Nationalist sentiment in Constantinople was not surprising, given the actions of the Allies and the Greeks, but it was clearly a boost to the cause of Mustafa Kemal and his new government. Increasing confidence about the control of the city by the Nationalists helped to reduce his many problems. In spring 1920, a Nationalist army commanded by Kâzim Karabekir finally defeated the Armenians (of the new Republic of Armenia), and established an acceptable frontier in the east.[17] Then, after the British forces had withdrawn from northern Syria, the French had fought a regular war with the Turks. Deploying their locally recruited 'Armenian Legion', the French had advanced northwards out of Syria to take over Cilicia, and had placed a garrison in Marash, north of the Taurus Mountain range. This garrison was rather isolated, particularly in the winter when the passes through the Taurus Mountains were closed. Also demobilisation had reduced the French strength, hence the recruitment of Armenians, and they were simultaneously fully occupied in Syria itself, where there was a rival Arab government established in Damascus – the French had to mount a regular campaign in May 1920 to remove this government. In March, Marash fell to the Turks, to the accompaniment of a massacre of the Armenian population, and in April, the garrison at Urfa surrendered, only to be massacred as they marched away – the employment of Armenians would be seen by the Turks as an additional insult. The French came to the conclusion that the resurgent Turks were an enemy too far and cut their losses, abandoning the attempt to control Cilicia and a strip of northern Syria; the new boundary, in the absence of any obvious natural features, was agreed to lie along the line of the railway, Germany's Berlin–Baghdad railway. The Nationalists were thus free of the French threat by May, and could switch their forces elsewhere. One of the towns taken in the campaign, Aintab, was renamed Gaziantep, 'gazi' being an honorary title for a victory over Christians and other infidels; it was a title that was awarded to Mustafa Kemal as well; Milne's prediction of 'a nation rising' was coming true.[18]

This could only energise the Nationalists further. Already in January, they had carried out the audacious raid for arms, capturing the French garrison (only nine Senegalese soldiers) at Akbash fort in the Gallipoli peninsula, and then removed the considerable contents of the armoury. Pressure developed from Nationalist forces at Eskishehir, on the main railway from the Anatolian interior towards Ismid and further on to Constantinople. Brigadier General Francis Montague-Bates, commanding at Ismid, reported this; when threatened, Bates refused to move, and a force of 400 marines, assembled from three battleships, was landed as reinforcements, using the destroyers *Speedy* and *Vidette*. Yet the Nationalists achieved their aim, for although the British force at Eskishehir was relieved without difficulty, it was then withdrawn, along with the rolling stock there, and the line was also blown up.[19] This was the final stage in the withdrawal of British forces from the Anatolian interior. The result was that the Allied forces were defending only the coast from now on, though the Greeks held a section stretching some distance inland. Meanwhile at Brusa, Christians were asking for protection against Nationalist attacks. As an early Ottoman capital, Brusa was an obvious Nationalist target, as well as being a major city and a route centre. A further boost for the Nationalists was a military convention agreed with the Soviet government, which firmed up their confidence that their eastern boundary was safe. The French were now withdrawing in Cilicia in the south, and soon made an armistice there.

On 11 August, the Allies presented to the sultan's government the final version of the preliminary treaty of peace, named from the Parisian suburb of Sèvres. It was remarkably punitive, proposing to prevent Turkey from possessing any substantial warships or any aircraft, and removing substantial quantities of its territory, leaving its army with so few men that it was rendered indefensible. The Zone of the Straits was to be controlled by an international commission; Italy and France, and Greece were to take control of areas of territory or to hold 'spheres of influence' over much of Anatolia. The British 'share', the Arab territories, was tacitly conceded without argument; the Turks had no liking for the Arabs. The text was published next day in British newspapers, and it was rejected absolutely by the Nationalists; the sultan's government argued vehemently against it as well, knowing full well that acceptance would doom them.[20] It was also extremely insensitive in its timing, given that most of the territory was at the time under the control of an armed and active Nationalist government, which rejected it, while the main Allied belligerents had been steadily reducing their armed forces for the past year and more – not to mention that France had already suffered a major defeat in its attempt to secure a slice of Anatolia, so that its sphere of influence was effectively null before the treaty was even proclaimed.

One result of the end of the fighting in Armenia and Cilicia was increased pressure on the Allied positions along the Straits. A group of Nationalists occupied Lapseki (Lampsakos) on the Dardanelles, which pushed the British command into contemplating a serious retaliation. A second battleship, *Resolution*, was sent to join *Royal Oak* at Chanak, the fort that could control the Dardanelles passage, but it had to come all the way from Rodosto in Thrace. Meanwhile, *Royal Oak* reached Lapseki from Chanak, where Captain Whitehead landed with the British commander at the Dardanelles, Colonel Baldwin, and met the *kaimakam* of the town. He told them it had been merely another raid, not a conquest; the Nationalists had collected 200 rifles, executed thirteen 'brigands', and then left. *Resolution* was on the way to support *Royal Oak*, though its assignment was also to replace it. It was a major reaction, considering the relatively minor Nationalist raid, and suggests great nervousness in the British command system.[21]

There was concern also at 'the situation' at Bandirma (Panderma), halfway along the southern Marmara coast, which was also a station on the railway that roughly paralleled the coast. A destroyer was stationed there, as was a British 'Control Officer', in this case, Captain Coke Harvey. The nature of the situation is not explained, other than the strategic importance of the place, but here again there are signs of British nervousness at the proximity of the Nationalists.[22]

At the northern end of the Marmara, Nationalists were close to Ismid (the withdrawal of the British garrison from Eskishehir had opened up a considerable area to Nationalist occupation). The sultan's government was attempting to develop a campaign against them, using a force called the Army of the Caliphate. Two Turkish ships, a gunboat and a torpedo boat (*Kemal Reis* and *al-Hissar*) had been released from internment at Constantinople so that troops and ammunition could be transported from Constantinople to Ismid for that army's use. The Turkish general commanding this force was living on board the *Yavuz Sultan Selim* (ex-*Goeben*) because no suitable accommodation was available in Ismid. Having completed their delivery, the two Turkish ships were re-interned.

These three incidents – at Lapseki, Bandirma, and now Ismid, indicated that the Nationalists had established control over most of Anatolia, with the exception of the coast of the Marmara, and of the Zone of Smyrna, which was occupied by the Greeks. Vice-Admiral Fremantle, commanding the British ships in both the Black Sea and the Marmara, investigated a week or so later. He came to understand, from Brigadier General Bates, that Ismid itself was under threat of attack, and he offered a battleship for artillery support if needed.

The attack came a week later, once again by irregular bands of Turks, without any obvious formal organisation. The battleship *Ramillies* arrived. Captain Aubrey Smith was told of several places where damage had been caused to the railway by saboteurs; he instituted a regular patrol of the Gulf of Ismid to prevent communications across the Gulf, but detected nothing. Captain Smith described this as 'the present peaceful state of affairs' in a report dated 6 June, but by the 14th, irregular Turkish forces were attacking. *Ramillies* fired to disrupt the attacks during the night. This was reported to de Robeck, who became concerned about the navy's ability to control the Bosporos, and removed the *Yavuz Sultan Selim* to Tuzla, not far from Scutari. By the 22nd, a week after the beginning of the attacks, Ismid was still safe, but there was fighting in the countryside around it.

A considerable naval operation took place in defence of Ismid, involving two battleships and several destroyers. This, being also in defence of Constantinople, has been described in the previous chapter, and it was in the end successful. But the fighting saw the end of the Army of the Caliphate, which was defeated by the Nationalist irregulars and retreated to the British lines; the survivors were allowed take refuge with the British, but only at the cost of surrendering their weapons. It was the effective end of the sultan's war against the Nationalists.[23]

This changed the military and naval situation. The strongest single military force in the region was now the Greek army. At a meeting at Lympne in Kent, the British and French prime ministers, Lloyd George and Alexander Millerand, agreed that the Greeks should be allowed to advance out from the Zone of Smyrna northerly, where the Allied forces were under such pressure at Ismid, theoretically as a relief force for the Allies.[24] The Greeks meanwhile had taken the existence of the Sèvres treaty (and opposition to it by the Turks) as a sign that they could take over still more Turkish territory. The prime ministers' informal agreement, ratified later by the Supreme Council of the Peace Conference, in effect ignited the Greek–Turkish War, which for the Turks is their War of Independence.

Thus, the early months of 1920 saw a change in the prospects of both Greeks and Turks. The latter had revived, and had repelled, both the French in the south and the Armenians in the north, and could now concentrate on the west, the Greeks. The Allies had effectively pulled out of the conflict, other than defending their positions. The Greeks, on the other hand, had suffered the blow of the re-assumption of power by King Constantine, and so the retirement of Venizelos. The king's return brought many changes to the army command, replacing experienced commanders with inexperienced.[25] The Greeks did have the advantage of a disciplined army buoyed up by recent victories – in the Balkan Wars, in the Great War – and by the annexation of territory in Thrace and at Smyrna. But that last was a victory still only provisional, dependent on defeating the active Turkish enemy.

Chapter 11

The Greek Disaster, and Smyrna

The Turkish pressure at Ismid, though not advancing, and so bearable, would no doubt be repeated at irregular intervals, each time causing casualties and damage. This was so if the similar conditions in the Smyrna Zone were anything to go by. The answer would be to defeat the Turks decisively and so drive them away, but the British – and all the Allies, for that matter – did not have the armed strength in Turkey to do this, nor probably the will. General Milne appealed to London for reinforcements, but the British government could not contemplate sending more troops to Turkey, nor could the French. Demobilisation and war weariness had gone too far.

De Robeck nevertheless reported on 16 June that Ismid was under attack, as was the railway between Ismid and Scutari, and that the Allies' hold on the Bosporos was endangered. He needed reinforcements for the army and more seaplanes. He was promised Greek troops by a special arrangement, and that two battleships, *Revenge* and *Royal Sovereign*, which along with the rest of the 1st Battle Squadron had been due to return to England for refit, would remain with him.[1] *Iron Duke* blew up all the Turkish guns on the Asian side of the Bosporos, and those on the Dardanelles were next to be destroyed. Despite having to hold Batumi and watch events in the Crimea, de Robeck's ships were now heavily concentrated in the Straits, and more were called in from Malta.[2]

It had happened that Greek Prime Minister, Eleftherios Venizelos was visiting London at the time the Ismid area was under this new attack (perhaps not at all by coincidence) and he offered a Greek division to help out. British Prime Minister David Lloyd George and French Premier Alexandre Millerand worked out a scheme whereby the Greek army in the Smyrna Zone would move north, along the line of the Panderma–Smyrna railway, so relieving the pressure on Ismid. This was accepted by the peace conference's Supreme Council, though the Italians, already at odds with the

Greeks, were not pleased about it. But there were only three Italian ships left at Constantinople; the others had left, as de Robeck pointedly reported.[3]

The British defence force in the Ismid position and the peninsula west of the city consisted of three battalions, one British – the Gordon Highlanders – and two Indian, including the 21st Punjabis, and a battery of the Royal Field Artillery. A line had been established across the peninsula very similar to that of the Chatalja Lines to the west of Constantinople, along a line of hills facing a flat plain. This was a good defensive position, and was flanked by the sea to both north and south where the navy could provide flanking support, but there were few reserves, no facilities for night operations, and no anti-aircraft defences. The navy also provided a force of marines, and readied a battalion of seamen to be landed if required; two seaplane carriers and two battleships were available for support.[4]

The Greeks moved out from the Smyrna Zone on 22 June, moving northwards, at a time when Ismid was under the most serious pressure – but which then ceased almost at once. The Greek forces did not merely head for Panderma, as had been suggested in the prime ministerial talks, but passed beyond the Milne Line. One division moved directly east along the line of the Cayster River to capture Aleshehir; other forces moved north along the Panderma railway line as far as that place, and then kept going in order to fulfil their promise to assist in the defence of Ismid.[5] The Greeks were taking the opportunity of assisting in the defence of Ismid to expand their territory.

On 30 June, de Robeck telegraphed to the Admiralty that he was about to give 'all possible assistance' to the Greek advance.[6] He immediately made plans to assist in supporting landings from the sea close to Panderma, and in the Gulf of Gemlik close to Bursa. A Greek convoy of transports carrying 7,000 troops, 1,000 artillerymen, and 4,000 mules, escorted by the Greek battleship *Kilkis*, was sent from Smyrna, and the troops were landed on both sides of Panderma. They had the support of British naval forces, the battleships *Benbow* and *Marlborough*, with destroyers, trawlers and lighters; a second naval force sailed from Constantinople. The seaplane carrier *Pegasus* flew off two planes for reconnaissance. In addition, two naval detachments were to demonstrate off Mudania in the north and Karabigha to the west to prevent Turkish reinforcements approaching along the coast road to dispute the landings. This was within the Greek area as defined by the Milne Line. The Turks facing Ismid seemed to have vanished; they were supposed to have gone to oppose the Greek advance.[7]

The Greeks in fact went a good deal further. Panderma had been the originally agreed target, within the Greek area as defined by the Milne Line, which was no doubt why the navy had been used to support the landings there. But the Greeks then advanced further, moving on to take Bursa, and halted only just short of Ismid. Their position was thus a useful addition to the defence for the latter city, which was what Milne had wanted when its defence was under serious pressure. The division also passed beyond the city as far as Adapazar, 30 kilometres or so east of Ismid, from which the crossing of the Sakarya River could be dominated. A division was then sent from Panderma across the Sea of Marmara to Rodosto in Thrace to establish a powerful Greek military presence beside Constantinople; the capture of Adrianople followed in a few days, and occasioned much Greek celebration.[8]

This was the operation that de Robeck had described in a message sent to both the Foreign Office and the Admiralty as 'rash and ill-advised', and it was a clear sign that the British and Greeks had different objectives, the Greeks in particular using the threat to Ismid to deliberately expand their operation in Asia Minor. De Robeck was principally concerned at this moment with the defence of Ismid and its peninsula, which was certainly threatened, and which was a forward defence for Constantinople. The Greeks were, however, using the crisis to move well beyond both the Milne Line and Ismid and to confront the Turks at Adapazar; in addition, they had advanced into Turkish Thrace, clearly threatening Constantinople. The Greek gamble in fact came off, which was a dangerous sign for later. A message came to the Admiralty from the prime minister who ordered de Robeck to support the Greek expedition. So he did.[9]

The Greek advance on Bursa was therefore supported by British landings at Mudania and Gemlik, small ports on the south coast of the Gulf of Gemlik, which were the ports for Bursa and Ismid. The landing at Mudania was on 4 July, and was a difficult operation. Two adjacent landings were intended, one on 'Goat Beach', which was opposed by a group of Turkish snipers hidden in an olive grove. They proved impossible to shift by bombardment from the ships and were eventually driven off and away by a sweep by marines through the grove. The second landing group made two attempts to land at their designated beach, but were so strongly opposed that those who had landed were withdrawn. Another attempt was then made to land at the railway pier, but this was beaten back also, by Turkish soldiers fighting from the railway buildings. This force then moved along the coast and landed behind the original force at Goat Beach.

These landings were supported by two battleships, *Revenge* and *Royal Sovereign*, two destroyers, *Venetia* and *Westcott*, the seaplane carrier *Pegasus*, a tug and two lighters. Vice-Admiral Fremantle landed to make a decision on the next move. He decided to ignore a possible threat from the west, and to advance with the whole force – about 800 marines and sailors – into Mudania town, which was taken by the early afternoon; the Turks did not resist further.[10]

Two days later, on 6 July, a similar landing operation took place to capture Gemlik, the small port at the head of the gulf of that name. About the same number of seamen and marines were used as at Mudania, but they came from different ships: the battleship *Marlborough*, three destroyers, *Sportive*, *Speedy* and *Montrose*, a tug and two lighters; marines and sailors were contributed by the *Iron Duke* and *Benbow* as well as *Marlborough*. Despite the warning provided by the earlier landings at Mudania, less than 20 kilometres away, opposition to the landings was slight, and the town was captured by 9 a.m. By this time, of course, not only had Mudania been captured, but it will have become known that the Greek army was approaching from the south; indeed that a Greek cavalry division was not far off. Both Mudania and Gemlik were taken over by Greek forces when they arrived. They had reached Bursa, to the south of the two towns, on 8 July, and took over at Mudania and Gemlik on 16 July.[11]

The landings in Thrace followed on 19 July. The operation was launched from Panderma, using the ships and men that had occupied the town earlier. The Greek battleship *Kilkis* escorted the Greek transports along with the cruiser *Averoff* and at least three destroyers. However, the main escort was clearly the British force, consisting of two battleships, *Ramillies* and *Royal Sovereign*, with the destroyers *Westcott* and *Vidette*. Besides the landing at Rodosto, other landings were to take place further along the coast at Ereğli and Sultankeui.

This operation turned into one that, in the end, was in effect commanded and conducted by the British. The seaplane carrier *Ark Royal* arrived to assist in reconnaissance. At Rodosto, the Greek 3rd Infantry Regiment was successfully landed, and there was no opposition. At the other two targets, however, the Greek ships were late in arriving and were clearly reluctant to begin landings, staying well clear of the shore; they were also decidedly inexperienced in such an operation. The British ships had been off the ports at the correct time, according to the plan. *Ark Royal*'s reconnaissance showed that people were leaving the two towns, and there was no sign of any armed opposition. Finally, *Revenge*'s captain persuaded the transports to close the shore and to begin landings, though they proceeded very slowly until British boats were provided. At Sultankeui, they were met by three men waving white flags. At Ereğli, two battalions were landed, again without being opposed. Investigations later showed that at both Rodosto and Ereğli, preparations had been made for resistance, but it seemed that the presence of the battleships (which were probably known to have fired at resisting Turks at Mudania and Gemlik) was sufficient to discourage the resisters. The point was made, however, that the Greeks in this operation were slow and that, had opposition appeared, they would have been in severe trouble. A week later, the Greek forces were in Adrianople. King Alexander of Greece had visited Smyrna and then Panderma, and was on hand to witness the landings at Rodosto. He received congratulations from Vice-Admiral Fremantle, whose praise must have been provided with tongue in cheek.[12]

A fortnight later, the sultan's representatives in Paris signed the Treaty of Sèvres, which he and his advisers had been considering and arguing about since May. This acceptance had been one of the aims of the Allies, so both the Greeks and the Allies in Paris could consider their operations a success. But the problem now was that the government representatives who had signed had control only of the city, thanks to Allied troops, and the Turks who had power over most of the country – the Nationalists – rejected it.[13]

The signing of the treaty effectively finished the sultan's regime, even without a ratification, which he refused to enact. The Allies found that the sultan's representatives' signatures were not worth anything, since the sultan no longer had control over more than a tiny fraction of his empire. The Nationalists in Anatolia were much boosted in manpower as men deserted the sultanate system and moved to support and work for them. The occupation by Allied forces of any part of Turkey was now rendered precarious, since the Turkish population was liable to undertake overt or covert operations by any means, from demonstrations to guerrilla attacks and armed uprisings.

The Greeks, of course, were not satisfied with their gains, which indeed had so far been very easily acquired. Slowly they continued to move forward, bit by bit. From Aleshehir, their troops advanced another 100 kilometres to Ushak, an uncomfortable post. They advanced along the railway due east from Smyrna, and ahead lay the main railway through Anatolia, which linked with the Smyrna line at Afyonkarahissar; to the north was another junction, Eskishehir, which linked with the main line between Ismid and Scutari, and by road and rail with Bursa. Both junction cities remained in Nationalist control. In the north, a Greek reconnaissance in force from Bursa in January 1921 penetrated close to Eskishehir, but then retired; the lack of strong opposition seemed helpful, but it was certain that a major attack would be seriously opposed.[14]

The political troubles in Greece during the winter of 1920/1 delayed their affairs in Asia, and gave the Turks the opportunity for further reorganisation, but in March 1921, determined Greek offensives moved out towards the two junction cities. The attack launched from Ushak captured Afyonkarahissar on 27 March; in the north, however, the Bursa army, whose staff anticipated an easy advance as far as Ankara, Mustafa Kemal's administrative centre, collided with a new Turkish force. This had been the army that had fought against the reconnaissance in January, and now, strengthened and properly drilled and organised, it stood to defend the same position, at Inonu, where the route from Bursa descended to the Eskishehir plain. What was different this time was that the Turkish army was commanded by Ismet Pasha, a colleague of Mustafa Kemal's and a well-experienced and skilled Great War commander. He had gathered together the various Turkish irregular forces and had then drilled them into a disciplined and obedient army. The Greeks from Bursa therefore had a very hard fight, but they were able to retire back to their original positions, having failed to take their immediate objectives; this left the Afyonkarahissar force rather exposed, and so it also retired, having held the town for no more than four days.[15]

De Robeck had found out about the intended Greek offensives when he was at Smyrna in February. By early April, only a month after the intended Greek offensive, when the Greek failure had become clear, he was certainly contemplating the possibility of a Greek 'retirement', and put several suggestions to the Admiralty, including the probability of the Greeks retiring to hold only Smyrna, which would leave the British to defend Ismid. He was sure that the army and the navy together would be able to hold the Straits and Constantinople, though he would need more naval reinforcements. A reply a fortnight later (the Greek retirement had stopped at their former positions) was that de Robeck should withhold facilities from the Greek forces as far as possible. This policy had been initiated when King Constantine had returned to the Greek throne at the end of 1920; no European power now supported Greece in its eastern campaign.[16]

In the summer of 1921, however, the Greeks renewed their attack and captured both their earlier objectives, the junction cities of Eskishehir and Afyonkarahissar, but then they marched on to find decisive defeat at the twenty-two-day battle at Sakarya, close to Ankara, in August. To gather sufficient forces they had withdrawn their troops from the Ismid area, and pulled their forces back to Bursa (devastating the territories they abandoned in the process).[17] A neutral area on either side of the Straits, called the 'Zone of the Straits', had been proclaimed by the Allies at Constantinople in the hope that it would be respected – but the Nationalists at least were highly unlikely to do so. De Robeck had made clear his opposition to the intentions of the Greeks as they began their late advance, and again contemplated an ultimate Greek 'retirement', so that he turned to consider what the navy would need in order to concentrate on defending the Bosporos and the Dardanelles.[18]

Defeated at the Sakarya battle, the Greeks retreated to their former line, but this time covering Eskishehir and Afyonkarahissar. Their troops suffered severely for several months from the winter conditions in the trenches; thanks to inefficient staff work, irregular supplies, and poor officers, the morale and health of the soldiers in their bunkers suffered very badly – this was one of the consequences of replacing the experienced commanders by the inexperienced and arrogant partisans of King Constantine.[19] The Nationalists meanwhile made an agreement with Soviet Russia, surrendering Batumi in exchange for a Treaty of Friendship and military supplies, and making agreements concerning the Caucasus and mutual trade.[20] This reduced the Turks' problems in the eastern area once again, and opened up the possibility of further agreements, at least once the Soviets were free of their own civil war.

Armistices or peace agreements were agreed with Italy and France in southern Anatolia, who withdrew from their claimed territories, and supplied the Turks with weaponry, happy to see the Turks defeating the Greeks and causing difficulties for the British.[21] And yet, despite this inter-Allied friction, which was hardly anything new, the occupation of Constantinople continued to be an amicable joint Allied operation, though the garrison was mainly British.

At least two of the ships of the (now Bolshevik) Black Sea fleet were in good enough condition to be handed over to the Turkish Nationalists, or so the British heard, but again this was a report of a report. On 17 August 1921, 'from a very secret source', it had been reported that a destroyer and a torpedo boat, and possibly other vessels had been agreed for delivery. Trebizond or Tuapse were suggested as destinations. De Robeck, in reporting this to the Admiralty, explained that he hoped to seize the ships, and Lord Curzon had agreed to this.[22]

De Robeck sent out two destroyers, *Montrose* and *Trinidad*, to search along the north coast of Anatolia 'from Rizeh to the Bosporos', but they could find no evidence that the ships had been handed over to the Nationalists, at least not yet. On the other hand, no one from either British ship was allowed to land except at one port, Teriboli, and no information could be acquired; all queries were to be referred to Ankara. Of course, the secrecy in itself was suspicious, and was probably intended to be.[23]

This unusual determination by the Nationalist Turks to refuse information was countered by a complaint that the British destroyers had stopped and searched a Turkish caique. The complaint was from the Nationalist foreign minister, Yusuf Kemal, and was delivered to the new British high commissioner, Sir Horace Rumbold. The complaint was passed to de Robeck, who replied at length. He pointed out that the political situation regarding Turkey was an armistice, and so Britain and the Ottoman Empire was still technically at war.[24] In fact, it may be that the Nationalists were testing the waters in view of the arrival of a new high commissioner, while de Robeck was perhaps conscious that he was now dealing with a civilian high commissioner and took the opportunity to lay out the naval point of view. The Turks, of course, were also maintaining the position that they were the legitimate Turkish government, having decreed the abolition of the sultanate.

In the course of the letter de Robeck mentioned that the Greeks were able to pass ships through the Bosporos to raid the Turks in the Black Sea, and the Nationalists were able to receive supplies of arms and ammunition by sea. Both Greeks and Turks had been 'able to reap the advantage of unrestricted imports of war material'.

Despite the failure of the two destroyers to locate the ships supposed to have been delivered by the Bolsheviks to the Turks (it was probably no more than a rumour), the Admiralty soon after accepted as a 'fact' that such transfers – not just mythical ships, but war materials, food, and other goods – were available to the Nationalists. Admiral Brock, who became commander-in-chief in the Mediterranean in May, was given permission to sink any Nationalist ship that reached the Straits, and to sink the battleship *Goeben* to prevent it from being taken, though he then reported that it and other Turkish warships were 'incapable' of steaming or taking offensive action.[25]

De Robeck, in the course of a summary of the position of the navy in the Turkish/Greek area at the time of his demonstration at Constantinople in September 1921, discussed the 'War in Anatolia' briefly, pointing out the lift given to the Nationalists by their victory, and that they would very likely lay some of the blame for the Greek invasion on the British. He had reverted to 'normal' naval strength in the Straits region – one battleship, one light cruiser, six destroyers and a seaplane base on shore, but this would not be sufficient if the Turks attempted to cross the Straits.[26]

He had also remarked in an earlier report that keeping open the passage through the Straits was 'a matter of national importance' for Britain, whereas it was not so to anyone else, especially not to France and Italy. He did not elaborate on this, nor explain what he meant, but it was apparently for him a matter of power rather than access. He reported that, although the military front was quiet, in the Straits area there was considerable 'brigand' activity, and attempts were being made to move weapons into the Greek areas for use by Nationalist supporters in that area. At Chanak, which was under British control, a Nationalist group that included 'all the principal Turkish officials' had just been broken up. At Karabigha, the British garrison had almost a full-scale battle with 'a powerful band of brigands'.

The Greeks' retreat in 1921 had halted at their positions before Eskishehir and Afyonkarahissar, and the war ceased to move through the winter of 1921/2, a stalemate that continued through into the spring. De Robeck was moved to the command of the Atlantic Fleet, and his position as commander-in-chief in the Mediterranean was taken by Admiral Osmond Brock in May. His first problem was the apparent threat of the Greeks to make an attempt on Constantinople in July 1922.[27]

The navy had been concerned about the Greeks' moves in Thrace earlier, but that problem had faded away fairly quickly. A month later, a much more serious threat came from the Turkish Nationalists, but from the other direction, from Asia Minor. On 26 August, the reorganised, rearmed and newly disciplined Turkish army launched an attack against the Greek lines around Afyonkarahissar. The attack was concentrated on one part of the southern half of the Greek line, and the northern half was largely ignored for several days. By 28 August, the southern Greek line had been penetrated, and the first Greek refusals to go on fighting took place. Over the next four days, the Greek army in the south disintegrated into a mob of refugees heading for the coast. They were accompanied by an increasing number of civilian refugees, and they left behind burning towns and villages, destroyed bridges, burnt fields and massacred 'enemies'.[28]

The headquarters of the Greek army at Smyrna lost contact with the armies in the field early on, and once the retreat was on, there was no way of restoring it. Messages from the Greek headquarters were always out of date, and orders were impossible to execute. A series of Greek surrenders took place; ironically, this affected most seriously those Greek units that had retained enough cohesion to make a stand, so that the defeated men who fled were protected by units that were then compelled to surrender. By the end of August, the Turkish army was coming close to Smyrna and the Greek forces were in total disarray.

In the north, it quickly became clear that their southern flank was exposed, and the order was given for the whole force to retire, with designated evacuation ports for each unit – Mudania and Panderma principally. (The Greek army had evacuated the Ismid area the year before.) There was therefore little serious fighting in the north, and much less devastation. Most of the Greek troops got away unhindered.

At Smyrna and its neighbourhood, however, matters were very different. The order to the Greek forces was that they were to pass by the city and move into the Chesme Peninsula to the south, where transports would be available, and two Greek battleships, *Kilkis* and *Lemnos*, would provide artillery support.[29] All the time the number of civilians among the retreating and disorganised troops increased. Many of the civilians headed for Smyrna, though those that chose to go to other ports probably had a better chance of escaping. By 1 and 2 September, it was clear even to the Greek headquarters that the whole position of the Greeks in Asia Minor was in total dissolution.

Behind the victorious Turkish army, which was now intent on driving the Greeks out of all Asia Minor, succeeding in this in a campaign that lasted only three weeks, the countryside and the towns were looted and buildings and villages left in flames, the damage being done as much by the Greeks as the Turks. The situation in the north was perhaps less unpleasant, for there the Greek retreat was more orderly, but in all areas the Christian population, Greek and Armenian, fled to the coast in advance of the Turkish arrival. It is worth pointing out here, in advance of the sack of Smyrna, that the practice of burning villages had been undertaken by the Greeks from the beginning of their invasion. In Smyrna in May 1919, at the start of the whole campaign, the Turkish quarter of the city had been sacked and looted, partly burned, and the Turkish population that had not been killed had fled. In the countryside within days of the invasion, Turkish villages were being burned, and the populations massacred or driven out.

Arnold Toynbee was reporting on events for the *Manchester Guardian*, and later described the events of 1921 in his book *The Western Question*. He compiled a partial list of the destructions – he used the term 'atrocities' – based on information he regarded as reliable. He listed at least 200 villages plundered, some of them burned and their inhabitants murdered, before July 1921; there was still more of this in the Greek offensive of July 1921. The Greek retirement from Ismid was accompanied by the burning of villages in the Yalova Peninsula, and the massacre or expulsion of the Turkish population.[30] The Turkish reply was, of course, to commit their own 'atrocities' when they captured the Greek villages. The destruction in the Greek retreat was committed by both Greeks and Turks, though it was the Greeks who committed most of the burning and looting during that retreat. There was clearly little or nothing to choose between the two sides in the matter of atrocities.

Since the restoration of King Constantine in December 1920, the Allies had severed any military and naval links with the Greek army, its navy and the government; in addition, they were still technically at war with the Turkish government of the sultan, and had no relations with the insurrectionary regime of Mustafa Kemal in Ankara. The French and Italians, as noted, had gone further and had arranged treaties and agreements with the Nationalist Turks, as had the Soviet Russians, whose own civil war was largely over by the end of 1921. Turks and Russians were both acting against the British, who had been leaders in the wars of intervention against both countries; the French and Italians tended to be competing with each other, and the French were adopting a generally anti-British position. Whatever their feelings, however, they both rallied to the defence of Constantinople when it was threatened by the Greeks. As the disaster for the Greeks in Asia Minor developed, the British had no responsibilities, other than basic humanity, to assist the refugees. The French and Italians, being effectively informally allied with the Turks, had still less, and had few ships in Aegean waters.

The Royal Navy, in the person of Admiral Brock, became fully aware of the 'development of [the] situation in Anatolia', on 2 September. Considering that the Greeks had been retreating for over a week, this was surely rather late, but the Greek headquarters were almost as much in the dark about matters in the interior as the watching British. It is obvious that the prospect of a general exodus of both Greek troops and Greek inhabitants of the city came as slowly growing surprise on all sides.

Brock turned his flagship, *Iron Duke*, around (he was on a show-the-flag cruise in the Adriatic) and ordered the battleship *King George V* (1911) to join him at Smyrna, though it was damaged when it struck a rock, and *Ajax* went to Smyrna instead. The Admiralty reacted also, but only after a few days. Its first priority was about controlling the Straits, and the Gallipoli Peninsula; then there was the likely problem of refugees – the Royal Navy would collect British subjects as it always did in such circumstances; other British ships available in the region would be directed to Smyrna to collect any others, British or otherwise.[31]

Brock arrived at Smyrna on 3 September, and saw the British consul general, Sir Harry Lamb, and the Greek high commissioner, Stergiadis, who 'appeared callous' – but this was just his habitual coldness, no doubt. The Greek authorities were primarily concerned to evacuate their army and its stores, and they ignored what was happening in the city. It turned out that the British in the city had contemplated the need for evacuation earlier, and Lamb had organised the requisition of four British-owned merchant ships that were in the harbour. This was partly to keep them out of the Greek army's hands, and partly to be able to take in the British refugees if necessary. Brock was in fact surprised that whole families were preparing to leave; he had thought that the men would remain behind to guard their property, but apparently, all of them intended to move. It was clearly understood among the Greek inhabitants that a massacre was in prospect when the Turkish forces got into the city; word of Turkish vengeance for Greek earlier atrocities had spread, but, as usual, the British did not feel they themselves would be threatened, though those who had been living in Smyrna were clearly apprehensive. The presence of an organisation able to take them off also calmed down the panic, until evacuation was essential.

The evacuation therefore began quietly and slowly. Ships had been available since 4 September, but then only one of them, SS *Mingary*, had enough evacuees on board to make a voyage worthwhile – it went to Cyprus. Turkish forces arrived in the city on the 9th; Stergiadis had left with his archives two days before; by then, the rest of the Greek administration had also disappeared. Neither the Greek administration nor the Greek army made any attempt to defend the city, or its Greek population. An Allied delegation set out to contact the Turkish military commander, Nureddin Pasha, to arrange a formal and controlled surrender of the city, but even then, it was probably too late to control what happened. Some of the earliest Turkish arrivals were irregulars, who set about looting and killing as soon as they arrived.

The British people living in the city finally decided to leave on the 10th, and were escorted by marines to the harbour, and loaded onto the second of the four ships, SS *Antioch*, but the Maltese and Cypriots in the city – British subjects, of course – who were generally much poorer than the 'English', had as yet barely moved, being reluctant to abandon what little they possessed. Mustafa Kemal arrived on the 11th, staying outside the city, and declared that the Nationalists considered themselves at war with Britain, which encouraged the reluctant British who were still in the city to go. When Sir Harry Lamb heard this from Kemal's own lips, he began actively encouraging all the British subjects still in the city to leave. Next day, many of the Maltese were evacuated onto the ships.

And that day, 13 September, fires started – or were started. How they began is, of course, disputed, but the Turks were now in control of much of the city, though the Turkish command was not in full control of its soldiers. There were plenty of stories of Turkish soldiers fire-raising, and preventing the city's fire brigade from working. The fires began in the Armenian Quarter, against which people there was a vicious Turkish hatred – Sir Harry Lamb claimed that they were deliberately started after a massacre of 2,000 Armenians, as a means of concealing and cremating the dead.

The quay was soon crowded with frantic, screaming and yelling refugees, both from the city and those who had been driven from the interior. The quay itself was cordoned off by Turkish soldiers at either end of the passage, and people were unable to get out except by water. *Iron Duke* received on board those who could get out to the ship in small boats, including an entire maternity hospital. The ship was soon crowded with shocked refugees, who had to be moved to other ships. But then, Admiral Brock ordered out boats from all ships to work at rescuing all they could. They were transferred to any merchant steamers that were available and sent off to Greece, the Aegean islands, Malta, or Cyprus. Brock took *Iron Duke* away on the 14th, having to attend to a problem at Chanak.

This account has been derived so far from Brock's rather colourless description of events, which at least is not too obviously partisan.[32] From the 14th, Rear Admiral Reginald Tyrwhitt, Brock's second-in-command, and commander of the 3rd Light Cruiser Squadron, takes up the story, but in just as narrow and colourless a way. He reports that most of the fires were out by the 15th, and that the barriers holding in the crowds on the quay had been removed and most of the people there had moved away. The Turks had organised the evacuations by now, placing Turkish soldiers to control those leaving, and shepherding them towards the evacuation points. They pulled out all men aged between sixteen and forty-five and sent them to work gangs in the interior. Tyrwhitt made some estimates of the damage (1 square mile burned out), deaths (1,000 at Bournabat suburb; 75 per cent of the Armenians killed), British property (all destroyed). His number for deaths is obviously a great underestimate.

The Turks gave permission for refugees to be collected in the Allied ships, but not in any Greek ship. The Greek ships in fact were moored off Lesbos, where they could receive refugees from other ships. Lesbos was also the target destination for many ships to unload the refugees they were carrying. Ships arrived every day to collect refugees in relatively small numbers. The battleship *King George V* took 120 and SS *Elpiniki* 59, but SS *City of Versailles* took 4,407 and SS *Worsley Hill* 3,153; HMS *Cardiff* carried 122. These are the estimated numbers in Tyrwhitt's report; he does not report other nationalities' merchant ships. (The warships did not have room for many extra people; the merchantmen did.) The refugees were being landed at places all around the Mediterranean, Piraeus, Mytilene, Malta, Cyprus and Egypt. The process was to be halted by the Turks at the end of September, but it continued thereafter for a few more days. By 5 October, the total removed from Asia Minor was estimated at about 220,000;[33] they were overwhelmingly women and children and the old. Men aged between 16 and 45 were retained by the Turks; most of them died fairly soon in the work gangs. The Turks were undoubtedly also concerned that surviving Greek men should not be available for reviving the conflict.

By the end of October, the crisis was over, the armies and navies had left, and recriminations could begin. Criticism had been voiced in Britain, presumably on the basis of newspaper reports, inaccurate as usual, that the British ships had been laggard in collecting and removing refugees. This bothered the Admiralty, who, as early as 29 September, asked Rear Admiral Wilmot Nicholson, commander of the 2nd Light Cruiser Squadron, to give a 'brief appreciation' of events, and estimates of numbers evacuated by ships of all nationalities.

He described the system as seen from a British ship.[34] The refugees were funnelled through by the American Relief Committee, which controlled the arrival of the ships and organised the relief effort both at Lesbos and in Smyrna. Traffic and loading at Smyrna itself was organised from HMS *Curacoa*, a light cruiser. It was estimated that *Curacoa* had handled 30,000 to 40,000 refugees daily. American 'barrier guards' inspected those claiming refugee status; several Turks were detected and refused entry; they were put ashore. All figures are, of course, estimates, but Nicholson suggested that the refugees totalled about 177,000; of these, 146,000 had been removed by British and American efforts. He claimed that the French destroyers and Italian ships collected only a few refugees each, mainly their own nationals. He gives 2,000 as the number of British nationals evacuated.[35] He did not include an estimate of those who made it to civilian ships without going through the 'official' process.

These are perhaps the nearest to accurate figures that can be found. Every book on the subject, or which refers to the subject, has a different total, quite often depending on the political allegiance of the author – Greeks exaggerate Greek casualties and blame the Turks, Armenians exaggerate Armenian casualties and also blame the Turks; the Turks won the war, which is justification in itself, but had suffered badly before Smyrna was attacked. The politicians in London, Paris and Rome generally escape any blame, though their decisions and orders had clearly contributed to the disaster. In the city, the fires destroyed the Greek, Frankish and Armenian quarters, leaving the Turkish and Jewish quarters relatively undamaged. The city, however, was finished as a community, social and economic, for two generations. The numbers of killed in the sack, the fire, the work gangs and the massacres are impossible to estimate; again, each of the commentators has his or her own number, but some tens of thousands must be supposed.

The advance of the Nationalist forces on land in September 1922 was also a presumed threat to Constantinople, which was an issue that so preoccupied Brock that he took his battleship away from Smyrna in the midst of the city's crisis. The threat to Constantinople compelled much attention to be directed at the apparent ease with which the Nationalist Turks could cross to Europe. The Black Sea was one of those ways. Brock had destroyers out patrolling the Thracian coast, on the lookout for 'motor caiques', which were said to be moving small bodies of troops to a Bulgarian port, where, presumably, they infiltrated into Turkish Thrace – the Bulgars, for once, were sympathetic to the Turks, after being allies in the Great War and fellow victims of the peace conference. On the other hand, the British patrols had met no such ship – it was probably more rumouring. Nevertheless, a destroyer flotilla was deployed to patrol along the coast from the northern entrance to the Bosporos westwards. The sack of Smyrna had not ended the general Turkish crisis.

The disaster at Smyrna was not intended by either side, but both committed actions that enabled it to happen. The Turks, of course, were the aggressors – but replying to earlier Greek aggression – and were more or less in control of the city when the fires began, which was the proximate cause of the panic and of the huge refugee crisis. But the Greeks had, quite deliberately, left the city to be taken by their enemies, neglecting to provide either defence or administration. No Greek attempt was made either to defend the city or to negotiate a peaceful surrender, which could have been possible. Since the Greek army was in control until the Turks arrived, its defence was their responsibility; this included the commissioner Stergiadis, who left on 7 September, and the high command of the army, who had left even earlier – men interested in the safety of their own soldiers, admittedly a reasonable concern. This was a city largely populated by Greeks that had vociferously welcomed the Greek army's landing; those Greek inhabitants were abandoned by the men they had welcomed. The greater blame thus lies with the Greeks for dereliction of duty, the lesser with the Turks, whose army command could not control all their men. And, of course, behind it all lay the centuries-long enmity between Greeks and Turks, and between Armenians and Turks, which meant that contact between them was almost invariably violent.

Chapter 12

Chanak

The battleship *Iron Duke*, carrying Admiral Brock, had been called away from the tragedy of Smyrna in September 1922 to attend to some problem at Chanak on the Dardanelles. This situation had already been the subject of messages back and forth between the admiral and the Admiralty, and once again, the issue was what to do if the Turkish Nationalists arrived in force on the Asian shores of the Bosporos and the Dardanelles, and the longer southern shore of the Marmara. The Turks would inevitably wish to reclaim Constantinople and Thrace from the Allies and from the Greeks. So, once again, there were two crises happening at the same time: that at Smyrna, and that centred on Chanak; the latter is the subject of this chapter.

De Robeck's judgment that the Straits were of 'vital importance to us', was repeated in different words in an Admiralty message to Brock on 8 September: 'the maintenance of the control of the deep water separating Asia and Europe was a cardinal British interest'.[1] Again, the statement was simply made, and not expanded nor explained, nor were the reasons for such a judgment laid out; it was evidently assumed to be obvious. The wording has the ring of an oft-voiced cliché, never yet seriously examined. It had not been so important in the past, when Russia was just as dangerous, for it was only the threat of the Russian Revolution that could have so frightened the Admiralty, and presumably the British government, into inventing a new area of concern on top of all the other such areas.

It is not too difficult to identify the reasons for this new belief – the navy was bothered about the possibility of hostile Russian naval vessels arriving out of the Black Sea and into the Mediterranean, and perhaps it was a result of fighting the Turks (and pre-war apprehensions about Russia having been increased). Possibly the Admiralty had now heard that the unfinished submarines at Nikolayev had been nearing completion; the rumour that Bolshevik ships had been handed on to the Turks would suggest that the

Soviet government had warships to spare in the Black Sea. In the end, of course, this presumption about the Straits was false, just as the rumours of the delivery of ships to the Turkish Nationalists were false, and when the time came for actually testing this belief, this 'cardinal British interest' could be abandoned without a qualm.

The 'Kemalists', as the Turkish Nationalists were colloquially now being termed in the naval messages, had now approached the shores of the Straits along their whole length. And so it became necessary to adopt a clear policy by which the naval officers could be guided. The Cabinet in London had discussed the issue on 7 September (the day Stergiadis abandoned Smyrna, and the day before Brock left Smyrna for Chanak). The conclusions were spelled out in the message sent to Brock the next day. Any attempt to occupy the Gallipoli peninsula should be resisted by force. Naval forces were to be increased. British troops should occupy the peninsula alongside the French who were already there.[2]

Brock pointed out that the essential part of the problem lay in the availability of transport, which the Nationalists would require if they were to cross in force from east to west. Ships and boats of all sizes were plentiful throughput in the Straits, so if the navy made an attempt to stop a crossing it would be easy to thwart. He suggested that *Pegasus*'s seaplanes could be used to inspect the several ports in the Marmara region. The Dardanelles could be patrolled by aircraft and destroyers day and night. He suggested that two additional destroyer flotillas would be needed, plus HMS *Argus*, the aircraft carrier, 'for observation'. The Admiralty quickly agreed to send *Argus*, and the Air Ministry agreed to supply the planes.[3]

The government accepted all this, and the prime minister said that Brock was not to destroy shipping unless all other controlling methods had failed. Apart from *Argus*, Brock was soon told that two destroyer flotillas were to be sent out, along with seventeen planes, together with *Sandhurst*, a repair ship that had been converted into a false battlecruiser during the war, and now had been returned to its original purpose. A frozen meat ship was being found also to help with supplies.[4] Brock was ordered to give the Admiralty some idea of the quantity and type of shipping in the Straits. In reply, he pointed out the many sailing ships in the port, of every type and size up to caiques, which was the general name given to the larger, seagoing vessels. In the Straits themselves there were 'innumerable' boats, caiques and ferries manned by Turkish citizens – and so probably loyal to the Nationalists, at least since the terms of the Treaty of Sèvres became public. He set out a plan for controlling the shipping, but emphasised that surveillance alone would not be enough. If the Nationalists did attempt to cross from Asia to Europe, British warships would have to be sent in, and would have to use force, which was an act of war, and a violation of the agreed armistice.[5] The problem was not confined to the Dardanelles, but included the need to control both the Bosporos and the Sea of Marmara, which increased the difficulties at least tenfold.

Brock suggested further that, in order to be complete, some sort of a blockade of ports of the larger size, and the Mediterranean and Asian coasts that were under Nationalist control should be set up – he mentioned Smyrna, Antalya, and Mersin. The Cabinet rejected this, probably because a blockade was regarded as a weapon of war, and that it would tie up a large number of ships.[6] There was also the issue of the warships the Nationalists had been rumored to have obtained, or were obtaining, from the Soviet Russians in the Black Sea, which included a submarine, possibly – this was all very vague. Finally, on 22 September, Brock set out his intentions regarding the control of transport, but added that it was impossible to clear the shipping from the Golden Horn, and that if the Asian shore (that is, the Ismid peninsula) fell into Nationalist hands, the city of Constantinople would inevitably also fall. Even if the Bosporos was cleared of shipping, more vessels could replace them in a short time, and if it was cleared, then immediate hardship would be caused to the people of the city, and the life of the community would be 'gravely upset'. Anyway, such an operation would take at least several days.[7]

Next day, Brock set it all out in a memorandum addressed to Tyrwhitt, who was his second-in-command and was responsible for the Bosporos area. He gave orders based on the discussions he had had with the Admiralty and the Cabinet. Tyrwhitt's 3rd Destroyer Flotilla, together with the 2nd, which was due to arrive next day, had to do three tasks: first, prevent Turkish soldiers getting into Europe by way of the Black Sea (where sailing ships were ubiquitous); second, control the Bosporos; and third, prevent ferries heading for the Princes' Islands from going on to Marmaran ports, which were under Nationalist control.[8]

Tyrwhitt in fact was occupied with the refugees at Smyrna on the 22nd and 23rd, when these instructions were sent to him. He had also received information from the Italian Admiral Pepe that the Turks were intending to attack Chanak, perhaps on the 23rd. Tyrwhitt noted that the Turkish forces were pulling out from Smyrna, by train, horse and foot, though their destination was not clear, but both were heading 'to the northward'. He transferred the local Smyrnan command to the rear admiral of the 2nd Flotilla and set off for Chanak, where he collected dispatches, and then sailed to Constantinople, to his new command.[9]

The defence of Constantinople depended largely on retaining control of the Ismid peninsula, and it seems that the Turks were unwilling to attempt an attack on the Maltepe Lines, across the eastern root of the peninsula. This had become well organised and developed during the past year. As Tyrwhitt understood from his talk with the Italian admiral, the next pressure point was going to be at Chanak.

This was at the crucial point of the Dardanelles. There were others, at Gallipoli, Lapseki, and so on, but Chanak (now Çanakkale) was at the most awkward passing point for any ships, and was the place from which control of the Strait could be directed. It was at the point called by the Allies the Narrows, where the channel was less than a kilometre wide; its current was correspondingly more powerful than elsewhere. Ships had to turn through 90 degrees at that point, then sail on for a short distance, and then, before reaching Chanak, between Chanak and Kilid Bahr, turn again the opposite way – clearly a process requiring careful and slow navigation. (Today, cruise ships the size of Great War battleships who call at Çanakkale approach very carefully, and warn their passengers in advance that it might be impossible to call there if the currents and winds are too strong or turbulent – the Strait is a wind funnel as well.)

A force in control of Chanak, and preferably Nagara Point further north as well, and positioning artillery of a reasonably heavy type there, could dominate the waterway. If the Dardanelles was thus blocked, an Allied force in the Sea of Marmara and at Constantinople would be isolated. (The navy hardly needed to be told this, after its experience there in 1914–15.) It was also recognised that, without control of the Ismid peninsula, which was very vulnerable to a strong Turkish attack, Constantinople could not be held – and the Allied military force in the city had been substantially reduced. (The Allies could rely on local Turkish militia forces to defend the city against the Greeks in Thrace, but they could hardly be expected to fight the Nationalist Turkish forces if they crossed from the Ismid peninsula.)

So, holding Chanak was vital to enable forces to get up to the Bosporos, Constantinople, and the Black Sea. It is also very surprising that it had not been mentioned in the discussions earlier. Perhaps it was another general assumption, never spelled out. The loss of Chanak would necessarily entail the loss of Constantinople, and the bottling up of any British forces in the Sea of Marmara and the Bosporos. All this had been the lesson of the fighting at Gallipoli; it is amazing that the lesson seems to have been ignored already, though, to be fair, Chanak had been garrisoned by the Allies since 1918.

The task of holding Chanak was primarily a military one, since the attack would obviously come by land; the naval role would be supportive and to use its guns. If the Turks gained control of the fort, their guns could dominate the Strait as they had in 1915. That meant it was the army's task to hold Chanak and its surroundings, though naval assistance would obviously be helpful, and the battleships' big guns had proved very useful in Crimea and at the defence of Ismid. So the navy's task would revert to patrolling the Straits and harassing caiques and ferry boats, and possibly bombardments. The army had a garrison in Chanak and one in Constantinople, with forces also in the Ismid peninsula and the Gallipoli peninsula. But the total available force was less than 8,000 men, so this was spreading the British forces very thinly. Marines and seamen's battalions could be expected as reinforcements from the ships, as well as other forces sent from elsewhere, and artillery support would come from the big ships, but a serious land attack, persistent and repetitive (as in the twenty-two-day Sakarya battle) would eventually win, especially if the ships could be driven away by land-based artillery forces scattered along the Asian coast (as in the Gallipoli campaign in 1915). This was all the condition of affairs at the Dardanelles, which the navy knew all too well.

It was clear that the centres of attention would now be Chanak and the Ismid peninsula. (Bursa had been surrendered to the Nationalists by negotiation between an Allied commission and the Nationalist commander; it had clearly been possible to negotiate with the Turks, which was encouraging; quite possibly, Mustafa Kemal had seen enough of war, and would opt for diplomacy when it proved useful.)[10] The Turks moved up to the Ismid peninsula defences, but it quickly became apparent that their main attention was fixed on Chanak, which was the vital strategic point. Turkish cavalry arrived in the neighbourhood, probably part of that force Tyrwhitt had noted as heading from Smyrna 'to the northward', and the garrison was soon being reinforced.

Chanak's garrison, before the crisis developed, consisted of the 1st Battalion of the Loyal Regiment. Colonel D.I. Shuttleworth was dispatched there as commander of the town and the surrounding area, and set about preparing and improving the defences, vigorous patrolling, and planting British flags along the line of the boundary of the supposedly 'neutral zone' of the Straits, though this neutrality had been self-proclaimed by the Allies, and was not recognised by the Turks.[11] The garrison was actually supposed to supervise two lines. First, the normal meaning of the term was a physical defence system, trenches, barbed wire, and all the apparatus that had been evolved on the Western Front in France. This line was fairly close to the town. The more distant line was the outer boundary of the zone, designed to keep the enemy away from the defence line; this line was too distant to be controlled by the garrison, and there was no indication that the Turks respected its neutrality. Theoretically, the neutral zone boundary was what should keep the Turks out, but in practical terms, the trenches and barbed wire entanglements were the main defence; the zone boundary could be easily crossed even inadvertently, hence Shuttleworth's flags.[12]

As it happened, and probably not by coincidence, Field Marshal Lord Plumer, governor of Malta, came through the Dardanelles on a visit to General Harington, his former chief of staff in France, and now the local commander-in-chief. He stopped off at Chanak, visited Shuttleworth, and sent a message – 'All well here' – to Harington. What exactly he meant is not obvious, but since the garrison was small, and by this time clearly inadequate, he could only be referring to Shuttleworth's capabilities.[13]

Plumer sailed on to Constantinople. While with Harington, they obviously discussed the difficult situation that now existed throughout the Straits. Harington was being harassed by messages from the War Office, one of which suggested that Chanak be evacuated and the defence of the Dardanelles consolidated at Gallipoli, a fatuous suggestion that was guaranteed, if it was implemented, to lead to a rapid defeat. Harington took Plumer into his office and showed him the War Office telegrams. At the end of half an hour's discussion, Plumer wrote out two telegrams of his own, one to the War Office, and the other to the prime minister, in which he expressed his full confidence in Harington and his plans, making clear that criticism from London, from whatever source, was unhelpful and unwelcome.[14] His messages carried much weight, of course, as a peer and a field marshal; they would not be ignored. Then, in his capacity as Maltese governor, he ordered two battalions to be sent from the island as reinforcements. He probably did not have the authority to do this, but the 1st Gordon Highlanders and the 2nd Royal Sussex Regiment did arrive – again, the weight of his authority was sufficient to ride over any problems of mere legality.[15] Harington himself sent a squadron of the 3rd Hussars, a battery of field artillery, and the 2nd Sherwood Foresters to Chanak from Constantinople, gambling that the Nationalist Turks did not have the manpower to make attacks at both Chanak and Constantinople.[16] The cavalry and the field artillery attempted to make the journey by land, but were blocked by a much larger force of Turks and had to go by sea in the end – such are the advantages of sea power.

At the same time, the British naval strength in the Straits was being steadily increased. Ships were sent mainly from Britain. The 2nd Destroyer Flotilla left Devonport on 16 September and arrived at Constantinople on the 25th; the aircraft carrier *Argus* made the same voyage two days later with a flight of seaplanes, and collected more planes at Malta on the way. (The Admiralty was warned that the Maltese air command might foil the plan by 'putting everything into the air at once then saying that they had nothing serviceable'; the ship did collect the allocated aircraft, however, and went on to Chanak, not to Constantinople.)[17] Three battleships were sent, *Revenge* from Devonport to Constantinople, arriving on the 28th; *Malaya* and *Ramillies* were sent from Portland and Sheerness to Chanak, arriving on the 30th. The 3rd Destroyer Flotilla also sailed from Devonport to Chanak, and arrived a day before the battleships. By the end of the month, therefore, Chanak had been substantially reinforced by several battalions of soldiers, and the navy had added an aircraft carrier, three battleships, and eighteen destroyers to those already there. In addition, *Curacoa* was at Smyrna, and *Caledon*, *Carysfort*, and *Ceres*, all light cruisers, were elsewhere in the Straits, usually watching the coast road.[18] It was certainly a formidable assemblage of sea power as well as military force. It will surely have given the Turks pause; they were, after all, now campaigning at the coast, well within reach of the ships' guns. The ships, however, were not just warships, floating gun platforms, but they could, as they had several times recently, contribute skilled infantry, marines, and seamen to the land fighting.

Other ships were also on the way, and arrived in the first week of October, as before, mainly going to Chanak. This included the 1st Destroyer Flotilla (with eight ships), another aircraft carrier (*Ark Royal*), a battalion of Royal Marines, and the navy transport *Elsdon*, with a supply of artillery pieces, 6-inch and 4-inch guns, intended to be mounted at Gallipoli.[19]

More infantry was gathered from around the Mediterranean. From Egypt (despite a recent uprising in the Delta, now suppressed, and a great political crisis) came the 1st King's Own Scottish Borderers, the 2nd Highland Light Infantry, and some batteries of medium and field artillery. This meant that, the size of the force having expanded, it required a higher ranked commander than Colonel Shuttleworth: Major General T.O. Marden was appointed. Two Guards' battalions, 2nd Grenadiers and 3rd Coldstreams, joined the Irish Guards who were already Constantinople to form a Guards Brigade. From Gibraltar came the 1st Duke of Wellington's and the 1st South Staffordshires. The several battalions were now grouped into three more brigades, one in the Ismid peninsula at Haidar Pasha, beside Scutari, and two at Chanak; the Guards reinforced the garrison at Constantinople. The RAF had now gathered seventy aircraft and two aircraft carriers. And, of course, the navy was steadily increased during the first two weeks of October.[20]

The Turks meanwhile had also been gathering their forces. Shuttleworth sent the 3rd Hussars under Captain Petherwick, who took the 3rd Hussars and a detachment of the Loyals out on a mounted patrol to deter the 'enemy' from approaching too closely. They went as far as Ezine, 40 kilometres from Chanak on the direct road from Smyrna.[21] It was obvious that the Turks would arrive from that direction, if they were coming. The Turkish forces may have outnumbered the Greeks in the campaign in Asia Minor, though not by much, and had won a famous victory and conquered the city of Smyrna, but they were still often less than well trained, and they were facing very well-trained and experienced British professional soldiers, men who, in most cases, had survived the fighting on various fronts in the Great War. The infantry were well positioned in prepared defences, in the approved Western Front style of triple trench lines, and were well backed up by naval artillery. By the end of September also, General Marden had a reasonable reserve, and his forces were being reinforced by land and sea almost every day from 21 September onwards.

However, the defence of Chanak and that of the Ismid peninsula were dealt a blow on the 19th when the French and Italian contingents in the defence forces were ordered to withdraw. Both commanding generals, Charpy and Mombelli, had joined in the defence force that manned the Chatalja Lines against the Greeks when they had menaced Constantinople, and had almost automatically responded when the Turks menaced the city from the other direction, and also at Chanak. But their governments balked at the possibility of finding their forces fighting the Turks, even in defence, and even where they were acting as an international force. But both governments had made formal and informal agreements with Mustafa Kemal's regime elsewhere, the French in Syria, the Italians at Antalya (and both were supplying weapons to the Nationalists). The two governments decided that the defence of the neutral Zone of the Straits – which is what was at stake in formal terms – was not their responsibility. Their troops were pulled out, with profuse apologies by the generals in command to Marden and Harington. Their contingents reverted to being the garrison at Constantinople, which would face them with still another dilemma if the Turks attacked the city.[22]

The confrontation of the Turkish cavalry and the Hussar detachment at Ezine on 23 September was, at least in retrospect, a decisive moment. Captain Petherwick had only thirty Hussars with him, and they faced several hundred Turks, growing to a force of an estimated thousand soon after. Petherwick feared to become surrounded and pulled back to a strong position above a stream, which ran in a steep valley; the only bridge had been destroyed, and the crossing was extremely difficult; this strong position, as much as the political responsibility involved for the Turkish commander in attacking the British force, stopped the Turks. In fact, had the Turks had orders to attack, Petherwick's force could have been pushed aside with relative ease and the Turks would have been able to push on to the base at Chanak, defended by only a battalion at that point. But they did not charge, and the commanders, both Petherwick and Shuttleworth, when he arrived, concluded that no order to attack had been given to the Turks, and that the Turkish commander was waiting for new orders from his superiors. It was also encouraging to see that the Turkish forces, composed in large part of the irregulars, were under clear control.

Shuttleworth was evacuating the civilians from the town, both those whose home it was and the many who had been driven in as refugees from the interior as the Turkish cavalry approached – the usual Christians, Greeks and Armenians, but also some Turks. They were moved out as quickly as possible, across the Strait to Gallipoli and its peninsula. The navy was set to constructing jetties to allow them to be embarked more easily, and marines and seamen's battalions were landed along the same jetties. By the 24th, Shuttleworth had five battalions in his command, quite sufficient to put up a serious and prolonged defence, if necessary. His successor, General Marden, had even more men, and had permission to fire if he felt it necessary for his troops' survival. And more ships, and more troops and more aircraft, were constantly arriving. Marden felt strong enough to send the town's *mutasarrif*, or mayor, to the Turkish commander (whom Shuttleworth himself knew and liked). The *mutasarrif* was known to be a Kemalist – Shuttleworth never names him, referring him to him only as the 'Kemalist *mutasarrif*'; he had had plenty of time to see how well the British were ensconced, a point he was expected to make to the Turkish commander. He stayed there for several days, then returned to the town.[23] It may be significant that, although it was estimated that by then the Turks had about 17,000 men before the town, little more than gestures of aggression were being made; of course, the British forces were soon approaching that number as well. When the *Ark Royal* arrived on the 26th, the Chanak force had available a mixed force of seventy aircraft, fighters, bombers, and reconnaissance craft, clearly outnumbering those with the Turks, which were estimated at fifty.

One wonders if Shuttleworth was a classicist, for it was in camp in the Troad, of which Chanak was a part, that the Persian Great King Xerxes, twenty-four centuries earlier, captured a Greek spy, and instead of executing him on the spot as expected, showed him round the Persian armed camp, and then let him go with his awe-inspiring, blood-chilling information of the huge size of the Persian host. The mission of the *mutasarrif* was clearly of the same sort, for it could be guaranteed that he would know and describe the strength of the British forces at Chanak.

At the Ismid confrontation, in the north, however, where there was relatively little activity – the Turks could hardly fight on more than one front at a time, and Chanak, sensibly, was clearly estimated as the most important. An enquiry from the Chief of Naval Staff at the Admiralty about the possible uses of the navy in dominating the roads along the coast from Ismid to Scutari provoked a reply that would discourage any optimism, particularly after the withdrawal of the French and Italian contingents.[24]

Rear Admiral Richard Webb, in command of the 4th Battle Squadron, loaned from the Atlantic Fleet, and positioned in the north facing the Ismid peninsula, had pointed out that the roads along the peninsula and even that along the centre, were within range of his naval guns, both those on the north and south coasts and the single road inland. But Brock answered the Admiralty enquiry by pointing out that the French and Italian withdrawal meant that the defence line which had been already organised, the Maltepe–Dudulu line, could no longer be held, since there were not enough British soldiers available in the area to man it. As a result, the peninsula was relatively open to attack, whenever the Turks should choose to move in. In that case, Constantinople, which had been infiltrated already by plenty of Turks, including some who were soldiers, would have to be abandoned, and the defence concentrated at Gallipoli.[25] He was envisaging an advance by Turkish troops from Ismid to Scutari combined with an uprising in the city, and the two Turkish forces connected by the innumerable ships in the Bosporos. But he was also conscious that the Turks could not risk another public massacre at Ismid, such as had occurred at Smyrna, still less one in Constantinople; yet any naval attack by ships without obvious excuse would produce anti-Christian reprisals, or compel the Turks to attack in self-defence. Both sides in the north were being compelled to hold their hands.

Meanwhile, one result of the defeat of the Greek army in Asia Minor was a plot among senior officers in the army camp at Lesbos. It was aimed at the overthrow of King Constantine, who was held partly responsible for the defeat because of his meddling with the army command. Two army colonels, and the captain of the battleship *Lemnos*, issued a proclamation, and scattered pamphlet copies of it over Athens from an aircraft.[26] Within days, by 27 September, Constantine had abdicated in favour his son Prince George, who himself lasted less than a year; he was dominated by the military junta of the conspirators, and was then succeeded by a republic. In the midst of this Greek crisis, Brock and the high commissioner at Constantinople, Sir Horace Rumbold, issued orders to prevent Greek ships carrying troops from entering through the Dardanelles.[27] It remained possible that the Greek government, whoever was comprised in it, would cling on in Thrace and make another move for Constantinople, in order to legitimise their position with the Greek population by a victory of sorts. Almost all the Greek warships had already left through the Dardanelles. Greece had no support from any of its former friends.

In Britain, the advance of the Turkish Nationalist forces to the Straits had occasioned one message from the British government, on 11 September, to Mustafa Kemal to warn him to, in effect, keep clear, and respect the boundaries of the neutral zone, whose delineation made the matter clear on the ground. A fortnight later, on 29 September, another, more forceful, message, which could only be interpreted as an ultimatum, was to be delivered by High Commissioner Rumbold and the commander-in-chief, General Harington. By this time, the Turkish forces had already breached the neutral zone boundaries in more than one place, especially near Chanak, and it looked as though an attack would be made on the Chanak defences, which would certainly be an act of war and, given the official existence of the armistice, might well have much wider repercussions amid Britain's European allies. Between these two messages, after a long Cabinet discussion on 15 September, the Great Powers were informed of Britain's determination to hold on to Chanak, and appeals went to the dominions asking for their help if new hostilities with Turkey broke out.[28]

The French and Italians, however, were still hostile to the British in this point; the United States had largely withdrawn from involvement and were deeply involved in a new presidential election, due early in November, while President Wilson had been incapacitated after a stroke. Of the dominions, only New Zealand offered troops, a brigade (which would take a couple months to be mustered and get to the scene of events), while Canada insisted that its parliament must be consulted before the government committed troops (quite possibly a pointed dig at the British government, which did not apparently intend to consult its own parliament). Australia was undecided and similarly delayed a decision, and General Smuts in South Africa used his travels on an inspection tour to avoid answering at all. Newfoundland gave moral support, but did not promise any troops. Britain, to the government's dismay, had no worthwhile support internationally or imperially, though Lloyd George probably thought he could get Greek support.[29]

Mustafa Kemal was now, after the overthrow of King Constantine, afraid that Britain and Greece would revive that anti-Turkish alliance. It was in response to this that he pushed his troops at Chanak to move into the neutral zone, probably positioning his forces for a quick assault on Chanak that would free them to face a Greek attack, which would almost certainly be directed at Constantinople. This initial disruption of the British position on 29 September was reported to General Harington and Sir Horace Rumbold. They decided that the message for Mustafa Kemal – the 'almost ultimatum', which had been forwarded from London – was now too inflammatory to be delivered. In addition, they decided that the Turkish encirclement was not to be resisted, though the defence lines were manned and ready, and Marden was told this.[30] The neutral zone had, in effect, been abandoned, and the earlier London message was thus ignored.

This was the moment, therefore, when the men on the spot seized the initiative. Harington had a means of communicating directly with the Turkish government through the French General Franklin-Bouillon, who was already trying to persuade Mustafa Kemal to agree to talk. On 1 October, a Turkish agreement to hold talks was signified, to be held at Mudania. It was to be between the two commanders-in-chief of the Turkish and British forces, Ismet Pasha and General Harington. Harington's failure to deliver the ultimatum sent by Lloyd George, which would undoubtedly have torpedoed the talks, was a crucial non-move in the contest.

Harington attended the talks with his colleagues in their Committee of Generals, Charpy and Mombelli (who had refused to support the British position). Ismet attended with his own staff, and a Greek general was figuratively present, sitting in a Greek destroyer nearby.

Harington described the talks in his autobiography published in 1940, on his death.[31] They met in a scruffy room – an 'awful room', he called it – and negotiated there for ten days. He kept the British government informed by telegraph, and Ismet was in repeated contact with Mustafa Kemal at Ankara. Both of the government leaders were obdurate, and there were, according to Harington, still twenty-eight points of difference between the two sides after a week of talks.

In London, Harington was being heavily criticised by Lloyd George and his supporters in the Cabinet, who wanted to issue a stinging rebuke, which would have almost certainly forced the general's resignation and brought an end to the talks, and so probably leading to fighting. Lord Curzon, the foreign secretary, refused to deliver the message, and then walked out of the Cabinet meeting; the prime ministerial rebuke was another message that was never delivered in this crisis. However, two further messages reached Harington as he was going into what he had decided must be the final meeting on 10 October. One was from General Marden at Chanak, who reported that he did not think he could hold out much longer and asked for permission to fire on the Turks, who were moving ever closer to his defences; Harington replied by giving him permission after a certain time. The other message was from London, and he did not look at it, but stuck both messages into his pocket. He had had enough of instructions from London, and yet he could certainly produce them if necessary. He was now at the end of his own resources for negotiation, and was despondent about the possible results. At Chanak, the Turks had moved right up to the British wire and looked ever more threatening.

Harington had been in Constantinople overnight, reporting to London as usual. In the morning of the 10 October, he travelled back to Mudania in the *Iron Duke*. He had sent Marden his permission to fire, and he had arranged with Admiral Brock about the control of the Straits – he was to clear the Bosporos within twenty-four hours and begin clearing the Straits of vessels, reconnoitre Ismid, and on the expiry of the ultimatum, which Harington would have to deliver, begin bombing the Turkish troops in Ismid and on the roads.

When he arrived at the jetty at Mudania, therefore, he was prepared to end the talks with his pocketed ultimatum after one more talking session. But he was met by Generals Charpy and Mombelli, who had stayed on during the night while Harington went across to Constantinople to report to London. They must have had long and serious discussions with Ismet Pasha, and they said they could see the possibility of agreement, so Harington went into the meeting in a more positive mood.

It turned out that concessions were possible from both sides in the talks, and the twenty-eight points of difference that had recently blocked progress were steadily reduced to just six. Two of these, as Harington said, were such that they could quite easily, and more appropriately, be referred to the peace conference, which was about to be set up; two more were conceded by Ismet ('won' in Harington's words) and then there were just two. These were the areas to be held by the British around Chanak during the ceasefire that would exist during the peace talks, and the number of Turkish gendarmes to be permitted in Constantinople. The two men marched up and down in that 'awful room' until Ismet suddenly said '*J'accepte*' on the issue of the territory to be held by the British troops at Chanak. Ismet accepted the British position, a rather larger area than he himself had been arguing for; he probably realised that Turkey would get all of the territory in the end, since British troops would not stay after the peace was signed. For the number of gendarmes in the city, the final point, this was settled by a short bargaining session and a handshake – the British wanted 7,500, Ismet argued for 9,000, Ismet accepted 7,500, and Harington added in an extra 500. General Harington remarked that neither side expected the number to be adhered to, so the actual number agreed was irrelevant, and it was clearly not worth a war.

How accurate Harington was in his recollection of his negotiations is not clear. He was writing almost twenty years after the events, and writing in self-justification as an old man; it may well be that he heightened the tension and exaggerated his own participation. It would be helpful to have an independent view of the events; nevertheless, it has to be accepted that before this session of talks any agreement looked very distant, and after it the tension distinctly relaxed; everyone could get on with negotiating a peace treaty. Harington certainly deserves credit for a successful negotiation, and for his defiance of the belligerent British prime minister.

General Marden received a stand-down message from Harington an hour and a quarter before he would have had to open fire. Harington was clearly afraid that the principals in London and Ankara would have second thoughts and start insisting on reopening the argument on minor details, just to exert their authority – a new version of the decision at the negotiation of the Turkish armistice, where the British kept the French out of the talks. He therefore insisted on the agreement being translated into several languages and then immediately signed, a process that took all night; and only then, when it was checked and signed, was it transmitted to London and Ankara. The Greeks refused to sign until instructed by their government to do so, several days later, but by the end of the night of 10/11 October, the rest had signed; by this time, no one had any time for the Greeks.[32]

The word of his success in the negotiations had clearly spread quickly, and Harington was cheered by the sailors on the ships in the harbour when he returned to Constantinople, and was greeted there with a twenty-one gun salute, clearly well deserved.

The main terms were that hostilities between Greeks and Turks should cease, and the Greeks must pull out of Eastern (Turkish) Thrace, though they would keep control of Western Thrace, originally the Bulgarian section. They would be replaced by the 8,000 (approximately) Turkish gendarmes, but no Turkish soldiers were to go into that area until the peace treaty was signed. The perimeter at Chanak would be stretched to 15 kilometres from the town, and in the Ismid peninsula it would be 40 kilometres from Scutari east along the peninsula. The Turks could not cross these lines, nor would the Allies erect any more fortifications. Allied forces would continue to occupy Constantinople and the Gallipoli peninsula until a peace agreement went into effect.

The Convention of Mudania, as it was called, went into force on 14 October, after the Greeks had signed. The navy reacted by lifting restrictions on shipping visiting Nationalist ports, and allowed Greek destroyers to pass through the Dardanelles once more.[33] On the 15th, with the agreement having been implemented, and the Turks having withdrawn to the stated distances at Chanak and Ismid, Admiral Brock set about redistributing his enormous fleet. The 'Ismid force' was to be broken up, patrolling of the Marmara and the Black Sea was ended, and the 'Dardanelles force' was reduced, but it was to be available to be reassembled for the present.[34] (So much, incidentally for the passage through the Straits and the Black Sea being a 'cardinal British interest'.)

The final results of the fighting since the Turkish advance had begun in August were disastrous for the defeated Greeks. The primary result was the conquest of western Asia Minor by the revivified Turkish army; this was generally hostile to the old sultanate regime, and was under a government that was clearly prepared to make agreements to reduce the number of its enemies. Mustafa Kemal's willingness to treat with his enemies individually – Russia, France, Italy – without giving much away, so that he had progressively isolated Britain, while inflicting a devastating military defeat on the Greeks, was a masterly military and diplomatic performance. Second was the removal of the oppressive Greek government, whether royalist or Venizelist. This so weakened Greece that it was compelled to make peace, in which it had gained some territory in Thrace and the Aegean islands, if not in the Asian mainland. The third result was the prospect of a final peace conference, between Turkey and the Great Powers, undistracted by other countries' problems, and in which Turkey would be in a very strong position. And, more distantly from the scene of the fighting, at least geographically, just as defeat removed the Turkish sultanate regime, and the Greek royal regime, so it did the same for the British wartime political coalition.

Lloyd George had finally annoyed too many of his colleagues, and now found himself without political support in his campaign to revive the war against the Turks. (This was, in a way, suitable, for his own political isolation mirrored that of Britain as a whole in this crisis.) In the process, he had angered both the Conservative Party and the imperial dominions, and had united the first against him and divided the second. Moreover, it became clear that the larger part of the Conservatives were not simply annoyed, but were withholding their support, beginning with Andrew Bonar Law, the deputy prime minister and leader of the Conservative Party. At a meeting of the Conservative MPs on 22 October at the Carlton Club in London, Law spoke in favour of withdrawing from the coalition government, and was supported by the meeting; the message went to Lloyd George, who had no alternative but to resign office at once. Next day, Bonar Law became prime minister. The Turkish victory had claimed another victim.[35]

Chapter 13

A Final Evacuation

Admiral Brock was so confident that Harington's Mudania agreement would hold that he re-embarked the sailors who had been landed for the emergency at Chanak and Gallipoli, and sent several of his ships to Malta for overdue docking and maintenance. But in the Straits, he still held two battle squadrons, two light cruiser squadrons, five destroyer flotillas, a submarine flotilla, and a few other ships. Dismissing four ships, therefore, was hardly a decisive reduction in his naval power, even if it was a useful display of confidence. Perhaps even more significantly, he reinstated leave arrangements, and proposed to go himself to Malta for a 'change'.[1]

Then a few days later, the admiral, presumably having thought through the implications of the Mudania Convention more thoroughly, sent a pessimistic report to the Admiralty. He did not believe that the Nationalists would respect the Mudania Convention, and detailed the potential problems that would result at Constantinople and the Ismid peninsula. This, of course, was normal procedure, to argue for the worst-case result. He then suggested, very much in a different vein, that as a '*beau geste*', as he put it, the British might evacuate Constantinople on the first day of the coming peace conference. The Admiralty was somewhat nonplussed to receive this, and wondered if it should be passed on to the Foreign Office; Admiral Beatty described it as 'not helpful'. The Foreign Office received a copy nevertheless, but did not agree with the notion; no diplomat would.[2]

Meanwhile, the Admiralty was considering a new redistribution of its ships, assuming that it would soon be free of the need to hold so many ships at the Straits. Its major concerns now came from two sources: the first was the possibility of a war with Japan (which had been cast loose by the ending of the Anglo-Japanese alliance, a result of the Washington Naval Agreement), and the second was the presumed need to combat the view that the Mediterranean was becoming a 'Franco-Italian lake', navally speaking. Calculations of the naval strength of all three countries were made, but it may be noted that the United States' navy was not considered. The Admiralty was already planning for future wars, but then that was its job.[3]

These considerations provoked a detailed exploration of the possibilities and the need for preparation. For all the constant reiteration that access to the Straits, and hence to the Black Sea, were vital British interests, more than once stated, or claimed, during the various Black Sea and Straits crises with Russia and Turkey, it is noticeable that the Straits are not mentioned once in this discussion of redistribution and the possibilities of future wars. The mantra that access was an essential for Britain had been dropped. It would seem that well in advance of the reconvening of the peace conference, about to assemble at Lausanne to make a new peace treaty with Turkey, the Admiralty at least had decided that the Straits and access to the Black Sea was no longer a cardinal requirement for Britain.

It was understood, however, that the existence of the new, or revived, peace conference required the great gathering of ships in the Straits to be continued while the conference was on, and that a garrison in Constantinople was necessary (just as the Turks maintained a considerable armed force close by the Straits area). The Mudania Convention had thus put the situation into a freeze. The new conference began late in November, and by mid-December, the prospect of an agreement was regarded as 'hopeful', in the Admiralty. Meanwhile, with little say in the proceedings, the navy indulged in exercises, and attended to details such as the evacuation of part of the Greek royal family after King Constantine had abdicated and moved into exile. They were collected from Phaleron Bay by HMS *Calypso* and taken to Corfu, where four royal princesses and a 'baby prince' – Prince Philip, later Duke of Edinburgh – were collected and all taken on to Italy.[4] It rather put these various events into a chronological perspective to realise that this man – Prince Philip – lived on until 2021, only three years before this book was published.

General Harington had already arranged to rescue Sultan Mehmed VI, whose attendants had almost universally turned against him in the palace as the fortunes of the Nationalists rose. By an elaborate operation, conducted by Harington with much enjoyment, the sultan was taken from his palace and onto the battleship *Malaya*, to be exiled at first at Malta, then into Italy.[5] He was succeeded by his cousin Abdul Majid II, who was caliph only, since the sultanate had been abolished by the Ankara government. The authority of the Ankara regime, therefore, was clearly being obeyed in Constantinople, even in 1922, even by the non-sultan, and with the Allied occupation still in position.

In the five years covered by this account, therefore, the Royal Navy had rescued and taken into exile three imperial families (Russia, Austria-Hungary, Ottoman), and a selection of Greek royalty. (King George V had intervened with the Admiralty on behalf of the Russians and the Greeks; the others had been rescued on naval initiative.)

The conference at Lausanne, which involved collecting together delegates from many countries, was slow to start, and lengthy when it got going, even leisurely; it was, that is, no longer seen as an urgent matter. It was accompanied by the usual arguments and side deals, walkouts and disputes, tantrums and rows, as well as the continued naval activity in Turkish waters. In February 1923, a Turkish attempt to exclude warships over 1,000 tons from Smyrna, presumably fearing that the conference would adjudge the city for Greece, produced a crisis, in which the warships of five nations deliberately entered the harbour in defiance of the Turkish ultimatum – Britain, France, Italy, the United States, and Holland.[6] Two of these navies had been neutral in the Turkish part of the Great War.

It was never altogether clear what exactly the Turks wanted in this minor crisis, other than to make a stand over their claim to sovereignty in Smyrna. This, of course, had been ceded to Greece by the Treaty of Sèvres, which was now in effect being revised at Lausanne, and no doubt the Turks wanted to make it absolutely plain that they possessed the city and were determined to keep it, no matter what the conference decided – this seemed to be the lesson of that little crisis of access. As such crises tended to do, the tension gradually faded, as attention shifted elsewhere. A further crisis between the Greeks and the Turks over their mutual boundary in Thrace blew up in May, provoking the development of a plan for action by the navy, which in the event did not need to be activated.

There were walkouts at the conference – by Lord Curzon in a self-consciously dramatic way – and interruptions – notably by the Turks, who left the conference on 4 February, and stayed away for two months. It is presumably no coincidence that the dispute at Smyrna began only two days after this walkout, as a Turkish assertion of their position at the city. But they returned to the talks when the Greek army, somewhat revived, was built up in western Thrace and threatened to move into eastern Thrace again and make for Constantinople; the Turks had been allowed their 8,000 gendarmes in western Thrace by the Mudania agreement, but it was reckoned that there were now 20,000 armed and organised Turks in that area, the extras having been recruited locally, and perhaps there were the same number of soldiers who had infiltrated into the city.[7] On the other hand, if fighting broke out, the Greeks might fight very hard to gain revenge for their previous defeat, and they had to face gendarmes, not a fully organised army, and they would have the advantage in heavier weapons. If they succeeded in taking eastern Thrace and the city, it was unlikely that the Turks would ever regain those territories; but it would certainly destroy the peace conference. Even after the Turks returned to the talks, which they did partly to defuse the pretensions of the Greeks in Thrace, three more months passed before an agreed text was produced and signed.[8] The continued existence of the Turkish armistice would have meant that the Allies were theoretically bound to join in, on the side of the Turks – not a comfortable prospect.

The terms of peace were, after all the fuss, generally straightforward, if at times ingeniously crafted to deal with awkward points. The Turkish boundaries were mainly agreed – except with the British mandate of Iraq, where Mosul remained in dispute between Britain and Turkey (and France) for several more years; Armenia and the Kurds were sacrificed – the former had in fact become a small Soviet republic, the latter were divided between three states. An exchange of populations was decided: Turkish Greeks were to go to Greece (there were not many of them left), and Turks in Greece to Turkey (a much larger number) – except in eastern Thrace and Constantinople, where Greeks were permitted to continue – a factor which has caused repeated problems over the succeeding century. Supervision of the passage of the Straits was assigned to Turkey, reasonably enough since it now governed both shores along their whole length. This involved an international agreement that was, in effect, a separate treaty; it governed who had the right to pass through, and gave Turkey the right to supervise and control the traffic, particularly the passage of warships.

As is usual, the provisions of the whole treaty have either continued in place, where they were of little importance, or have been altered piece by piece over the years – the Straits Agreement, for example, was reworked into the Montreux Convention of 1936, and the Mosul agreement was settled by Turkey's acceptance that Iraq should hold the territory – though Turkey has continued to harbour ambitions to re-expand into the territories beyond its southern frontier ever since (and has succeeded in parts along the Syrian border).

The Treaty of Lausanne was ratified late in August 1923, and the British presence in the Straits, its ports and cities, became redundant. With plenty of time to prepare for departure, the Turks could be in no doubt that the evacuation – yet another evacuation, to add to those of the Russians, the Greeks, the Turks, and others – would go ahead. The British, as ever, made a military ceremony out of it, with a parade in front of the Dolmabahçe Palace on 2 October. Most of the navy's ships had left by that time. Admiral Brock retained two squadrons, each of one battleship, a light cruiser, and a flotilla of destroyers, at Constantinople and at Chanak until the army had left. The ships stayed on in the interval between the treaty's signature and the evacuation, and they then collected the garrisons.[9]

This ended what must be considered one of the most extraordinary episodes in British naval, military, and imperial history. Only in the aftermath of such a conflict as the Great War, as a result of which every polity between the Rhine and the Pacific had fallen into dissolution, could small groups of British troops, each little more than a couple of battalions strong at the most, have had such effects as in Central Asia and the Caspian Sea. But the entrance of the British fleet into the Black Sea is unique in British maritime history (with the exception of the Crimean War). It is all a clear signal that Britain, as a result of the victory gained in the Great War, was for a brief moment the single world superpower; but note that such an exalted position was held only briefly and temporarily, and without any permanent result, other than an extension of the military and economic exhaustion of Britain – and, of course, the eventual evaporation of its empire. There were occasional ambitions visible in British imperial circles to acquire still more colonies, as in the African and Middle Eastern mandates, and even, ambitiously and only fleetingly, as protectorates over the Central Asian khanates.

But the British interventions simply delayed the inevitable. The Russian Empire was reconstituted as Soviet Russia, and the new Turkish state came into existence without serious British hindrance or involvement, and despite French and Italian ambitions. The Ottoman Empire shed its Arab appendages and emerged vigorous, as the Turkish Republic, from the Greek challenge in Asia Minor, which had, to be sure, been encouraged by some of the British, for a time. The limits of British imperial power were already visible in these adventures, their results, and the British withdrawal from all these areas. Characteristically, it was the navy that was the first to penetrate through the Straits into the Black Sea, and the last to pull out from the central point of all this activity, the city of Constantinople.

This peace treaty, of Lausanne, ended the Great War in the Near East. The aftermath of the fighting had lasted as long as the fighting itself, four and a half years. It had caused about 500,000 people to be driven from their homes, mainly Greeks and Russians, but almost every other nationality in the area had suffered as well; also, fatal casualties amongst Asiatic Greeks, Turks, Russians, Caucasians, Central Asians, and others had been perhaps as many. It had been a remarkably difficult route to re-establishing peace.

The city of Constantinople was another casualty of the Great War, or rather of the subsequent armistice. It suffered a huge influx of poverty-stricken refugees, which enhanced its already heavily cosmopolitan population, at least for a time. It also suffered the indignity of a foreign military occupation, for the first time since the Ottoman conquest in 1453. It was an experience that left the population stunned for a time. Then further indignities followed. It was demoted from its status as the capital city of the Turkish state, in favour of its bleak country cousin, Ankara. Then it was compelled to abandon its traditional (Christian/Roman) name, and become Istanbul. For all these changes it is obvious that the Allies' victory in the war and the, mainly British, occupation of the city was to blame. The withdrawal of the Allied forces late in 1923 was the beginning of Istanbul's new life.

Notes

Introduction

1. It may be pointed out that the Ottoman Empire was the only enemy state that saw its capital city occupied by enemy forces – this did not happen with Berlin, Vienna, Budapest, or even Sofia. The Turkish reaction to this suggests that Allied restraint over other capital cities – if that is what it was – was sensible.

Chapter 1: *Shark* as Bait

1. Paul G. Halpern, *A Naval History of World War I*, London, 1994.
2. ADM 53/59982 – 83, logs of *Shark*, June to October 1918; I discussed this voyage in my *13 Sharks*, Barnsley, 2016, where it is 'Shark XI'.
3. J.D. Grainger, *The Forty Sieges of Constantinople*, Barnsley, 2022; it is worth noting that the Ottoman Empire had been at war continuously since 1911, and the Allied siege of Constantinople was the second in that period, the first by the Bulgarians (now recent Ottoman allies).
4. Ibid.
5. For a brief view of the city during the war, see Charles King, *Midnight at the Pera Palace: The Birth of Modern Istanbul*, New York, 2014, Chs. 2 and 3.
6. TNA, ADM 53/59984, log of *Shark*, November–December 1918.
7. Accounts of the navy in the Black Sea, sometimes with references to associated events, are in Stephen Roskill, *Naval Policy Between the Wars*, vol. 1, London, 1968, and Paul G. Halpern, *The Mediterranean Fleet, 1919–1929*, Navy Records Society, 2011.
8. The best account of the Black Sea war are in Halpern, *Naval History*, Ch. 8, and Arthur J. Marder, *From the Dreadnought to Scapa Flow*, 5 vols., Annapolis, MD, 1961–1970.
9. Donald W. Mitchell, *A History of Russian and Soviet Sea Power*, London, 1974, Ch. 16.
10. Mungo Melvin, *Sevastopol's Wars: The Crimea from Potemkin to Putin*, Oxford, 2017, pp. 368–72.
11. Mitchell, *Russian and Soviet Sea Power*, pp. 344–7; Melvin, *Sevastopol's Wars*, pp. 372–85.

Chapter 2: Armistice – and Control of the City

1. David Fromkin, *A Peace to end all Peace: Creating the Modern Middle East, 1914–1922*, London, 1989, pp. 360–4.
2. J.D. Grainger, *The Battle for Syria, 1918–1920*, Woodbridge, 2013.
3. Ibid.
4. Paul G. Halpern, *The Royal Navy in the Mediterranean 1915–1918*, Navy Records Society, 1987, doc. 262, Captain George Chetwode to Admiral Kelly, 20 October 1918.
5. Ibid., docs. 265 and 266, exchange of letters between George Clemenceau and David Lloyd George.
6. Ibid., 260, Admiralty memorandum on naval strength.
7. Ibid., list on p. 572.

8. Ibid., docs. 258, 260–266.
9. Ibid., docs. 266–269.
10. Ibid., doc. 267, Calthorpe to Admiralty, 38 October; Roger Ford, *Eden to Armageddon, World War I in the Middle East*, London, 2009, pp. 385–97 has a good account from the Turkish point of view (though he calls Amet 'Aget').
11. Margaret MacMillan, *Peacemakers*, London, 2001, pp. 378–9.
12. The terms are printed in Sir James Edmonds, *The Occupation of Constantinople*, part of the *Official History of the War* but not completed; the various parts that had been gathered by Edmonds were transcribed by Neil Wells, and published by the Naval and Military Press, Uckfield, 2010; the terms are noted on pages 1 and 2 and appendix 1, pp. 36–8.
13. C.C.R. Murphy, *Soldiers of the Prophet*, London, 1920 (reprinted 2010); part of this is about Murphy's travels; the last chapter, 'Constantinople in 1918', concerns the city and the armistice.
14. Andrew Mango, *Ataturk*, London 1999, p. 195.
15. Edmonds, *Occupation*, pp. 3–5.
16. This is clear from Edmonds, *Occupation*.
17. King, *Pera Palace*, p. 41.
18. Ibid., Mango, *Ataturk*, pp. 195–6.
19. King, *Pera Palace*, pp. 37–42.
20. Edmonds, *Occupation*, pp. 6–8.
21. Ibid., p. 9.
22. Edmonds, *Occupation*, pp. 6–8.

Chapter 3: The Central Asian Railway

1. F.M. Bailey, *Mission to Tashkent*, 2nd edn., Oxford, 1992.
2. Described in detail by Peter Hopkirk, *On Secret Service East of Constantinople: The Plot to bring down the British Empire*, Oxford, 1995; Colonel Murphy, in *Soldiers of the Prophet*, describes his own travels through the area before and during the war.
3. F.J. Moberly, *Operations in Persia 1914–1919* (Official History of the Great War), London, 1987, pp. 320–1, 333–5.
4. C.H. Ellis, *The TransCaspian Episode*, London, 1963, Ch. 1; Moberly, *Operations in Persia*, pp. 347–9; Geoffrey Wheeler, *The Modern History of Soviet Central Asia*, London, 1964, Ch. 6.
5. Moberly, *Operations in Persia*, pp. 334–5, 349.
6. Lord Curzon, in his younger days, had been one of the first Westerners to travel this railway; see 'superior person' in Fitzroy Maclean, *A Person from England and Other Travellers*, London, 1956, republished 1984, pp. 283–306.
7. Malleson's new instructions: Moberly, *Operations in Persia*, p. 357; Ellis, *TransCaspian*, pp. 26–8.
8. Ellis, *TransCaspian*, pp. 58–65, with British and Russian references.
9. Moberly, *Operations in Persia*, pp. 371–3.
10. Ibid., Ellis, *TransCaspian*, pp. 66–70.
11. Ellis, *TransCaspian*, p. 78.
12. Moberly, *Operations in Persia*, pp. 394–6; Ellis, *TransCaspian*, pp. 78–9.
13. Ellis, *TransCaspian*, p. 80.
14. Ibid., Moberly, *Operations in Persia*, p. 298.
15. Moberly, *Operations in Persia*, pp. 419, 423–4.

16. Ellis, *TransCaspian*, pp. 131–2; Moberly, *Operations in Persia*, pp. 424–44.
17. Moberly, *Operations in Persia*, pp. 403–407.
18. Ibid., pp. 444–6.
19. Ibid., pp. 447–8.
20. Ellis, *TransCaspian*, pp. 152–3.
21. Ibid., pp. 154–5; Moberly, *Operations in Persia*, p. 430.
22. Ellis, *TransCaspian*, pp. 158–9.

Chapter 4: The Oil of Baku

1. Daniel Yergin, *The Prize, the Epic Quest for Oil, Money & Power*, London, 1991, pp. 57–63, 132–3.
2. Ibid., pp. 129–31.
3. It had been part of a Transcaucasian Federation (or 'Commissariat') for a time, composed of Georgia, Armenia and Azerbaijan, but this had collapsed from internal tensions in May 1918; see Firuz Kazemzadeh, *The Struggle for Transcaucasia, 1917–1921*, New York, 1951 (reprinted 2023), Ch. 7.
4. Ibid., pp. 179–82.
5. The main sources for these events include L.C. Dunsterville, *The Adventures of Dunsterforce*, London, 1920; M.H. Donohoe, *With the Persian Expedition*, London, 1920; Moberly, *Operations in Persia*; Ronald P. Minez, *At the Limit of Complexity: British Military Operations in North Persia and the Caucasus*, ed. Elizabeth J. Brown (n.d.).
6. Donohoe, *Persian Expedition*, p. 2.
7. F.M. Bailey, *Mission to Tashkent*, Oxford, 1992.
8. In 1989–91, with the break-up of the Soviet Russian state, this ambition revived in Turkey with talk of Kazakhstan becoming united with Turkey; it did not happen, but that it was discussed was noticeable.
9. Peter Hopkirk, *Setting the East Ablaze: Lenin's Dream of an Empire in Asia*, London, 1984, Ch. 11 describes 'The Last Stand of Enver Pasha'; he put his life where his beliefs were, and died fighting for his version of a new Turkish Empire.
10. Dunsterville, *Dunsterforce*, p. 4; Donohoe, *Persian Expedition*, pp. 61–2; Moberly, *Operations in Persia*, pp. 270–1, for example.
11. Donohoe, *Persian Expedition*, pp. 70–2.
12. Moberly, *Operations in Persia*, p. 283; Dunsterville, *Dunsterforce*, Ch. 7.
13. Anthony Wynn, *Persia in the Great Game: Sir Percy Sykes, Explorer, Consul, Soldier, Spy*, London, 2003, pp. 248–312.
14. Dunsterville, *Dunsterforce*, p. 133.
15. Moberly, *Operations in Persia*, pp. 290–1.
16. Dunsterville, *Dunsterforce*, pp. 137–8.
17. Moberly, *Operations in Persia*, pp. 289–90, 300.
18. Dunsterville, *Dunsterforce*, pp. 137–8.
19. Ibid., pp. 155–63, 196–7.
20. Ibid., pp. 164–6.
21. Donald Rayfield, *Edge of Empires: A History of Georgia*, London, 2012, pp. 327–31.
22. Dunsterville, *Dunsterforce*, p. 202.
23. Ibid., p. 212.
24. A.H. Brun, *Troublous Times: Experiences in Bolshevik Russia and Turkestan*, London, 1931.
25. Dunsterville, *Dunsterforce*, pp. 193–8.
26. Ibid., pp. 207–208.

27. Ibid., pp. 208–209, 211–13.
28. Ibid., p. 235.
29. Ibid., pp. 218–26, 229–96; withdrawal, pp. 303–13.
30. Neither Dunstable nor Donohoe record this – they had left the city before the massacres took place; it is discussed in Minez, *At the Limits*.
31. Dunsterville, *Dunsterforce*, p. 239.
32. Moberly, *Operations in Persia*, p. 365.

Chapter 5: The Royal Navy Caspian Sea Flotilla

1. Moberly, *Operations in Persia*, p. 366.
2. F.J.F. French, *From Whitehall to the Caspian*, London, 1921.
3. Dunsterville, *Dunsterforce*, p. 219.
4. Ibid., p. 311.
5. Moberly, *Operations in Persia*, p. 365.
6. Dunsterville, *Dunsterforce*, p. 178; Moberly, *Operations in Persia*, p. 370.
7. Moberly, *Operations in Persia*, p. 365; British conjecture by now was that Enver aimed to set up an expanded Azerbaijan stretching as far north as the Terek River and as far as Enzeli to the south-east.
8. Moberly, *Operations in Persia*, pp. 370–1.
9. Ibid., pp. 369–70.
10. Ibid., pp. 387–8, 420.
11. Rayfield, *Edge of Empires*, pp. 330–1.
12. Quoted in Keith Jeffrey, *Field Marshal Sir Henry Wilson: A Political Soldier*, Oxford, 2006, pp. 247–9.
13. Charles King, *The Ghost of Freedom: A History of the Caucasus*, Oxford, 2008, p. 167.
14. French, *From Whitehall*.
15. Ibid., pp. 119–25, 134–5.
16. Moberly, *Operations in Persia*, pp. 418–24.
17. Ibid., p. 423.
18. John Guard, 'The Royal Navy in the Caspian Sea 1918–1920', and available through Wikipedia; references here are necessarily unpaginated.
19. Guard, 'Navy in the Caspian'.
20. Ibid.
21. Ibid.
22. Moberly, *Operations in Persia*, p. 42; Guard lists the ships.
23. John Robert Ferris, *Men, Money, and Diplomacy: The Evolution of British Strategic Foreign Policy, 1919–1926*, Ithaca, NY, 1989, provides a clear account of the government's dilemma(s).
24. French, *Whitehall*, p. 12.
25. Moberly, *Operations in Persia*, pp. 444–8.
26. Guard, 'Navy in the Caspian'.
27. French, *Whitehall*, pp. 188–9.
28. Norris's report is in Halpern, *The Mediterranean Fleet*, doc. 29; a Wikipedia article, 'The Battle of Alexandrovsky Fort' is brief, as is the account in Guard, 'Navy in the Caspian'.
29. Guard, 'Navy in the Caspian'.
30. Guard, 'Navy in the Caspian'.
31. Ibid.
32. Halpern, *Mediterranean Fleet*, doc. 53, 15 January 1920.

33. B.McL. Ranft, *The Beatty Papers*, vol. 2, (1916–1927), NRS 1993, doc. 34, 6 January 1920.
34. Commodore Norris wrote an article describing his exploits, 'The Royal Navy on the Caspian, 1918–1919', *The Naval Review*, 1919–1920; Wikipedia, '1920 Royal Navy mission to Enzeli'.

Chapter 6: Into the Inhospitable Sea

1. Peter Kenez, *Red Advance, White Defeat, Civil War in South Russia 1919–1920*, Washington, DC, 2004, pp. 142–6; George Stewart, *The White Armies of Russia: A Chronicle of Counter-Revolution and Allied Intervention*, pp. 154–5; George A. Brinkley, *The Volunteer Army and Allied Intervention in South Russia: A Study in the Politics and Diplomacy of the Russian Civil War, 1917–1921*, Notre Dame, Indiana, 1966, pp. 37–50; Rayfield, *Edge of Empires*, Kazemzadeh, *Struggle for Transcaucasia*.
2. Melvin, *Sevastopol's Wars*, pp. 370–6.
3. For a clear account of the North Russian interventions, see Clifford Kinvig, *Churchill's Crusade*, London, 2006, which also includes brief references to South Russia; for the Baltic anti-Bolshevik and anti-German campaigns after November 1918, see Geoffrey Bennett, *Cowan's War*, London, 1964.
4. Halpern, *Royal Navy in the Mediterranean*, doc. 180.
5. Halpern, *Mediterranean Fleet*, doc. 1, Calthorpe's letter of proceedings.
6. Michael Jabara Carley, *Revolution and Intervention: The French Government and the Russian Civil War, 1917–1990*, Kingston and Montréal, 1983, pp. 111–18.
7. Halpern, *Mediterranean Fleet*, doc. 1, Calthorpe's report, 12 December 1918, is the source for this and what follows; see also Melvin, *Sevastopol's Wars*, pp. 385–8.
8. Carley, *Revolution and Intervention*, pp. 118–21.
9. Halpern, *Mediterranean Fleet*, doc. 1, Calthorpe's letter of proceedings, 12 December 1918.
10. Halpern, *Mediterranean Fleet*, doc. 2, Seymour's letter of proceedings, 25 January 1919.
11. Ibid.
12. Halpern, *Mediterranean Fleet*, doc. 2, Calthorpe to Admiralty, 18 January 1919.

Chapter 7: British Control

1. Halpern, *Mediterranean Fleet*, doc. 2, Calthorpe to Admiralty, 18 January 1919.
2. Halpern, *Mediterranean Fleet*, doc. 3, Seymour to Calthorpe, 25 January 1919.
3. Ibid., docs 4 and 5, Calthorpe to Admiralty, Malta, 18 February 1919, and Admiralty to Calthorpe, 1 March 1919.
4. Ibid., doc. 6, Calthorpe to Admiralty, Constantinople, 22 March 1919.
5. Carley, *Revolution and Intervention*, p. 161.
6. Ibid., pp. 168–71.
7. Stewart, *White Armies*, pp. 171–2; Carley, *Revolution and Intervention*, pp. 170–1; Kenez, *Red Advance, White Defeat*, pp. 190–1.
8. Halpern, *Mediterranean Fleet*, doc. 8, Seymour to Calthorpe, 8 April 1919, doc. 9, Admiralty to Calthorpe, 8 April 1919, and doc. 10, Calthorpe to Admiralty, 18 April 1919.
9. Halpern, *Mediterranean Fleet*, doc. 8, Seymour to Calthorpe, 8 April 1919.
10. Melvin, *Sevastopol's Wars*, pp. 391–2.
11. Halpern, *Mediterranean Fleet*, doc. 10, Calthorpe to Admiralty, 18 April 1919.
12. Ibid., doc. 11, Seymour to Calthorpe, 19 April 1919.
13. Ibid., doc. 12, Calthorpe to Admiralty, 21 April 1919, and doc. 13, Calthorpe to Vice-Admiral Amet, 20 April 1919.
14. Ibid., doc. 14, Seymour to Calthorpe, 1 May 1919.
15. Ibid., Carley, *Revolution and Intervention*, pp. 174–81; Melvin, *Sevastopol's Wars*, pp. 394–6.

16. Halpern, *Mediterranean Fleet*, doc. 14, Seymour to Calthorpe, 1 May 1919.
17. Melvin, *Sevastopol's Wars*, pp. 396–7.
18. Halpern, *Mediterranean Fleet*, doc. 16, Seymour to Calthorpe, 5 May 1919.
19. Ibid., doc. 22, Commander Richard Down to commanding officer, HMS *Calypso*, HMS *Forrester*, Arabat Bay, 13 May 1919.
20. Kenez, *Red Advance, White Defeat*, pp. 36–9.
21. Halpern, *Mediterranean Fleet*, doc. 15, Calthorpe to Admiralty, 1 May 1919.
22. Ibid., doc. 27, Calthorpe to Admiralty, 25 May 1919, and doc. 28, Commodore Fitzmaurice to Admiralty and Mediterranean Commander-in-Chief, HMS *Centaur*, 25 May 1919.
23. Ibid., doc. 34, Commodore Fitzmaurice to Admiralty and Commander-in-Chief, Malta, HMS *Centaur*, 16 June 1919.
24. Ibid., doc. 40, Fitzmaurice to Calthorpe, HMS *Centaur*, 14 July 1919.
25. Ibid., doc. 32, Calthorpe to Admiralty, 9 June 1919.
26. Ibid., doc. 37, Calthorpe to Admiralty, 29 June 1919.
27. Melvin, *Sevastopol's Wars*, pp. 397–8.
28. Halpern, *Mediterranean Fleet*, doc. 31, Seymour to Calthorpe, 6 June 1919.
29. Ibid., doc. 39, Seymour to Calthorpe, 6 July 1919.

Chapter 8: British Withdrawal

1. Halpern, *Mediterranean Fleet*, doc. 29, Norris to Seymour, 25 May 1919.
2. Halpern, *Mediterranean Fleet*, doc. 17, Admiralty to Commander-in-Chief Mediterranean and Commodore Aegean, 7 May 1919, doc. 19, Admiralty to Captain C.T.M. Fuller, 8 May 1919, and doc. 20, Admiralty to C-in-C Mediterranean, 11 May 1919.
3. MacMillan, *Peacemakers*, p. 438.
4. Mango, *Ataturk*, p. 218.
5. Halpern, *Mediterranean Fleet*, docs. 45 and 47, Seymour to De Robeck, 30 August and 18 September 1919.
6. Ibid., doc. 43, Seymour to de Robeck, 19 August 1919.
7. Ibid., doc. 47, Seymour to de Robeck, 8 September 1919.
8. Ibid.
9. Ibid., docs. 51, 54, 55, De Robeck to Admiralty, 15, 25, and 28 January 1920.
10. Ibid., doc. 52, Admiralty to de Robeck, 15 January 1920.
11. Ibid., doc. 54, de Robeck to Admiralty, 25 January 1920.
12. Ibid., doc. 57, de Robeck to Admiralty, 30 January 1920.
13. *Volya* decayed at Bizerta along with the rest; its 16-inch guns were removed in 1942 by the Germans and installed in the Channel Islands to defend that German conquest; they do not seem to have been used.
14. Stewart, *White Armies*, p. 343.
15. Ibid., pp. 343–7.
16. Halpern, *Mediterranean Fleet*, doc. 53, Admiralty to do aerobic, 15 January 1920.
17. Ibid., doc. 57 (preparations), de Robeck to Admiralty, 30 January 1920; doc. 61, Lieutenant Commander Knox-Little to Senior Naval Officer, Odessa, 9 February 1920; doc. 62 (Odessa), Captain Reinhold to de Robeck, 13 February 1920, and doc. 65 (Novorossiisk), Seymour to de Robeck, 9 March 1920.
18. Ibid., docs. 57 and 62, as above.
19. Ibid., doc. 57, as above.
20. Ibid., doc. 57 (as above), p. 141, note 1.
21. Ibid., doc. 176, the aerobic to Admiralty, 2 September 1921.

22. Ibid., doc. 96, de Robeck to Lord Curzon, 27 April 1920.
23. Ibid., doc. 136 – a banquet – Seymour to de Robeck, 11 July 1920.
24. Ibid., doc. 89, Fremantle to Admirals Madden and de Robeck, 21 April 1920.
25. Ibid., doc. 91, Lord Curzon to de Robeck, 23 April 1920; and doc. 96, de Robeck to Lord Curzon, 27 April 1920.
26. Ibid., doc. 136 (note 23).
27. Ibid., p. 213, note 1; also doc. 57 (note 17).
28. Wikipedia, '1920 Royal Navy mission to Enzeli'.
29. Stewart, *White Armies*, pp. 373–4; Halpern, *Mediterranean Fleet*, doc. 145, Admiralty to de Robeck, 10 August 1920.
30. Halpern, *Mediterranean Fleet*, doc. 162, Rear Admiral G. Hope to de Robeck, 12 November 1920; docs. 163–5, de Robeck to Admiralty 13, 14 and 15 November 1920; doc. 166, Captain C. Seymour to de Robeck, 18 November 1920; doc. 167, de Robeck to Admiralty, 23 November 1920; Stewart, *White Armies*, pp. 376–7.

Chapter 9: Constantinople Occupied

1. The refugee numbers and origins are hardly systematically dealt with, but the following references will give an idea of the issue, and the varied approaches to it: Edmonds, *Occupation*, p. 19; King, *Midnight*, fifth chapter 'Moscow on the Bosporos', and *The Black Sea*, Oxford, 2004, pp. 211–12; Philip Mansel, *Constantinople: City of the World's Desire, 1453–1924,* London, 1995, pp. 398–401.
2. E.R. Hooton, *Prelude to the First World War: The Balkan Wars, 1912–1913*, 2014.
3. Report by the admirals in January and February 1920 are principally concerned with refugees, and again in November 1920; Halpern, *Mediterranean Fleet*, docs. 281–8 (mainly on French operations); Melvin, *Sevastopol's Wars*, pp. 412–18; Mitchell, *Russian Sea Power*, pp. 346–7; Brinkley, *Volunteer Army*, pp. 271–3.
4. Mango, *Ataturk*, p. 219.
5. Mango, *Ataturk*, Ch. 11; Edmonds, *Occupation*, pp. 9–11.
6. Halpern, *Mediterranean Fleet*, doc. 24, Acting Captain H.L. Boyle to Commodore Fitzmaurice, 17 May 1919, and doc. 25, Calthorpe to Admiralty, 20 May 1919.
7. Ibid., doc. 24 (see above).
8. Edmonds, *Occupation*, pp. 7–8.
9. Mango, *Ataturk*, pp. 206–207, 223, note 14.
10. King, *Midnight*, p. 56; Wikipedia, 'The Occupation of Istanbul', quoting British Foreign Office documents.
11. Wikipedia, 'Occupation'.
12. Edmonds, *Occupation*, p. 7.
13. King, *Midnight*, p. 42.
14. William N. Still Jr, *Victory without Peace: The United States in European Waters, 1919–1924*, Annapolis, MD, 2018, Chs. 7–10; Robert Shenk, *America's Black Sea Fleet: The US Navy amidst War and Revolution, 1919–1923*, Annapolis, MD, 2017.
15. Edmonds, *Occupation*, pp. 16–17, and Appendix III.
16. Mango, *Ataturk*, Ch. 11; Edmonds, *Occupation*, p. 10.
17. Edmonds, *Occupation*, pp. 19–31, quoting Milne's letter.
18. Ibid., p. 11.
19. Mango, *Ataturk,* p. 264.
20. Edmonds, *Occupation*, p. 11.
21. Halpern, *Mediterranean Fleet*, doc. 64, Admiralty to de Robeck, 5 March 1920.

22. Edmonds, *Occupation*, pp. 12–15; King, *Midnight*, pp. 74–5.
23. Wikipedia, 'Occupation'.
24. Halpern, *Mediterranean Fleet*, doc. 67, Admiralty to de Robeck, 15 March 1920.
25. Halpern, *Mediterranean Fleet*, docs. 72 and 73, de Robeck to Admiralty, 25 March 1920.
26. Edmonds, *Occupation*, Appendix IV gives these details.
27. Mango, *Ataturk*, pp. 246–7; King, *Midnight*, pp. 75–8; Roderic H. Davison, 'Turkish Diplomacy from Mudros to Lausanne', in *Essays in Ottoman and Turkish history, the Impact of the West,* Texas, 1990, pp. 206–41.
28. Halpern, *Mediterranean Fleet*, docs. 115–17, de Robeck to Admiralty, 16–17 June 1920 (one document).
29. Ibid., doc. 119, Admiralty to de Robeck, 19 June 1920.
30. Ibid., docs. 123–5, de Robeck to Admiralty, 20 and 22 June 1920.
31. Ibid., docs. 126–7, de Robeck to Admiralty, 22 June 1920.
32. Ibid., doc. 129, Admiral Fremantle's Report of Proceedings, 25 June 1920.
33. Ibid., doc. 131, de Robeck's orders for the operation, 1 July 1920, and doc. 132, de Robeck to Admiralty, 7 July 1920.
34. Ibid., docs. 133 and 134, de Robeck to Foreign Office and Admiralty, 8 July 1920.
35. Halpern, *Mediterranean Fleet*, doc. 132, de Robeck to Admiralty, 7 July 1920, a lengthy appreciation of the political, military, and naval situation.
36. Edmonds, *Occupation*, p. 18.
37. Ibid., pp. 18–19.
38. Michael Llewellyn Smith, *Ionian Vision: Greece on Asia Minor 1919–1922*, London, 1976, pp. 149–50, 184–8; Edmonds, *Occupation*, p. 17.
39. Halpern, *Mediterranean Fleet*, doc. 168, de Robeck to Admiralty, 28 February 1920.
40. Ibid., doc. 172, de Robeck to Admiralty, 23 June 1921.
41. Ibid., doc. 179, de Robeck to Admiralty, 1 October 1920.
42. Ibid., doc. 180, Excerpt from the Diary of Lieutenant C.H. Drage, 2–21 November 1921.
43. Ibid., docs. 184–8, Admiralty (Keyes) to Brock, 29 July 1922; Brock's reply, 31 July, and Balfour's comments, 1 August.
44. Ibid., docs. 184–7.
45. Ibid., doc. 188; Sir Charles Harington, *Tim Harington Looks Back*, London, 1940, p. 109.

Chapter 10: Smyrna, Greeks, and Turks

1. See, for example, my *The Battle for Palestine, 1917*, and *The Battle for Syria 1918–1920*, Woodbridge, 2006 and 2013.
2. C.M. Woodhouse, *Modern Greece: A Short History*, 4th edn., London, 1986, pp. 194–205.
3. MacMillan, *Peacemakers*, pp. 442–3.
4. Halpern, *Mediterranean Fleet*, doc. 17, Admiralty to Commander-in-Chief Mediterranean and Commodore Aegean, 7 May 1919, and doc. 24, Acting Captain H.L. Boyle to Commodore Fitzmaurice, 17 May 1919.
5. Ibid., doc. 19, Admiralty to Captain C.T.M. Fuller, 8 May 1919, and doc. 20, Admiralty to C-in-C Mediterranean, 11 May 1919.
6. Ibid., doc. 24 (Boyle's report) and doc. 25 (Calthorpe's).
7. The most competent account of events in Smyrna on the day is in Michael Llewellyn Smith, *Ionian Vision: Greece in Asia Minor, 1919–1922*, London, 2nd edn., 2022, Ch. 5.
8. Halpern, *Mediterranean Fleet*, doc. 24 (see note 4).
9. Still, *Victory Without Peace*, p. 220.

10. Llewellyn Smith, *Ionian Vision*, pp. 99–103; see also Arnold Toynbee, *The Western Question in Greece and Turkey: A Study in the Contact of Civilisations*, London, 1922 (reprinted 2012), pp. 160–167.
11. Llewellyn Smith, *Ionian Vision*, p. 124.
12. Ibid., pp. 120–1.
13. Halpern, *Mediterranean Fleet*, doc. 179, de Robeck to Admiralty, 1 October 1921.
14. Ibid., doc. 38, Calthorpe to Admiralty, 4 July 1919, and doc. 39, Seymour to Calthorpe, 6 July 1919.
15. King, *Midnight*, p. 211; the turnout for the demonstration was estimated at 200,000 Turks.
16. Halpern, *Mediterranean Fleet*, doc. 59, a report by de Robeck to the Admiralty of Milne's warnings.
17. Mango, *Ataturk*, pp. 290–4.
18. Ibid., pp. 295–6.
19. Halpern, *Mediterranean Fleet*, doc. 82, Vice-Admiral Freemantle to Admirals Madden and de Robeck, 31 March 1920.
20. Edmonds, *Occupation*, Appendix IV, for the list of the relative articles for his purpose (pages 44 – 47).
21. Halpern, *Mediterranean Fleet*, doc. 103, Vice-Admiral Freemantle to de Robeck, 14 May 1920.
22. Ibid.
23. Ibid., doc. 105, Vice-Admiral Freemantle to de Robeck, 26 May 1920, doc. 108, Captain Aubrey Smith to de Robeck, 6 June 1920, and doc. 113, Captain Aubrey Smith to Vice-Admiral Fremantle, 15 June 1920.
24. Llewellyn Smith, *Ionian Vision*, p. 135.
25. Ibid., pp. 186–8.

Chapter 11: The Greek Disaster, and Smyrna

1. Halpern, *Mediterranean Fleet*, doc. 190, Admiralty to Brock, 2 September 1922.
2. Ibid.
3. Ibid., doc. 193, Admiralty to Air Ministry, 11 September 1922, doc. 194, Air Ministry to Admiralty, 12 September 1922, and doc. 196, Air Commodore J.M. Steel to Rear Admiral Chatfield, Air Ministry, 15 September 1922.
4. Ibid., doc. 199, Admiralty to Brock, 16 September 1922.
5. Ibid., doc. 197, Admiralty to Brock, 15 September 1922, and doc. 200, Brock to Admiralty, 17 September 1922.
6. Ibid., doc. 202, Brock to Admiralty, 18 September 1922, and doc. 203, Admiralty to Brock, 19 September 1922.
7. Ibid., doc. 210, Brock to Admiralty, 22 September 1922.
8. Ibid., doc. 215, memorandum by Brock, 22 September 1922 to 9.
9. Ibid., docs. 229 and 230, Tyrwhitt to Brock, 19 and 24 September 1922.
10. Mango, *Ataturk*, p. 344; for Bursa's importance to the Turks, see David Walder, *The Chanak Affair*, London, 1969, p. 101.
11. Sir Charles Harington, *Tim Harington Looks Back*, London, 1940, p. 136.
12. Walder, *Chanak*, pp. 191–2, for the layout of the neutral zone.
13. Harington, p. 135; Walder, *Chanak*, p. 204.
14. Walder, *Chanak*, pp. 206–207.
15. Ibid., p. 207.
16. Edmonds, *Occupation*, p. 26.

17. Halpern, *Mediterranean Fleet*, doc. 194, Air Ministry to Admiralty, 12 September 1922, and doc. 196, Steel to Chatfield (note 3).
18. Ibid., docs. 201 and 204, Admiralty to Brock, 18 and 19 September 1922.
19. Ibid., doc. 220, Admiralty to Brock, 26 September 1922, and doc. 244, Admiralty Memorandum of Forces sent to the Mediterranean, October 1922.
20. Ibid., 244.
21. Harington, pp. 137–40, the report of Shuttleworth, describing Petherwick's actions.
22. Walder, *Chanak*, p. 222.
23. Harington, pp. 139–40.
24. Halpern, *Mediterranean Fleet*, doc. 217, Admiralty to Brock, 25 September 1922.
25. Ibid., doc. 216, Admiralty to de Robeck (now C-in-C, Atlantic Fleet, 24 September 1922.
26. Llewellyn Smith, *Ionian Vision*, pp. 337–41; Woodhouse, *Modern Greece*, pp. 206–208.
27. Halpern, *Mediterranean Fleet*, doc. 240 and note 2, Brock to Admiralty, 10 October 1922.
28. Walder, *Chanak*, pp. 215–16.
29. Ibid., p. 253. (New Zealand); Newfoundland was sympathetic, but offered no troops; the others in effect refused.
30. Harington, p. 142.
31. Ibid.
32. Harington, pp. 142–53, including contemporary documents in his possession.
33. Edmonds, *Occupation*, pp. 27–8.
34. Halpern, *Mediterranean Fleet*, docs. 240, 241, 245, Brock to Admiralty, 10, 12 and 15 October 1922.
35. Walder, *Chanak*, pp. 321–7; Kenneth O. Morgan, *Consensus and Disunity: The Lloyd George Coalition Government, 1918–1922*, Oxford, 1979; Robert Blake, *The Unknown Prime Minister*, London, 1955, pp. 444–58.

Chapter 12: Chanak

1. Halpern, *Mediterranean Fleet*, doc. 115, de Robeck to Admiralty, 16 June 1920.
2. Ibid., docs. 125, 127 and 128, de Robeck to Admiralty, 22 and 25 June 1920.
3. Llewellyn-Smith, *Ionian Vision*, pp. 135–6.
4. Halpern, *Mediterranean Fleet*, doc. 125, Report of Proceedings by Vice-Admiral Fremantle, 28 June 1920.
5. Llewellyn-Smith, *Ionian Vision*, p. 136.
6. Halpern, *Mediterranean Fleet*, doc. 130, de Robeck to Admiralty, 30 June 1920.
7. Ibid., doc. 131, do aerobics orders for supporting the Greek operation, 1 July 1920.
8. Ibid., doc. 141, Vice-Admiral Fremantle to de Robeck, 27 July 1920.
9. Ibid., doc. 137, Admiralty to de Robeck, 12 July 1920.
10. Ibid., doc. 138, Vice-Admiral Fremantle to de Robeck, 13 July 1920.
11. Ibid., doc. 139, Captain Charles D. Johnson to de Robeck, 22 July 1920, and doc. 140, Vice-Admiral Fremantle to de Robeck, 16 July 1920.
12. Ibid., doc. 141, Vice-Admiral Fremantle to de Robeck, 27 July 1920; and doc. 142, Captain Aubrey C.H. Smith to Vice-Admiral Fremantle, 21 July 1920.
13. MacMillan, *Peacemakers*, p. 460.
14. Llewellyn-Smith, *Ionian Vision*, pp. 136 and 198–9.
15. Ibid., pp. 215–18; Toynbee, *The Western Question*, pp. 233–5.

16. Halpern, *Mediterranean Fleet*, docs. 170, de Robeck to Admiralty, 9 April 1921, and doc. 171, Admiralty to de Robeck, 26 April 1921.
17. Llewellyn Smith, *Ionian Vision*, pp. 242–52; Toynbee, *The Western Question*, pp. 235–54.
18. Halpern, *Mediterranean Fleet*, doc. 178, de Robeck to Admiral Beatty, 22 September 1921, and doc. 179, de Robeck to Admiralty, 1 October 1921.
19. Llewellyn-Smith, *Ionian Vision*, pp. 264–8.
20. Mango, *Ataturk*, p. 310; Kazemzadeh, *Transcaucasia*, pp. 325–7.
21. Mango, *Ataturk*, pp. 309 and 327.
22. Halpern, *Mediterranean Fleet*, doc. 174, de Robeck to Admiralty, 17 August 1921, and doc. 175, Foreign Office to Admiralty, 17 August 1921.
23. Ibid., doc. 176, de Robeck to Admiralty, September 1921.
24. Ibid., doc. 177, de Robeck to Sir Horace Rumbold, 12 September 1921.
25. Ibid., doc. 184, Admiral O. de B. Brock to Admiralty, 26 July 1922.
26. Ibid., doc. 179, de Robeck to Admiralty, 1 October 1921.
27. Halpern, *Mediterranean Fleet*, doc. 184 (note 25); Llewellyn-Smith, *Ionian Vision*, pp. 299–301; Edmonds, *Occupation*, p. 25.
28. Llewelyn-Smith, *Ionian Vision*, pp. 310–16.
29. Ibid., pp. 316–23.
30. Toynbee, *Western Question*, Chapter VII, entitled 'The War of Extermination'.
31. Halpern, *Mediterranean Fleet*, doc. 189, brought to Admiralty, 3 September 1922.
32. The capture, sack, and fire of Smyrna has been described several times, by the correspondents at the time, such as Ernest Hemingway and George Ward Price, and in later accounts by, amongst others, Giles Milton, *Paradise Lost: Smyrna 1922*, London, 2008, Marjorie Housepian Dobkin, *Smyrna 1922: The Destruction of a City*, London 1975, and Mansell, *Levant*. This account of the navy's actions is based on official reports by several officers, printed in Halpern, *Mediterranean Fleet*, doc. 228 (Brock), doc. 229 (Tyrwhitt) and doc. 195 (Lieutenant A. Duckworth), which are customarily ignored.
33. Halpern, *Mediterranean Fleet*, doc. 268, Nicholson's report, dated 12 March 1923.
34. Halpern, *Mediterranean Fleet*, doc. 223 (the Admiralty's request for an accurate accounting) and doc. 227 (Nicholson's reply, with the figure of 177,000 rescuees).
35. Ibid.

Chapter 13: A Final Evacuation

1. Halpern, *Mediterranean Fleet*, doc. 245, Brock to Admiralty, 15 October 1922.
2. Ibid., doc. 247, Brock to Admiralty, 19 October 1922.
3. Ibid., doc. 246, Memorandum by Brock, 15 October 1922.
4. Ibid., doc. 252, Captain H.A.B. Williamson to Rear Admiral Tyrwhitt.
5. Harington, pp. 158–60.
6. Halpern, *Mediterranean Fleet*, docs. 255–68, exchanges of messages between Brock and the Admiralty in February 1923, with reports by Captain C.A. Scott of the cruiser *Calypso* at Smyrna; doc. 168 is Rear Admiral Nicholson's Report of Proceedings at Smyrna, 12 March 1923.
7. MacMillan, *Peacemakers*, pp. 463–6.
8. Edmonds, *Occupation*, pp. 28–9.
9. Ibid., p. 29; Walden, *Chanak*, pp. 350–1.

Bibliography

Bailey, F.M., *Mission to Tashkent*, 2nd edn., Oxford, 1992.

Bennett, Geoffrey, *Cowan's War*, London, 1964.

Blake, Robert, *The Unknown Prime Minister*, London, 1955.

Brinkley, George A., *The Volunteer Army and Allied Intervention in South Russia, a Study in the Politics and Diplomacy of the Russian Civil War, 1917–1921*, Notre Dame, Indiana, 1966.

Brun, A.H., *Troublous Times, Experiences in Bolshevik Russia and Turkestan*, London, 1931.

Carley, Michael Jabara, *Revolution and Intervention: The French Government and the Russian Civil War, 1917–1919*, Kingston and Montréal, 1983.

Davison, Roderic H., 'Turkish Diplomacy from Mudros to Lausanne', in *Essays in Ottoman and Turkish History, 1774–1923, the Impact of the West*, Texas, 1990.

Dobkin, Marjorie Housepian, *Smyrna 1922: The Destruction of a City*, London, 1975.

Donohoe, Major M.H., *With the Persian Expedition*, London, 1920,

Dunsterville, L.C., *The Adventures of Dunsterforce*, London, 1920.

Edmonds, Brigadier General Sir James E., *The Occupation of Constantinople 1918–1923*, transcribed by Neil Wells, Uckfield, 2010.

Ellis, C.H., *The TransCaspian Episode, 1918–1919*, London, 1963.

Ferris, John Robert, *Men, Money, and Diplomacy: The Evolution of British Strategic Foreign Policy, 1919–1926*, Ithaca, NY, 1989.

Ford, Roger, *Eden to Armageddon, World War I in the Middle East*, London, 2009.

French, Lieutenant Colonel F.J.F., *From Whitehall to the Caspian*, London, 1921.

Fromkin, David, *A Peace to end all Peace: Creating the Modern Middle East, 1914–1922*, London, 1989.

Grainger, John D., *The Battle for Syria, 1918–1920*, Woodbridge, 2013.

Grainger, John D., *13 Sharks: The Careers of a Series of Small Royal Navy Ships, from the Glorious Revolution to D-Day*, Barnsley, 2016.

Grainger, John D., *The Forty Sieges of Constantinople: The Great City's Enemies and its Surival*, Barnsley, 2022.

Grainger, John D., *The Battle for Palestine, 1917*, Woodbridge, 2006.

Grainger, John D., *The Battle for Syria 1918–1920*, Woodbridge, 2013.

Guard, John, 'The Royal Navy in the Caspian Sea 1918–1920', available through Wikipedia.

Halpern, Paul G., *A Naval History of World War I*, London, 1994.

Halpern, Paul G., *The Mediterranean Fleet, 1919–1929*, Navy Records Society, 2011.

Harington, Gen Sir Charles, *Tim Harington Looks Back*, London, 1940.

Hooton, E.R., *Prelude to the First World War: The Balkan Wars, 1912–1913*, 2014.

Hopkirk, Peter, *On Secret Service East of Constantinople: The Plot to bring down the British Empire*, Oxford, 1995.

Hopkirk, Peter, *Setting the East Ablaze: Lenin's Dream of an Empire in Asia*, London, 1984.

Jeffrey, Keith, *Field Marshal Sir Henry Wilson: A Political Soldier*, Oxford, 2006.

Kazemzadeh, Firuz, *The Struggle for Transcaucasia (1917–1921)*, New York, 1951 (reprinted 2023).

Kenez, Peter, *Red Advance, White Defeat: Civil War in South Russia 1919–1920*, Washington, DC, 2004.
King, Charles, *The Ghost of Freedom: A History of the Caucasus*, Oxford, 2008.
King, Charles, *Midnight at the Pera Palace: The Birth of Modern Istanbul*, New York, 2014.
Kinvig, Major General Clifford, *Churchill's Crusade: The British Invasion of Russia 1918–1920*, London, 2006.
Llewellyn Smith, Michael, *Ionian Vision: Greece in Asia Minor, 1919–22*, London, 1976, 2nd edn. 2022.
Maclean, Fitzroy, *A Person from England and Other Travellers*, London, 1956, republished 1984.
MacMillan, Margaret, *Peacemakers: Six Months that Changed the World*, London, 2001.
Mango, Andrew, *Ataturk*, London, 1999.
Mansel, Philip, *Constantinople: City of the World's Desire, 1453–1924*, London, 1995.
Mansell, Philip, *Levant: Splendour and Catastrophe on the Mediterranean*, London, 2011.
Marder, Arthur J., *From the Dreadnought to Scapa Flow*, 5 vols., Annapolis, MD, 1961–1970.
Melvin, Major General Mungo, *Sevastopol's Wars: Crimea from Potemkin to Putin*, Oxford, 2017.
Milton, Giles, *Paradise Lost: Smyrna 1922, The Destruction of Islam's City of Tolerance*, London, 2008.
Minez, Major Ronald P., *At the Limit of Complexity: British Military Operations in North Persia and the Caucasus 1918*, ed. Elizabeth J. Brown (n.d.).
Mitchell, Donald W., *A History of Russian and Soviet Sea Power*, London, 1974.
Moberly, F.J., *Operations in Persia 1914–1919* (Official History of the Great War), London, 1987.
Morgan, Kenneth O., *Consensus and Disunity: The Lloyd George Coalition Government 1918–1922*, Oxford, 1979.
Murphy, C.C.R., *Soldiers of the Prophet (1921)*, London 1920 (reprinted 2010).
Norris, David, 'The Royal Navy on the Caspian, 1918–1919', *The Naval Review*, 1919–1920.
Ranft, B.McL. (ed.), *The Beatty Papers*, vol. 2, (1916–1927), NRS, London, 1993.
Rayfield, Donald, *Edge of Empires: a History of Georgia*, London, 2012.
Roskill, Stephen, *Naval Policy Between the Wars*, vol. 1, London, 1968.
Shenk, Robert, *America's Black Sea Fleet: the U.S. Navy Amidst War and Revolution, 1919–1923*, Annapolis, MD, 2017.
Stewart, George, *The White Armies of Russia: A Chronicle of Counter-Revolution and Allied Intervention*, Uckfield, 2009.
Still Jr, William N., *Victory without Peace: The United States Navy in European Waters, 1919–1924*, Annapolis, MD, 2018.
Toynbee, Arnold J., *The Western Question in Greece and Turkey: A Study in the Contact of Civilisations*, London, 1922 (reprinted 2012).
Walder, David, *The Chanak Affair*, London, 1969.
Wheeler, Geoffrey, *The Modern History of Soviet Central Asia*, London, 1964.
Woodhouse, C.M., *Modern Greece: A Short History*, 4th edn., London, 1986.
Wynn, Anthony, *Persia in the Great Game: Sir Percy Sykes, Explorer, Consul, Soldier, Spy*, London, 2003.
Yergin, Daniel, *The Prize: The Epic Quest for Oil, Money & Power*, London, 1991.
Wikipedia, 'The Battle of Alexandrovsky Fort'.
Wikipedia, '1920 Royal Navy mission to Enzeli'.

Index